AF608048

The Appalachian Photographs of EARL PALMER

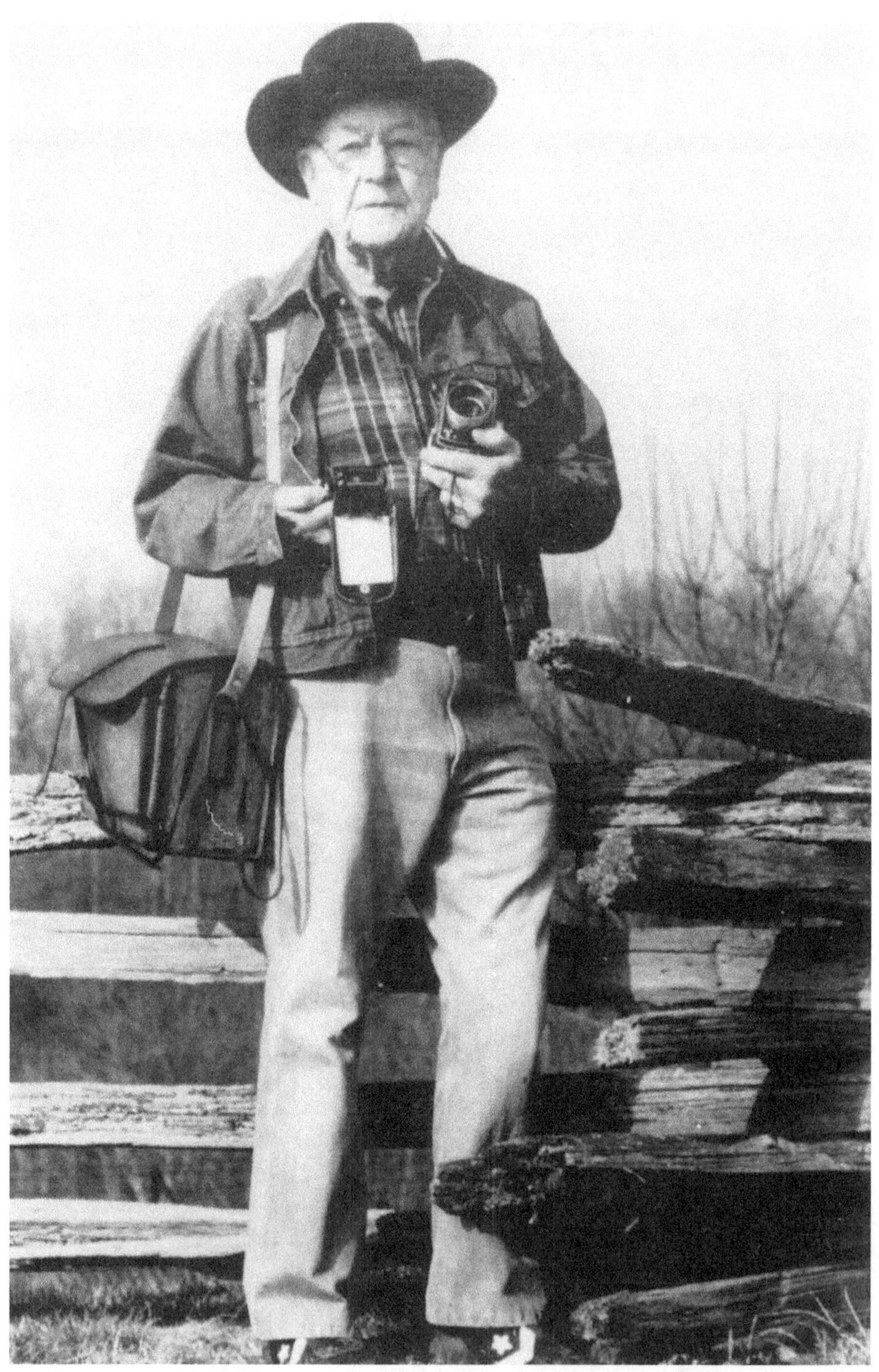

The Appalachian Photographs of EARL PALMER

JEAN HASKELL SPEER

THE UNIVERSITY PRESS OF KENTUCKY

Frontispiece: Earl Palmer, 1984. Photograph by Evelyn Palmer

Scholarly publisher for the Commonwealth,
serving Bellarmine College, Berea College, Centre
College of Kentucky, Eastern Kentucky University,
The Filson Club, Georgetown College, Kentucky
Historical Society, Kentucky State University,
Morehead State University, Murray State University,
Northern Kentucky University, Transylvania University,
University of Kentucky, University of Louisville,
and Western Kentucky University.

Editorial and Sales Offices: Lexington, Kentucky 40506-0336

Library of Congress Cataloging-in-Publication Data

Speer, Jean Haskell, 1947-
The Appalachian photographs of Earl Palmer / Jean Haskell Speer.
p. cm.
Includes bibliographical references.
ISBN 0-8131-1695-3 (alk. paper)
1. Appalachian Region, Southern—Description and travel—Views.
2. Appalachian Region, Southern—Social life and customs—Pictorial works. 3. Mountain whites (Southern States)—Pictorial works.
4. Palmer, Earl, 1905- . I. Palmer, Earl, 1905- . II. Title.
F217.A65S72 1989 89-24772
975—dc20 CIP

This book is printed on acid-free paper meeting
the requirements of the American National Standard
for Permanence of Paper for Printed Library Materials.

♾

Contents

To my mother and father and sister,
with whom I wandered the mountains in my childhood

Preface

The first time I saw some of Earl Palmer's photographs I was captivated. As a folklorist interested in the traditional culture of Appalachia, I was struck by Palmer's images of the folklife of mountain people. There were photographs of farm life, mountain cabins and rail fences, quilting, basketmaking, gathering mountain herbs, boiling molasses, stirring apple butter, and making moonshine. But it was not only the subject matter that drew me to the photographs. I had seen and even made photographs of mountain folk culture many times before. I was struck by the quality of the photographs, the range of subject matter, the apparent age of some of the photographs, and the story they seemed to tell about Appalachia.

I didn't know Earl Palmer then, but I wanted to know him. Some years later I had an opportunity to meet him when, in 1985, he asked the art department at Virginia Polytechnic Institute and State University whether they would be interested in his collection of photographs. They in turn contacted me in the Appalachian Studies Program and we arranged a visit with Earl. During that first visit I was overwhelmed by the historical and cultural significance of his collection of photographs (and by its sheer size) and by the powerful and complex personality who had made it. I decided then that here was a scholarly opportunity not to be missed by a folklorist in Appalachia—a chance to work with a native-born photographer of his own traditional culture who was himself a rich repository of mountain folklore and a masterful storyteller.

I asked Earl if I might visit him regularly and tape-record our discussions about his life and his work. He was eager to begin our collaboration and so we embarked on what is now three years of work and still continues. This book is not the culmination of our work together but an introduction to Earl and his photographs of Appalachia.

Earl has spent a lifetime, as he puts it, "conjuring" Appalachia, creating a rich and complex Appalachian vision in pictures. He believes the highest and best vision of Appalachia is rooted in its past, made manifest in its traditional culture and in those persons who remain emblems of the past in the present. In fact, Earl's photographs may be said to constitute a kind of mountain manifesto, a public declaration of his intention to create a particular Appalachian world.

Earl has photographed Appalachia according to his world view. He has seen the mountaineer as both historically real and eternally mythic. He has made a photographic record of what has been real, if now only remembered, and he has created a vision of Appalachia's past as he wishes it to be remembered. Earl has understood the power of the photographic image to preserve and to persuade, especially to build a rhetorically powerful argument through repeated and consistent images.

The photographs chosen for this volume from Earl's collection of twenty to thirty thousand negatives represent the mainstream of his work. They include some of his most critically acclaimed and popular photographs, some historically and culturally valuable photographs, and photographs that illustrate Earl's concept of "Appalachianness." The photographs were made over a period of more than fifty years from 1936 to 1988. Geographically, they represent the heartland of Southern Appalachia, covering portions of Kentucky, West Virginia, Virginia, Tennessee, and North Carolina. In his photography, Earl has used a variety of cameras, ranging from a 4 x 5 view camera to a Rolleiflex to several types of 35mm cameras. He does his own developing work in his fully equipped basement darkroom.

Dates for the early photographs are usually estimated. For many years, Earl did not regularly record dates of his photographs. His explanation for this omission is that early in his career he had no idea anyone would ever have an interest in his photographs that would require thorough documentation. It has become clear to me, however, that the photographs have a timeless quality for Earl; the subjects, not the time period, are crucial to him.

For most of his photographs Earl writes extensive captions that are intended to be evocative more often than informational. They are narratives that mix historical fact with Earl's imagination in short vignettes about mountain life. Because writing is nearly as important to him as photography, I have included his captions here, sometimes in abbreviated form. Where further information was available and seemed needed, I have added it, and have provided identification for the photographs Earl did not caption.

My biographical-critical essay is drawn primarily from transcripts of taped interviews with Earl over a three-year period from 1985 to 1988. My research as an ethnographer of Appalachian culture has helped me place Earl's work in the larger context of cultural studies about the region. I am not a photographic critic, but I have tried to understand these photographs and their creation through the work of such photographic critics as Susan Sontag, Roland Barthes, Christopher M. Lyman, Mark Roskill and David Carrier, Charles Alan Watkins, and others.

In the essay, I have tried to describe how Earl and his photographs fit into a tradition of intellectual and cultural ideas about Appalachia and into a particular photographic tradition. Daniel Lindley, in a study of the photographs of Walker Evans, comments: "The photographs have a continuing power to engage us whether we know anything of the circumstances surrounding their creation or not. In essence, it is not what the photographs bring to us that is ultimately persuasive. It is what we bring to the photographs; and what we bring is what makes these photographs matter." Earl's photographs, too, have a power to engage us without knowing the circumstances of their creation. But I have tried to provide a context for the photographs to explain their means of persuasion, to enrich what we bring to them, to make them matter more or differently.

Writing the essay proved more difficult than I originally thought because there are so many audiences for this book and Earl's work—Earl himself, those who unconditionally love the photographs and their vision of Appalachia, and those who have a professional and scholarly interest in photography and in Appalachia. I have tried to be sensitive to the needs of each audience and fair to Earl Palmer.

Throughout this book, all quotations from Earl are taken from our taped interviews or from my field notes of other conversations we have had. Long quotations are documented with accession numbers that correspond to tapes and transcripts (PSP 10-86A; *P*almer-*SP*eer, October 1986, side A). The original tapes and the transcripts have been deposited in the Appalachian Collection of the Carol M. Newman Library at Virginia Polytechnic Institute and State University in Blacksburg. The photographs in this book and many other Palmer photographs and artifacts are also part of the collection. The director of special collections, Glenn McMullen, and the archivist for the Appalachian Collection, Laura Katz, have been a tremendous help to me.

Earl has given freely of his photographs because he wants to see them used in research, teaching, and for exhibition long after he is gone. He says, "It would hurt me [if the photographs were not used]. I believe I'd awaken from my sleep if I passed on and I thought nobody could repair to them."

This book would not have been made without the generosity and encouragement of Earl Palmer and his wife, Evelyn. They made me feel like family in their home and nurtured me with good food, good talk, lots of laughter, and a sprinkling of tears. Others who have assisted me and urged me on with the work include Jerry Crouch, editor of the University Press of Kentucky, who believed in the project and me and understood the patience required for birthing a book; Evalin F. Douglas, managing editor of the Press, whose good judgment strengthened the book; Robert Graham of the Department of Art and Art History at Virginia Polytechnic Institute and State University, who first took me to meet Earl; my colleagues in the Appalachian Studies Program, the Center for Programs in the Humanities, the Department of Communication Studies, and other friends from VPI&SU, especially Elizabeth C. Fine, Robert Denton, Dorothy and Les McCombs, Virginia and Bill McWhorter, Jim and Phyllis Long, Bernice Born, who helped me solve a multitude of problems, and Ed Born, Rick Griffiths, and Norma Montgomery, who typed my manuscript cheerfully (as she does everything); and two of my former students, Henry Cobb and Katherine Schmitt, who were perceptive and devoted beyond expectation.

The poem from Jesse Stuart's *Man with a Bull-Tongue Plow* quoted in the introduction is used with permission of the Jesse Stuart Foundation, P.O. Box 391, Ashland, Kentucky 41114.

Finally, my deepest thanks to my husband, Wayne, a fine photographer and storyteller in his own right, who has made a lifetime commitment to the mountains and to me.

Loyal Jones, a native-born teacher and scholar of Appalachian studies, warns that in Appalachia "we are still trading our real treasures—values, religion, songs, land, essence—for new and untried things, without knowing that what we lose may be irreplaceable. It behooves us to make shrewd trades, like our horse trading forebears. Else we shall awake one day to find that what our fathers and mothers cherished is but a memory or a fading image on old photographs." Earl Palmer's photographs capture those cherished memories and fading images.

Introduction

One of the most ambitious photographic projects in American history was being widely publicized in 1905, the year Earl Palmer was born. Edward Curtis had begun *The North American Indian,* a project that consumed Curtis's whole life, resulted in twenty published volumes of photographs, and started a still unfinished critical controversy about the relationship between photographs and reality. According to Christopher Lyman's study of Curtis, Curtis set out to document "the vanishing race" of the North American Indian but succeeded in reinforcing the mythological "imagery of Indianness."[1] To achieve the desired impression, Curtis frequently posed his subject, provided costume and props, and retouched photos to remove elements of acculturation and modernity. The project provoked controversy about whether his photographs were ethnographic documents or creative art.

Lyman believes that much of what has been produced as documentary photography is highly subjective, including many of the acclaimed Farm Security Administration photographs of the 1930s. He argues that to point out their subjectivity is not to challenge their importance as documents but rather "to clarify *what kind* of documents they appear to be after close inspection of the evidence surrounding their creation."[2]

After explicating the context for the production of Curtis's photographs, Lyman concludes that what photographers frequently document, especially in a large body of work, is an *attitude* or attitudes that are powerful parts of the photographer's cultural environment, just as Curtis's photographs of "Indianness" documented an important part of his environment.

Like Curtis's photographs of American Indians, Earl Palmer's photographs of Appalachian mountain people are not ethnographic documents. They are not documentary photographs. But they are significant and revealing cultural documents. To appreciate Palmer's photographs, we need only look at them. To understand them, we need to ask why they are significant, what they reveal, what kind of cultural documentation they provide, particularly what attitude or attitudes about Appalachia they reflect. The answers to these questions lie in the relationships among Palmer's personal life, his attitudes toward photography and writing, his vision of Appalachia, and the interplay between commerce and culture.

PAST AS PROLOGUE

> People robbed of their past seem to make the most fervent picture takers. . . . Everyone who lives in an industrialized society is obliged gradually to give up the past.
>
> —Susan Sontag

When Earl Palmer was growing up in Straight Creek Hollow, a mining camp in eastern Kentucky where he was born in 1905, he was unaware of Edward Curtis and his work on the American Indian. Nevertheless, in his approach to photographing Appalachia in the years after 1905, Palmer was comparable to Curtis. Like Curtis, Palmer wanted to capture in photographs his perceptions of a people, his own people in the mountains, his own imagery of Appalachianness. Palmer has said: "I don't photograph the city or the seashore. I'd be lost out west or at the seashore; I wouldn't know how to go about taking pictures there. The only thing I know is I was born here in these mountains and that's all I know. I don't know anything else but that—the mountains and their people and their way of life that they lived is all the glory I want for me" (PSP 10-86B).

Palmer's approach to photographing Appalachia and his sense of what constitutes Appalachianness have been the result of many forces in his life. Some of these forces have been personal—the result of an Appalachian childhood, kinship ties, his early education, and his philosophy about how to live one's life. Other influences have come from his professional life as a mountain storekeeper, banker, and free-lance photographer. His perceptions of mountain life have been influenced largely by a set of cultural attitudes about Appalachia that developed in the late nineteenth and early twentieth centuries. These cultural notions center on Appalachia's isolation, the picturesque qualities of the region, and her rugged, self-sufficient people and their traditional folkways.

When Earl was born in Straight Creek Hollow, part of the mountain region had already begun a transition from a subsistence, agrarian society to a culture of town-dwelling industrial workers. Earl's father, who died when Earl was less than a year old, was a part-time coal miner and owner of a small dog-and-pony circus that traveled through the mountain coal communities. Earl's mother, widowed and hard pressed to make a living in her small store, had little to pass on to Earl but stern values of hard work, a moral life, and the necessity for education. Earl says, "Mother was a slam-bang, hard driver and the driving didn't appeal to me." When she sent him down the mountain to live with a foster family and attend school, he went willingly. But he spent his summers on his mother's small farm "busting clods of dirt." Earl seems never to have forgiven his mother for refusing all her life to tell him anything about his father, how he died, or even where he was buried. This missing piece of his past still makes him say in anguish, "I'll take that one with me."

If Earl's early memories of his mother are bittersweet, he expresses only fondness for his foster parents, David and Martha Lewis. His foster father, a carpenter and Civil War pensioner, taught Earl to live off the land. "My foster father took me to the woods often. We'd go in the spring and cut beech trees for that inner cambium, you know, that's so sweet you can chew it. I had an early love . . . was raised up, born into the woods, in moonshine country." Earl's foster father may have given him his love for mountain land, but it was his foster mother who set him on his photographic journey. As Earl loves to tell it, she helped him save the signatures from twenty-seven Arbuckle coffee containers to redeem for a simple camera when he was only seven. He was bitten forever by the shutter bug.

Inspired by the romantic and glamorous figure of his long-lost father (and also by his mother's dirt clods), Earl often ran away from home in the summers of his adolescent years to join circuses passing through the mountains. Even now, in his eighties, he attends a performance by a traveling circus every year. "The Lewises and the gypsies raised me," Earl says. "Mother gave me away." Earl's memories of the circus gypsy camps are of flickering fires, wily horse traders, and moonlight dances. "Those gypsy girls were graceful and pretty, I thought then." To Earl's way of thinking, he was "indelibly stamped," perhaps had genetically inherited "a strain of gypsy blood in my veins," a trait that has made him forever restless (a self-styled roaming cameraman) and unafraid of a strong personal style in photography and writing.

The wellspring of Earl's talents for self-expression may have been his gypsy blood, but he discovered and developed those talents through his schooling. From his childhood days, Earl was an avid reader, storyteller, and speaker, interested in the power of words and poetic expression. He remembers that his teachers always asked him to read aloud and perform recitations and he gladly complied: "I want the jaybird, she called me, to read that. . . . She called on me to read and recite most of the time. I liked that." Even now Earl tells with gusto the stories he most loved from his childhood, stories that provide clues to understanding the body of his photographic work.

One of many favorite and vividly remembered stories is from the McGuffey Readers on which he was weaned: A sultan wanted to buy some cloth from a boy working for his master. When the boy refused to cut the price, the sultan said, "Off goes your head." To which the boy replied, "I cannot change from what I've been ordered to do." The sultan then praised the boy and said, "A child of your caliber can be in my kingdom one day." For Earl, loyalty continues to be a virtue of the first order.

A similar message is at the heart of another story Earl tells often and with relish, one he calls "Stick To Your Bush." Earl tells it this way:

> The child went out one day to pick berries
> and his father said, "Son,
> now the other children will see larger berries,

and they'll be running from bush to bush
but you stick
to your ONE bush
and pick it dry."
And the child did
and he came in that night with a basketfull of berries.
An object in life
To stick to your bush.

Don't be nomadic,
A lot of people are too nomadic
Failures in life because of being a nomadic person,
moving from pillar to post that you've heard.
The still sow drinks the slop. [PSP 8-86B]

Earl tells these two stories often in discussions of his photographs, as though they are emblematic of his own purpose and persistence as a chronicler of mountain life. He is partial to the notions of stewardship and "being a good custodian" of what life offers. In photographing Appalachia, Earl believes he has "stuck to his bush," dedicating himself to the work for more than fifty years. This story also seems to express a latent confict Earl feels between his attachment for his native mountains and his impulse toward wanderlust. One of the clear messages of his photographs is admiration for the strong rootedness to place he attributes to mountain people.

When Earl was fifteen, he ran off in the summer with a circus but left it after a time and spent the remaining summer months at Berea College. When he ran away the following summer, his mother took action:

> Mother got me back, went down to the Lewises and got me back to the house and penned me up and said, "You're going to school somewhere." So Mother had a little country store, loaded up the delivery wagon with an old horse named Prince and we drove 16 miles to Barbourville, a little Methodist school. We drove halfway that night, spent the night in a little church stretched out on wooden pews. The next night we drove into Barbourville with some hams and shoulders mother had, some sidemeat, and she traded that in on my tuition and said, "Son, it's up to you." That was in 19 and 21. [PSP 8-86A]

Earl attended Union College in Barbourville for two years, where he found a mentor in George Murray Klepfer, a retired *Saturday Evening Post* editor. Klepfer wrote in Earl's memory book, "You'll always have hard work to do, Earl. The only way to make hard work 'easy' is to do it well. Realize all your own assets every day and cultivate the habit of happiness over other people's successes. Faithfully yours, George Murray Klepfer, 1922." Earl left Union after two years and spent a year at Eastern Kentucky Normal School (now Eastern Kentucky University) earning a teaching certificate. At Eastern Earl learned the fundamentals of photography and improved his writing. He credits his biology teacher, "Bug" Smith, with teaching him "the rudimentary things about developing and printing" photographs.

Finding money to attend school was difficult. Earl had a half-sister who sent him five dollars a month while he attended Eastern, but he still found it necessary to work during the summer months. One summer he worked in a coal mine at Black Mountain, Kentucky, where he learned much of the lore and lingo of mining that he uses in writing captions and stories to go with his photographs. His mining experience gave him a profound admiration for coal miners and the wisdom to see that coal mining was not his destiny. He remembers vividly his own brush with death in the mine's darkness:

> I was with a man who was killed one night, within six foot of him. Ben Higgins . . . who went to school with me incidentally. I worked on track. Ben was in charge of the track and I was his helper and we ran our trip into a safe hole, a heading. We was pushing the trip up—in mining you're not allowed to push anything, you can pull it, not push it—and it buckled and hit a set of side timbers and let a roof seam fall in. He was in the motor and I was in the supply car about two cars back. And when the hill seam fell in, I stopped the trip right there, and I was unharmed. The slate fall got him and not me. Oh, he lived about a month . . . but I didn't mine any more after that. [PSP 8-86A]

Instead, Earl earned his teaching certificate. But he found teaching jobs scarce and the pay low. So in 1923 he went to work for the A&P grocery chain. He rose quickly to a management position in 1926 in Evarts, Kentucky, just as the mine wars began erupting there that would earn the town the name of "Bloody Evarts." Earl worked at several stores in coal communities in eastern Kentucky during intense periods of labor strife and he tells gruesome stories of the violence he witnessed. He remembers his store clerk killed in front of his store in Evarts. He made photographs of a bullet-riddled car in which several law officers were killed in 1941 at the Fork Ridge Coal Company in Kentucky.

News clippings from the 1920s and 1930s and notices in A&P's own newsletter indicate that Earl quickly acquired more and more responsibility with the company. He spent a short time away from the mountains in Nashville, Tennessee, managing a store there in 1935. But he quickly returned to his native soil. When World War II began he was manager of a store in Middlesboro, Kentucky. It was there that a fateful incident occurred that gave rise to the body of Earl's photographic work represented in this book.

During the Depression years and the war rationing years that followed, Earl often befriended mountain people and coal miners and their families in the communities served by his grocery stores. It was not unusual for him to "find" fresh meat for them or to make supplies available willingly to moonshiners. Earl has always felt compassion for moonshiners; he believes they are the "salt of the earth" and have a right to "make a dollar or two to keep the wolf from the door or from having pups in the backyard." His compassion cost him his career with the store chain that had provided his livelihood for twenty years. In 1943 he was indicted in a federal court for selling sugar to a moonshiner. He vividly recalls the night he was caught:

> The night I delivered sugar to Ed Clark—he had a syndicate of stills—he backed a fox hunter's truck up to the back of the store with a canvas over it and we loaded the sugar. He paid me for 30 bags, about 300 pounds, hard [hardened sugar could not be sold in the store for ration coupons]. He started to go off, I started to close the door, I heard a crash—a black man was driving Clark's truck—then looked out there and two or three men jumped out of this little black car and were looking at the damage. The black man knew the dangers of transporting illegal sugar so he had rammed the car. They had the alley blocked on either end and caught me when I come out. . . . They follered Ed Clark from where he was moonshining, followed his truck to the store, let him in the alley, then blocked it. I said, my God, how deep are your rivers. That black man had rammed that car, spun it around, and went on down Cumberland Avenue into the night with his sugar. So next morning federal marshals came to the store to question me and I said, "I'm an employee of A&P, I can't answer anything." Said, "We counted you with 30 bags." "Well, I didn't see anybody at the back door." I found out years later, there's an old, cheap house of ill repute butted up against the alley and they had taken a room there and could see as we put the sugar in the truck that rainy night, could see through the window. [PSP 10-87B]

The management of A&P disavowed any knowledge of Earl's activities, though he insists he worked at their direction to get rid of unsalable sugar. He was indicted on numerous counts of illegal merchandising but, according to his ironic story, worked a trade with the judge for probation in return for some bootleg whiskey. But what hurt more than the sentence was his feeling that the A&P management, to whom he had been loyal for twenty years, had been disloyal to him, had failed him. "Talk about mad . . . I got mad at the A&P officials who defrauded me when I was trying to help them get rid of sugar by moving it to the moonshine trade. You know, your loyalties are not easily given in life, if truthfully awarded to a person. . . . You don't subscribe loyalties and retract them—I don't."

So Earl made an important decision. He left A&P to run his own general store in Cambria, Virginia, a small community wedged between the Blue Ridge and Allegheny Mountain ranges. He says this was "the best move I ever made—it turned me loose on photography." Earl had already been working as a free-lance photographer for some years. He started selling photographs and stories to the Sunday supplements of newspapers as early as the 1920s and found both the income and the creative outlet satisfying. By the 1930s he was an enthusiastic photograher interested in improving his camera skills. In the mid-thirties, when he was living in Nashville, he met E.F. Carroll, who taught Earl much of his photographic technique. Earl learned about Carroll at a local camera shop where, he says, he was "praying with the Christians about the different cameras." Carroll, owner of Carroll Engraving Company and a photographer for Sears Roebuck, tutored amateur photographers in shooting and developing their photographs. It was from Carroll that Earl learned more sophisticated darkroom techniques and increased his sense of photographic aesthetics.

Earl credits Carroll with giving him the rules he has always followed for composing his photographs. He says Carroll told him "Earl, when you approach a scene, look at it, look behind it, particularly behind it, each side and walk around it. If what's behind it or beside it doesn't contribute to what you want, don't photograph it. Don't photograph a house dead on, show it at least has a side to it. Let nothing happen in the edge of your print, nothing going on out there." Earl believes that following these rules has given his work a signature: "A lot of people who know my work say they can tell my work from anybody else's because I don't have anything going on out in the edges. . . . I've always concentrated my work close in."

Earl also acknowledges the influence in these early years of photographer Joe Clark. Clark was born a few years before Earl in Claiborne County, Tennessee, near the Cumberland Gap and near Earl's home. When Clark migrated out of the mountains to Detroit as a young man, he began to sell photographs of mountain life to newspapers and magazines hungry for images of the "strange land and peculiar people" of Appalachia. Clark soon became a well-known photographer, a staff photographer for *Life* magazine, and ultimately the creator of twelve books of photographs, with such titles as *A Few Grains of Corn from the General Store, White Lightnin'*, *Tennessee Hill Folk,* and *Up the Hollow from Lynchburg.*

Earl was acquainted with Clark and impressed with Clark's success as a photographer of mountain subjects. Even a quick look at some of Clark's early photographs (as, for example, in *Tennessee Hill Folk*)[3] reveals Earl's debt to and kinship with Clark. The two photographers share much subject matter (plowing with a bull-tongue plow, mountain farmsteads, gristmills, moonshining), composition style, and sometimes even the same people (both photographers have pictures of Aunt Nora Treece; both were friends with and photographed author Jesse Stuart). But there are differences. Oddly enough, Clark has far more photographs of mountain stores than storekeeper Palmer, probably because Clark made many more interior photographs than Earl prefers to do. Clark (perhaps because of his Detroit experiences) is more willing to photograph the influences of modernity on rural mountain life, and less apt to concentrate on archetypal folk cultural traditions. One photograph reveals the divisions between these two photographers who are similar in so many other respects: Clark photographed a Tennessee hill family, clearly middle class, making music in their front yard, with one son playing an electric guitar and the other a set of snare drums. Earl would not photograph such a scene because it would not fit his conception of appropriate mountain music (traditional, nonamplified string instruments).

Perhaps revealing some degree of competitiveness between the two photographers, Earl quickly points out that Clark "did advertising photography, which I've never done" and "his work closely resembles mine, but he was never a writer; I try to put words and pictures together." But Earl never hesitates to mention Clark among his photographic mentors.

When Earl returned to storekeeping in mountain communities in the late 1930s, after his sojourn in Nashville, he began to take photographs of the people and places and lifestyle he most admired: the rural, self-sufficient life of many mountain people that was giving way to industrialization, commercialism, and relative urbanity even as he captured it on film. The parents of his first wife, Alice, whom he married in 1934, epitomized the serenity and self-sufficiency he so admired in rural, mountain people. He made a series of photographs of the Bowmans on their farm near Berea, Kentucky, and declares they were "solid people." He speaks of his father-in-law with such reverence that it seems Robert Bowman became a second surrogate father (with foster father David Lewis) for the father Earl never knew. As Earl describes his father-in-law, his respect for Bowman's rural wisdom and elegant economy of living are clear. Bowman exemplified the traits in mountain life for which Earl would make visible metaphors.

Another of the early subjects that helped shape Earl's particular approach to photographing Appalachian life was the preacher and buggy maker, Winton Bolton. According to Earl, Bolton made horse-drawn buggies "right under the pinnacles" of what is now Cumberland Gap National Historic Park. Earl photographed Bolton in various stages of buggy building—carving a fallon (the curved part of a wheel), making the floor and sidings of the buggy, forging iron for a buggy part, standing beside a finished buggy (pp. 95-97). Earl, who was already selling photoessays to newspapers, recognized the commercial and historical value of recording a craft process in serial photographs. He has continued this habit throughout his photographic career and thereby increased the usefulness of his collection to historians, folklorists, and other students of the processes of traditional culture in Appalachia.

In typical Palmer fashion, Earl found Bolton interesting and admirable not only for his skill as a craftsman but for the principles he espoused and his mountain eloquence. Bolton was a Missionary Baptist preacher as well as a buggy maker, and Earl has one striking photograph of Bolton presiding over a creek baptizing (104). Earl says of Bolton:

> I made a story on him. He was an advocate for a dry country; he didn't like whiskey. He spent his lifetime fighting the forces of the damage that whiskey can inflict on mountain people. And he was an old-time preacher. The story is told that he went to the cemetery one day and said, "Lord, I've brought John in to be with you." Said, "John and I roamed around together a lot when we were young, had many escapades as younguns." Said, "I loved him in life and love him in death," and said, "Lord, I'm going to leave him with you tonight." [PSP 10-87B]

Whether the story is apocryphal or not, it became one model for Earl's own dramatic and sentimental oral and written style.

During a period of rapid change in the economy and culture of the mountains, Earl astutely realized the timeliness of recording an old-time preacher and buggy maker like Bolton. The last of the old-time loggers caught Earl's attention too and he photographed not only steam sawmills and logging operations powered by horses, but the haggard faces of the "wood hicks" and the accouterments of their trade—their tools and their clothes (63-66).

Looking for subjects for photographic stories brought Earl into contact in these early years with some influential persons and significant institutions in the history of Appalachia. He made his first trip to visit the Frontier Nursing Service, founded by Mary Breckinridge, in the 1930s. FNS nurses traveled on horseback to bring health care and midwifery to the mountain people of eastern Kentucky. Earl became a good friend of Mary Breckinridge and her nurses and took some remarkable photographs of the nurses going about their work, which he sold to the magazine *New York Lying-in Hospital* and to a publication produced by the Belgian government. When the war years came, Earl provided the nurses with scarce and highly prized cigarettes and chocolates from his store in Middlesboro. When Mary Breckinridge published her book *Wide Neighborhoods* about this pioneering mountain health service, she asked Earl Palmer to do the cover photograph.[4] Earl says, "Mary Breckinridge was instrumental in my getting lots of pictures of mountain things I wouldn't have gotten save for her." In these early days Earl also traveled to Caney Creek Junior College (now Alice Lloyd College) in Pippa Passes, Kentucky, and has both photographs and pleasant memories of the time he spent with the students.

Savoring the success he was having as a free-lance photographer and seeing his career with A&P coming to a close as a result of the sugar fiasco, Earl took a correspondence course from the New York School of Photography and received a certificate from them in 1943. This became a pivotal year for Earl. He left A&P, moved to Virginia, and started his own business. He now felt even more confident of his abilities as a photographer. The "mom and pop" store he operated with his wife gave him more time to pursue photography and his new home in the Blue Ridge mountain section of Appalachia gave him new subjects. The only negative note was the loss of much of his early photographic work in the move. Earl does not know what happened to most of his pre-1943 photographs.

Earl prospered in Virginia, building a solid business and a solid reputation in the community that earned him six terms as mayor of his small town. In his roles as storekeeper, local politician, bank board member, and civic group activist, Earl came to know more and more mountain people and often served as their advocate in times of crisis or distress. He helped more than one person who was in trouble with the law over illegal whiskey distilling, worked for tax relief for the poor, helped secure free eye care and other health care for those in need. All this work made Earl a trusted friend to many in the region and opened doors for photographs otherwise hard to obtain.

Earl's move to Virginia and his decision to pursue photography more vigorously coincided with the postwar boom in automobile travel and tourism, the growth of popular photographic magazines (*Look, Life*), and an intense interest in the American past, traditions, and local culture that seems to follow all major wars in which

America participates. In a scenic region opening to unprecedented numbers of tourists, this intersection of cultural forces offered many opportunities for free-lance photography: national magazines, travel magazines published by every major automobile company, newspapers interested in regional cultures, postcards and calendars promoting tourism, and publishers of regional books all offered outlets for Earl's work.

Earl's photographs and stories about the region quickly earned him a berth as a regular supplier of mountain material to *Scenic South*, a magazine published by Standard Oil Company (Kentucky Division); *Dodge News*, published by the Chrysler Corporation; *People and Places*, published by De Soto; and to *Travel Magazine* and *Mountain Life and Work*. Throughout the 1950s and 1960s, most of his work went to these publications. His photographs and stories about the mountain south proved so popular that at least two of the magazines did special feature stories about Earl himself.[5] One of these features, in *Dodge News* in 1955, said this:

> A great share of gorgeous photography that you see in magazines, in displays, and as backdrops for advertisements is created by "traipsin' photographers"—men and women to whom the call of the outdoors is irresistible, and to whom the camera is an art medium. Typical of these is Earl Palmer of Cambria, Virginia, homespun philosopher, nature lover, and chronicler of mountain life in America today. A camera fan since he was eight [seven, according to Earl] years old, Palmer decided upon photography as a vocational pursuit only a few years ago.
>
> Now 49, Palmer owns a small, crossroads general store, but he breaks his "storekeepin" frequently to traipse off through the Great Smoky Mountains to "shoot" beauty and human interest with his camera. Palmer needs no other reason than his own artistic bent to pack camping and photo equipment into his car, turn the store over to his wife, and take to the open road.[6]

Earl's photoessays for these travel magazines covered such subjects as mountain mill-days, the preparation of regional foods, herbs and wildflowers and the medicines made from them, folk toys, quilting, broom-making, making apple butter, curing hams, hunting wild honey, and interesting places to visit in the mountains, such as the Cumberland River Gorge in Kentucky, the Blue Ridge Parkway, "Bloody Harlan," or the exhibition coal mine at Pocahontas, Virginia. As Earl's skills and reputation grew, so did requests for his work. He regularly provided photographs and stories for the Metropolitan Newspaper Syndicate and National Geographic called on him for assistance with a book on herb medicines, *Nature's Healing Arts*.[7] Earl's work also appears in books on railroading and on moonshining, and in a study of the C&O Canal.

Earl's work on these projects took him all over the Appalachian region and introduced him to the famous, the not so famous, and even the infamous among mountain residents. One of the famous, who became one of Earl's dearest and most admired friends, was the Kentucky writer Jesse Stuart. They met in 1953 when

Standard Oil commissioned Earl to do a story on Stuart and make photographs of him (20). Thereafter they exchanged letters and visits, and Stuart often used Earl's photographs of him for his book jackets. Among Earl's prized possessions is a copy of Stuart's book *Taps for Private Tussie,* in which Stuart wrote: "To Earl Palmer, camera genius, who photographs a region for the outside world. With all good wishes, Jess Stuart."

Another of Earl's cherished possessions, a wooden replica of the famous Mabry Mill on the Blue Ridge Parkway, was a gift from Newton Hylton, "the finest mountaineer I ever knew," he says. Earl met Hylton in the late 1940s when exploring and photographing the Blue Ridge Parkway and its environs. Hylton typified the Appalachian mountaineer to Earl. He was a subsistence farmer, a blacksmith, a leather tanner, a banjo maker and player, a woodcarver, a wheelwright, an herb gatherer, a man of few dollars and few words but a man of enormous dignity. Hylton worked as a blacksmith for Ed Mabry in the 1930s and built a new wheel for the National Park Service restoration of Mabry Mill in the 1940s. A 1976 park service publication about the Blue Ridge Parkway described Hylton this way:

> Out in the blacksmith shop, busy pumping the hand bellows, "puttin' the fire" to his forge, is . . . Newton Hylton. In 1956, at 84, Uncle Newton worked a complete season in the shop, 8 hours every day except Monday. Cars make him "seasick," so he walked 6 miles to and from work.
>
> Making some horse shoes, he remarked, "These here shoes won't never see a horse, I don't reckon. The ladies use'm to hang behind doors. Men folks use'm for pitchin' horse shoes." And then in a tone that means both modesty and pride he'll say, "I can't get along like a young feller, but I don't slight my work none." Then his hammer will strike the glowing iron in just the right way and in just the right place.
>
> Old soldiers, and old mountaineers as well, eventually fade away. Mr. Hylton, whose tart humor and generous good will is embodied in our "Uncle Newt" [a mythic folk character used in the guidebook to explain, in dialect, local place-names and mountain lore], passed on to his reward in 1958.[8]

The National Park Service, like Earl, saw Newton Hylton as the quintessential Appalachian mountaineer; they explain that their "Uncle Newt" character "was born out of love and admiration for the mountainesque local color he represents."[9]

But if the Park Service felt it had captured Hylton's spirit in verbal depiction, Earl was less sure it was possible. "Nothing I could say would really tell you who Newt Hylton was," Earl says. That may be why he felt it necessary to record Hylton in depth on film (3-15). There are probably more photographs of Hylton in Earl's collection than of any other single subject. And it seems fitting that the young man Earl is now tutoring in photography and attitude, "to take my place in the annals of things," is Hylton's great-grandson.

In addition to the famous and not so famous, Earl has known and developed a fondness for a few of the more notorious inhabitants of the mountains. Thomas

Jefferson Cupp, for example, was an old-style moonshiner who regularly packed a pistol and who died after falling in a mountain creek during a liquor delivery. Though Earl has known some moonshiners who were addicted to alcohol and prone to violence when drinking, he believes they have generally been honest men making a living the best, or perhaps the only, way they knew how. Earl is intrigued by the mystery of moonshiners, their betwixt-and-between status. To Earl moonshiners represent that "tolerated margin of mess" identified by folklorist Barbara Babcock-Abrahams, outside the boundaries of the normal social order but necessary to it.[10] Moonshiners, he says, are part of the "warp and woof" of mountain life.

Earl's photographic journeys throughout the mountain region quickly earned him a reputation as the "Blue Ridge Mountain's Roamin' Camera Man," a title he uses to adorn his business stationery. He spent what time he could spare away from his store traveling the highways, but mostly the byways, of Appalachia from the late 1940s until the 1970s. To his way of thinking, "the charm of the countryside is off the mainstream—people feel it's incumbent to paint and fix up if they're on the main road." As a way to find appropriate subjects for his photographs and background material for his stories, Earl often made his first stop in a small mountain community at the local general store. His own storekeeping experience told him that the storekeeper would know the local scuttlebutt because, as Earl says, "the all-wise storekeeper lends an ear as if hearing stories for the first time." He had perfected this practice himself, which has resulted in the vast store of local knowledge he possesses.

To win the trust of persons he hoped to photograph, Earl has traded on his own gregariousness and good humor, his identification with mountain people from his own roots, and generosity. Uncomfortable with formality, Earl says of his expeditions, "I've never gone city-like to 'em—I go in jeans. I take little things with me to trade and, if they've got anything to sell, I buy, unquestioning of price. I never bargain with a mountain man for anything he has to peddle." With this philosophy, Earl has amassed a now valuable folk art collection, including many items seen in his photographs—ox yokes, baskets, chairs, brooms, the Mabry Mill model made by Newt Hylton, and even a complete "coffeepot" moonshine still. (All these artifacts are now on permanent display at Virginia Polytechnic Institute and State University.)

Earl also swaps and collects oral traditions as readily as artifacts. In a memory as precise as his camera, he has collected colloquial sayings, anecdotes, stories, full-blown tall tales, and a host of other mountain wit and wisdom in his travels. Like a mountain stream tumbling over a rocky precipice, he can mesmerize you with the volume, speed, turns, and twists of his talk. Every photograph evokes a story, in which Earl can recount in vivid detail the encounter that produced the photograph or some related anecdote. He can recite effortlessly from memory nearly every poem and moral fable he has ever read or heard, and every caption he has ever written for his photographs. Earl believes he has tried to record faithfully in his speech and writing what he calls "the language of our people, the lingo, the nomenclature, I would say. I like to put down what they said. I don't embellish it. I like to keep it native." But, he admits, "If they didn't say it exactly, I try to envision what they might have said, so that in my writing I picture what they deleted."

Earl appreciates how much he has profited from the willingness of his mountain neighbors to be photographed and written about for commercial publications and public exhibitions of his work. He has never been interested in maintaining aesthetic distance between photographer and subject. Instead he has formed enduring friendships based on reciprocity with nearly every person he has ever photographed. Today he is often in contact with the second or third generation of a family he photographed years ago. Earl attributes these lasting relationships to his unstinting commitment to the people he has photographed, to the recognition and help he feels he has given in return for fascinating photographs. He honestly boasts, "I've always disarmed mountain people by being kind and considerate and promising, 'you help me and I'll help you. You'll have pictures of this occasion.' And I've never in any instance left a man without some sign of my having been there. I've always kept the promise to send some pictures back unfailingly—I've done that. So the pictures are scattered from here to Hades."

Keeping in touch with those he has photographed has given Earl proof that his work has often brought recognition or much needed help to families featured in his work. For example, about thirty years ago, Earl discovered some finely crafted baskets in one of his usual haunts, a mountain community store. He asked the storekeeper for directions to the home of the basketmaker (79-81). The storekeeper told Earl the baskets were made by a family who lived "up Turkey Cock Creek, but the road's so bad you can't get down there, Earl." But Earl resolved to get there somehow. As he tells it:

> I drove up to the county line. There was a huge beech tree there where I turned up a muddy road. There was one sump hole, a mud hole, and I could only get the car so far before it stalled. So I walked in. The father was a moonshiner who looked at me quizzically, so I told him what I wanted. It was a family with three girls, named after the Dionne quintuplets. They were very cooperative. And the story was first published in *Dodge News*, then the Metropolitan Newspaper Syndicate, then *Scenic South*. It created an insatiable demand [for baskets] for them to supply. And it's a true story that it made it possible for one girl to go to college. [PSP 6-87A]

Earl also recalls a photoessay he published about a mountain woman who cured and sold hams in her country store[11] (67). She had a lucrative local business, but after Earl's story about her, she had orders pouring in from Maine and Florida and Pennsylvania. "One man down in Florida was so thankful for her hams that he said, 'I'm going to send you a hog rifle, an old time rifle,' and he did. Said he was a gun collector and wanted her to have this gun, just thanks."

By the 1970s, many of the travel magazines for which Earl worked had stopped publication. Their demise, coupled with Earl's own fatigue with assignment work and his advancing age, made him turn to exhibition photography. With exhibitions, he could travel less and his work could be seen by more people in his own region, from whom he could receive immediate, personal reaction to the photographs.

Just as Earl was considering slowing down his pace, retiring from storekeeping, and doing local and regional exhibitions of his photographs, he was devastated by the death of his wife, Alice. Her death after more than forty years of a warm and companionable marriage sank him into a bout of depression that lasted two years. Earl feels he might never have worked again if not for the love and help of his friends, including Evelyn Chrisman, who became his "good wife" in 1981. As Earl returned to work—both photography and part-time work in a local grocery store—and neared the age of eighty, he discovered a new audience with an insatiable appetite for his photographs and stories of an Appalachia he had known for more than fifty years.

Earl's reentry into an active life coincided with the growth spurt in what some have called the "Appalachian studies industry." The social upheavals of the 1970s spawned a cultural identity movement in Appalachia that resulted in academic programs in Appalachian studies at colleges and universities in the region, the formation of new organizations and associations devoted to Appalachian advocacy, and an explosion of interest in Appalachia in the arts and in the media. An important part of this social movement included building the record of Appalachia's past as prelude to planning for its future. Earl's own life and experiences as well as his photographs supplied some of the missing past and he found himself swept into the rising stream of Appalachian interest.

At an age when many people are "put on a shelf," as Earl says, he is busier and more in demand than ever. His photographs now hang in colleges and universities, banks, hospitals, town halls, state and national parks, restaurants, a mountain vineyard, and even a funeral parlor. He has been honored by receptions and awards, including the Laurel Leaves Award given for outstanding contributions to Appalachia. He still regularly fills requests for photographs for book jackets, newspaper articles, and magazines. Television commentator Charles Kuralt found himself "on the road" to Earl's house for consultation and, of course, photographs. Students and scholars and other admirers make regular pilgrimages to the "Palmer estate" as Earl jokingly calls his home.

To ensure the continuity of his accumulated wisdom about photography and Appalachia, Earl in recent years has taken Newton Hylton's great-grandson, Dale Belcher, as his protégé. The young man accompanies Earl on his photographic jaunts, serving as driver and companion and devoted disciple. Earl, in turn, gives Dale camera gear, tips on technique, and a vast tradition of lore about Appalachia. He says he has chosen Dale as a worthy successor because he is "pure mountain."

Earl is pleased but undaunted by his success, which he feels is the natural result of what he calls "the magic of believing."[12] Earl's philosophy is simple but fervently held: you can attain whatever you desire in life if you believe in it, if it is "conscionable," and if you are a good steward, a good custodian of what you attain. Earl quotes a Biblical passage in which Jacob desires striped cattle, an apparent impossibility. But Jacob believed God when he instructed him to take limbs from trees and strip their bark in stripes and place them near the animals' watering place. The cattle conceived before the striped limbs and brought forth cattle "ringstraked, speckled, and spotted" and Jacob himself waxed exceedingly rich from his wondrous venture. If Jacob could get striped cattle, Earl has had no trouble believing a mountain boy from a coal camp with no formal photographic education could come to be a well-known, well-loved, and admired photographer of traditional Appalachian culture, attaining his wildest ambitions. Earl sums up his life this way: "I'm essentially a mountain man, a mountain photographer, and I profess no other life than that." And Earl himself waxed exceedingly rich—in the fullest sense of that word—from his wondrous venture.

CONJURING APPALACHIA

> Our imagery through whatever medium shows us what we and our culture want to see.
>
> —*Christopher Lyman*

How does Earl define what it means to be a mountain photographer? Through the years he has developed clear and very firmly held ideas about the vision of Appalachia he wants to preserve on film and present to the public. His view of Appalachia, his native land, is a complex mixture of his own cultural experience and definitions of his culture conceived by writers and various agents of social change in the mountains, including educational institutions, the media, and the commercial marketplace for cultural artifacts, including his photographs.

Earl grew up in the midst of major social upheaval in the mountains. He was what anthropologist Victor Turner would term a liminal person, on the threshold between the fading agricultural world and the booming industrial world of the eastern Kentucky coalfields.[13] He had a foot in each world, working on his mother's small farm and mining coal. He prepared himself for the changes coming to Appalachia by getting an education, learning photography, and taking up a professional career with a national chain of grocery stores. Earl anticipated what Jack Kirby concludes about Appalachia in his book, *Rural Worlds Lost*. The premodern life that still existed outside the mining town in Earl's youth "was dying. Paved roads at last arrived, along with the automobile. The little stores disappeared. Older children, then entire families drifted away, usually out of the highlands altogether. Those who remained lived by cash, the pickup truck, and the Piggly Wiggly."[14]

Like many mountain residents, Earl adapted to the changes and prospered, but he lamented the scarring of the land and the people in the wake of too much, often uncaring, modernity. According to Ron Eller and Kirby and other recent writers on

Appalachia, by the 1930s much of the Appalachian world in which Earl lived presented "a tragic portrait of postindustrial ruin and agricultural dislocation."[15] Earl could see this "tragic portrait" daily across the counters of his stores in numerous mountain communities as he traded and commiserated with families from the coal camps and local farms, the unemployed, and those who had no other business than moonshining or craft work to sustain them. But in his photography Earl, for the most part, chose not to make portraits of tragedy but of the dignity he saw in the faces and lives of his mountain neighbors. He emphasized the mythos of preindustrial pastoralism and satisfying self-sufficiency over postindustrial ruin and agricultural dislocation for his portrayal of Appalachia, though he has photographed both. Earl chose to photograph what seemed to him "all that is native and fine," a choice that sounds simple but is a complicated exercise in the politics of culture.

David Whisnant, in a stimulating analysis of the cultural politics that have shaped perceptions of Appalachia, says ruefully, "To this day there are a thousand people who 'know' that mountaineers weave coverlets and sing ballads for every one who knows that millions of them have been industrial workers for a hundred years, have organized unions and picketed state and national capitols in pursuit of their constitutional rights, and have laid their bodies in front of strip-mine bulldozers and overloaded coal trucks. Or that, today, they shop at the K-Mart and Radio Shack, drive Cameros, and watch as much television as people anywhere."[16]

This emphasis on the folk cultural aspects of mountain life, described so well by Whisnant, Eller, and others, stems from a widely held but not widely understood belief that Appalachia occupies a cultural space more than a geographic space in American life. Popular notions about Appalachia have less to do with the realities of life in the region than they do with a mythology created about the region in American literature and popular culture. At the end of the nineteenth century, the southern Appalachians became a magnet for religious missionaries and social reformers, capitalists with money to invest in coal, timber, and related industries, and tourists, many of whom were writers interested in the local color of the region. While all of these groups figured in some measure in developing a mythology about Appalachia, most cultural historians credit the local color writers with widespread dissemination of the belief that Appalachia was an isolated, homogeneous folk culture unchanged by time or circumstance.[17] Writers such as Mary Noailles Murfree and John Fox, Jr., created a fictional Appalachian world in which the finest Anglo-American stock lived the life of our pioneer forebears, blissfully ignorant of the tides of change in the American mainstream or stubbornly unwilling to adapt to the changes. In any case, the mountaineer became entrenched in the American mind as the quaint embodiment of cherished American values: independence, pride, self-reliance, loyalty.

Although the concept "Appalachia" today carries even more cultural baggage with it, the static view of an unchanging Appalachia that was shaped by the local color writers still is a predominant part of American folklore about the mountain region. It is the image to which Earl had the most access and which most influenced his vision of Appalachia. Earl was growing up in the mountains just at the time the local color writers (and the folk art revival movement) were most influential.[18] He attended mountain schools just at the time those institutions were directed by persons who adhered to what has been called the "Anglo-Saxon thesis," a belief that mountaineers were Anglo-Saxon stock undiluted in America from the time of its earliest settlement. Earl's bookshelves even now are lined with early copies of John Fox, Jr.'s novels (*The Trail of the Lonesome Pine, The Little Shepherd of Kingdom Come)*, Muriel Sheppard's *Cabins in the Laurel* (which combined text with Bayard Wootten's photographs of the region), Horace Kephart's *Our Southern Highlanders*, and the works of other local color writers. Earl knows these fictional works and their images of Appalachia rather than current fiction written about the region or the revisionist criticism directed at earlier portrayals of mountain life, including critical studies of photographers such as Wootten and Doris Ulmann.[19]

Earl's vision of Appalachia has also been influenced by the stories and more particularly the poetry of his friend Jesse Stuart. Earl has one glass-enclosed bookcase that is a kind of shrine to Stuart's work. It houses signed copies of Stuart's books, packets of letters in longhand sent to Earl from Stuart's W-Hollow farm in Kentucky or his travels abroad, and Earl's memories of their musings together. (Stuart, like Earl, had a fondness for the "stick to your bush" story in the McGuffey Reader and often told it as an important influence on his life just as Earl does.[20]) Stuart has been characterized as a poet of the soil; perhaps nowhere is this more striking than in his *Man with a Bull-Tongue Plow.* This work, one of Earl's favorites, has been called "a celebration of man as 'bronzed figure' of the earth."[21] One of the poems in this volume expresses a point of view typical of Stuart that has become typical of Earl's photographic expression:

Walking among her hills, breathing her air;
Plowing her soil, feeling her wind and sun
That stream as gold and silver in the fair
Blue days of Spring and summer corn-field haze.
Surely, I am eternal mountaineer.
People have lived here all of their days,
Plowed the same soil, felt the same wind and sun.
They have been sons and daughters of the soil
And made their living by honest toil.
This flesh will not go down eternal dust;
At least, I proffer to the gods and trust
It won't—but I do think that his flesh must
Return to the earth eternal mountain dust.[22]

Many literary critics see Stuart's mountain farm as the central metaphor in his work, a symbol for a morally sound, preindustrial paradise that could have been America's inheritance. Instead, Stuart grieved over what he saw as moral decay and a decline in the quality of existence in the rest of the country. He wrote about what might have been and criticized what was. He was a poet with a purpose.[23]

It is difficult even for Earl to say how much Stuart influenced his own vision of Appalachia and the expression of that vision in his photographs. Because Earl already was making photographs expressive of mountain rurality before he met Stuart, it seems likely that he saw in Stuart a kindred spirit and wise teacher (one of Stuart's legendary roles); Stuart gave him greater confidence in his view of Appalachia, his writing, and his sense of purpose. Like Stuart, Earl sees the mountaineer as both historically real and eternally mythic. He has created a visual metaphor to match Stuart's literary one of Appalachia as the embodiment of a harmonious universe. As Earl himself says, "The mountain man—whatever he does or has done, wherever he's gone or amounted to—that's been the subject, that's been the song of my life."

One of the most apparent features of Earl's photographic collection is the consistency of his rhetorical vision, the strong argument he presents that Appalachia is a place of serenity that spawned a culture of remarkable self-sufficiency. His photographs of the Appalachian landscape are serene and seductive, enticing the viewer to see Appalachia as a land of majesty, mystery, and changeless beauty; mountain lands marred by industry or urbanization figure minutely in his work and are used primarily as evidence of the disharmony brought on by modernization. Earl's photographs of mountain people show men, women, and children who look into the camera forthrightly and comfortably, with faces that may be somber or wistful but seem unstressed or, more often, with smiles and decidedly good humor in their eyes and the crinkles of their faces. Earl's photographs of traditional mountain culture depict an industrious folk who live by their wits and by the work of their hands, who find pleasure and artistic satisfaction in the creation of largely functional artifacts.

Earl's visual metaphors for mountain life emerge clearly in his categories for organizing his vast collection of photographs. They range from seasonal landscape photos ("snow scenes," "spring") to vernacular architecture ("barns," "gristmills," "cabins") to material culture ("quilting," "handcrafts") to traditional customs and activities ("plowing," "gathering mountain herbs," "moonshining") to portrait studies of individual mountaineers (Newton Hylton, Thomas Jefferson Cupp). His photos also include some well-known regional residents such as dulcimer-maker Jethro Amburgey, writers James Still, Harry Caudill, and of course, Jesse Stuart. He has photos of Civil War monuments (a tribute to his foster father) and important mountain landmarks and institutions (Mabry Mill, Kingdom Come School, Hindman Settlement School).

Conspicuously absent or rare in Earl's photographs are urban scenes, contemporary architecture, nontraditional mountain industries and occupations, trailers, and satellite dishes—all of which, especially the last two, are ubiquitous in the mountains today. "If there is any modernization in a scene," Earl says emphatically, "I pass it up. Color and drama departed with modernization." Racial and ethnic minorities are also absent from the Appalachian scene he depicts. All these are elements that do not fit Earl's conception of Appalachia. He also avoids scenes of conflict, decay, disease, and death; these do not meet his definition of appropriate photographic material. He says, for example, he has never photographed hog-killing, a persistent Appalachian ritual, because he doesn't like to see anything being killed. And he will describe in graphic detail his memories of corpses stretched out on "cooling boards," care of the bodies, and other traditional funeral practices, but he never photographed them: "I don't picture grossly things."

Some of the photographs in Earl's collection, like some of Jesse Stuart's poems, focus on trouble in the mountain paradise—loss and grief brought on by modernization, moral decay, and disharmony between land and people. One photograph shows a forlorn little church sitting atop a strip-mined knob; another captures the desolate expressions of a haggard miner and his pregnant wife standing before a closed mining office; still another photograph leads the eye to a sign in front of a strip mine with the chilling message, "If you're found here tonight, you'll be found here in the morning." When Earl talks about these pictures, he says they show "the dark side of the mountain" and calls them "too ugly, too informative."

Earl's inner vision of Appalachia is the touchstone by which he makes judgments about what to photograph, how to make the photograph, how to print it, and what to say about it. He chooses images he describes as "packed with Appalachia" and rejects those that "don't look the part." At one mountain festival he attended recently, he refused to photograph the musicians, insisting "the fiddlers were not exemplary, not representative of mountain musicians in my book, didn't fit. They didn't look the part, had collars and ties on, didn't stir my imagination any." Describing a beautiful young woman he had photographed, Earl remarked, "I wouldn't put her around an apple butter kettle because she doesn't look like she belongs at the end. I try to use mountain people that look the part, that they know what they're doing." Settings for photographs also must look right. When preparing to shoot a moonshiner at work at his still, Earl checks to see "if there's any debris around there in the form of tarpaper, roofing rolled up, or anything that doesn't look the part, doesn't look like it belongs there. I'll very carefully remove that." While such discontinuities are part and parcel of the documentary photograph, they are complicating intrusions when one is trying, as Earl does, to create mythic icons in a body of photographic work.

Earl searches for human subjects who fit his image of the mountaineer: "A man who lives down to earth with the sod, who measures life in terms of the soil, still a spawn of the earth so he actually belongs there and doesn't leave it." For Earl there is a clearly demarcated line between celebrating a person "born in overalls" and denigrating mountain people and their life style. He says emphatically, "I've never asked a mountain person to put on ragged clothes or patches—those people on 'Hee-Haw' make me gag. I try to portray a person in his best light. I've always stuck to realities."

Earl chooses his realities carefully, however, to comply with his own deeply held belief that "if you photograph unsubstantial people you get unsubstantial photographs." To illustrate this axiom he tells a story of accompanying a friend, a public health nurse, on a visit to the Smoky Mountains to see a Cherokee client of hers. Earl went with high expectations of taking some wonderful photos of a strong and noble Cherokee woman. He left without snapping a frame when he saw her as a "fat squaw in dire poverty" who seemed to him complacent about her plight and her squalor. The ignoble savage is not part of Earl's rhetoric of Appalachia and this evidence had to be rejected. Earl also points out that he won't take photographs of poor people in the mountains "getting the dole. I might hurt someone."

Some might chide Earl for consciously ignoring important economic and social realities in Appalachia. But for him, although these situations may be real, they are not constitutive of Appalachianness, of what is authentic in Appalachian culture. This is what Earl means when he says, "I like authenticity if I can get it, whatever it takes. AUTHENTICITY."

When Earl says "whatever it takes," he means it quite literally. Earl works in what photographic critic A.D. Coleman calls "the directorial mode," in which the image-maker has the right "to generate every aspect of the photographic image, even to create a 'false' reality if required."[24] Daniel Lindley identifies this approach to photography as a rhetorical stance in which the photographer works as mythic hero: "The photographer consciously works at creating a reality . . . of his own making. . . . He sometimes looks at the world and actually sees it changed by his manipulations. . . . He is a creator of his own particular genesis, making things over to suit an inner vision."[25]

Earl uses many of the techniques common to pictorialism, a photographic movement that peaked in the 1920s but remained influential in the 1930s when Earl was first starting to make photographs. Although Earl rejects the soft-focus technique so common to much of early pictorialism (evident in the Doris Ulmann photographs of Appalachia made in the 1920s and 1930s), he follows many of the pictorial practices used by one of his mentors, Adolph Fassbender. Fassbender was a prominent German photographer who fled the growing Nazi regime in prewar Germany, but not before the Nazi government had confiscated most of his photographic plates to retrieve the platinum, gold, and silver on which the photographs were cast. Fassbender came to the United States and started over. He published a book of photographs in 1937 that has shaped Earl's approach to photography even to the present day. Earl keeps Fassbender's book in a secret hiding place and reveals it like a sacred text only to the most serious viewer.

Fassbender's book, *Pictorial Artistry: The Dramatization of the Beautiful in*

Photography, was given to Earl as a gift from his store clerks when he made the decision to leave Kentucky for Virginia and a career as independent store owner and regional photographer in 1943.[26] In the preface, Fassbender contends that "the dreamy diffusion period [in pictorialism] has passed," but he advocates the use of other pictorialist practices and a pictorialist philosophy outlined by the early English photographer, Henry Peach Robinson (1858): "Any dodge, trick, and conjuration of any kind is open to the photographer's use. It is his imperative duty to avoid the mean, the bare, and the ugly, and to aim to elevate his subject matter to avoid awkward forms and to correct the unpicturesque. A great deal can be done and very beautiful pictures made by a combination of the real and the artificial in a picture."[27]

Fassbender's photographs in the book are mostly rural scenes of Bavaria, Nova Scotia, and Pennsylvania. Each is accompanied by Fassbender's own description of the scene (in romantic prose), a statement about the composition techniques he used to capture it, the technical problems he encountered, and the fundamental data on the shooting and developing of the photograph (type of camera, lens, film, exposure time, etc.).

Fassbender's work became Earl's textbook for teaching himself how to be a photographer. It cemented his commitment to regional photography focused on folkways.[28] Earl's captions for his photographs have much the same flavor as Fassbender's descriptions of his photographs and Earl records the same technical information that Fassbender provided. He used ideas from Fassbender's book in lighting, composition, and developing. Some years later Earl attended a workshop conducted by Fassbender in Roanoke, Virginia, and went on a photographic field expedition with him.

With Fassbender's influence, it is not surprising that Earl uses the sharp focus more common to the documentary tradition that emerged in the 1930s in combination with such standard pictorialist practices as posing, the use of props, and retouching.[29] The effect of Earl's use of these techniques is twofold: It gives the body of his work a remarkable consistency of vision and at the same time creates complex ambiguity for the viewer of the photographs. How much in the photographs documents reality in Appalachia or even the reality of Appalachia's past? How much has been created according to the photographer's inner vision of Appalachia?

The semiotician Roland Barthes tells us that understanding a photographic message depends upon our cultural knowledge of the codes the photographer imposes on the photographic image. These codes, which represent the rhetoric of the photograph, carry with them connotations that help us read the cultural meaning of the photographed image as the photographer intends. Barthes identifies six connotative codes (trick effects, pose, objects, photogenia, aestheticism, and syntax) but, for now, we need only be concerned with three that have the most bearing on Earl's work: trick effects, pose, and objects. Using any or all of these procedures in creating a photograph, Barthes remarks, "allows the photographer to *conceal elusively* the preparation to which he subjects the scene to be recorded."[30] Earl himself says, "The simplest pictures I've ever taken tell a simple, straightforward story without embellishment *that can be noticed.*"

Trick effects, for example, may not be detectable in a photograph to most viewers and so may convince viewers that what they see is simply what is or what was in front of the camera. As Barthes explains, trick effects "utilize the special credibility of the photograph [as a picture of reality] in order to pass off as merely denoted a message which is in reality heavily connoted."[31] Earl unabashedly uses an array of trick effects in his photographs to preserve what he feels are the correct connotations for Appalachia. If he photographs an example of vernacular Appalachian architecture, say a log cabin or a gristmill, that over the years has lost its roof or had its original roof replaced by a tin roof, Earl prints the photograph and then "fixes" the image. Using retouching pencils or sable brushes, he replaces the missing or the tin roof with a shake shingle roof to match, if not the original, at least his concept of the correct original (21). He eliminates the denotations of decay or modernity and provides instead a connotative code for the enduring and timeless quality of Appalachianness. As Earl says, "I never pass an abandoned house; I embellish it."

Probably the most frequent code Earl uses is the split rail fence, a logical choice because these fences are indeed widespread in the Appalachian landscape. Earl has interjected split rail after split rail onto scenes where no fence existed (21, 36). For him, rail fences have come to connote the essence of Appalachia. To him they seem to be ever-present remnants of an earlier time in the mountains when material culture seemed more consonant with the natural order of things; that is, rail fences were made by hand from local, natural materials and constructed in accordance with the natural contours of the land. No wonder Earl insists that "rail fences, now, there's something you can treat." Earl is conscious, too, that the rail fences and other stereotypical Appalachian metaphors he adds to the photographs operate as cultural codes. Describing a photograph of a quilting party, Earl points out a rail fence in the background and says, "If I can move those quilting frames in front of a rail fence, now, the rail fence will locate my story. That's the reason I had that fence out there. And a log cabin will locate my picture; that's the connotation."

Pose, the second of Barthes' codes of connotation, carries meaning for us because of a store of attitudes about what certain body poses are supposed to convey in our culture. Edward Curtis, for example, used pose as a central means of creating his imagery of Indianness. He often posed Indians in warlike stances (and in warrior's costume) long after the western Indians had given up warfare. In Lyman's critique of Curtis he charges that "subjects presented themselves to the camera more as what Curtis imagined they *should* be than as what they *felt* or actually were.[32] It is only in the photographs from the end of Curtis's career that the subjects "appear to have more to say about their presentation before the camera so that the resulting images are much closer to the ideal of cooperation between the photographer and subject which we think of in contemporary documentary photography . . . allow[ing] the subjects a decent chance to express themselves as they chose."[33]

The poses of human subjects in Earl's photographs reflect some middle ground between Curtis's extremes. They combine what Earl finds appropriate to his image of Appalachianness with a strong feeling that the subjects themselves have participated in deciding how to look and what to do in front of the camera. In the majority of Earl's photographs of mountain residents, the subjects do not look at the camera but are absorbed in the activities in which they are engaged—basketmaking, chairmaking, quilting, moonshining, and so on. One senses that the activities, if not routine, are at least common and familiar parts of their lifestyle and that they are pleased to be photographed doing what they enjoy. This away-from-the-camera pose gives Earl's photographs part of their documentary appearance because it seems to put the photographer in the role of ideal observer who "happened to see" this scene of mountain life and capture it for posterity.

On the contrary, however, Earl just "happened to see" only a minority of the scenes that appear in his collection. He arranged for most of his quilting pictures after searching out a community where quilters got together weekly at a local community center. For his photographic session, Earl advertised locally that he would give small cash prizes for quilts in several categories at the next quilting gathering. With such incentives Earl was able to get photographs of women involved in the work of quilting, the conviviality of a shared "carry-in" (potluck) lunch, and the display of some of their most favored quilts (83-86). His photographs record truthfully and beautifully some of the small rituals and intergenerational qualities (87) of the quilting tradition in Appalachia. In documentary fashion, the women wear their ordinary attire and bring their food in whatever is at hand. But to read these photographs as documentary would be wrong, for pose is carefully controlled.

Earl spurns the fake costuming of the hillbilly television type, but he will use costume elements to attain the image he wants. Of the quilting pictures he says, "I always asked the women to wear bonnets. Working with magazines, I had to keep my story in the woods." "Keeping my story in the woods," Earl's euphemistic phrase for preserving Appalachianness to his own and his publisher's satisfaction, extended from the right look of the women (bonnets) to the right place for the photograph to be posed. Earl moved the quilting frames, the food, and the quilters out-of-doors and in front of weathered barns or sheds or rail fences. He admits, "That's a little improvisation right there. I had to keep my story in the woods."

Making apple butter, like quilting, is a mountain tradition as strong as ever in many communities today. Earl has fine photographs of the component parts of the traditional process—from stirring the apples in copper kettles to pouring it thickly into jars to testing its taste (107-10). (Earl notes, "Some people used to use drunkard drops, cinnamon candy that took whiskey off your breath, to keep the apple butter from looking punkiney [pumpkin-colored].") For some of these photographs he visited local apple butter stirrings he knew were going to occur; for others he arranged the photographic session. He says, "I have two kettles. I buy some apples, make some [apple butter], just for pictures."

Earl's motives for arranging events and choosing subjects sprang partly from his desire to be commercially successful with his photography. Selling photographs to travel magazines in the boom period of automobile vacations of the 1950s and 1960s, Earl lined up activities he thought would be uniquely Appalachian and attractive to tourists. Being commercially successful (i.e., published) as photographer and writer is a major criterion by which he measures his work and the work of others. He discounts criticism of his work by those who haven't had his commercial success, saying sarcastically, "The man who knows the most about photography and who can help you the most is the person who's never been published . . . ha! . . . listen, the cold steel is publication of your work. I don't consider a person to have arrived until his pictures have been sold and exhibited." Assignment work from the magazines also made it possible for Earl to pay models. This is how he awarded prize money for quilts or bought materials for a moonshiner to bring his still into peak operating condition to be photographed. Children figure in many of his photographs, about which Earl says, "I'd always carry children with me. I don't go without models." On occasion, the models included Earl's pet dog, Skippy.

Earl frequently manipulates the composition of the person and setting to be photographed to meet one of his aesthetic requirements: that his photographs give an impression of liveliness, even movement. As he composes, Earl devises ways to add life to what may photograph as "dull and lifeless." For example, in photographing his good friend Goode Rakes working at a still, Earl got Goode to give up his "inveterate rolling of gosh awful cigarettes" and substituted a more appropriate-looking pipe. As Earl explains, "He didn't smoke a pipe, but to make sure he did, I put some tobacco and then dampened it slightly so that smoke would curl up from his pipe while he smoked. And to make sure—ordinarily the moonshiner hides most of his smoke, because smoke is telltale—but to make sure about the smoke, I doused a few wet leaves on the fire, just a few wet leaves to show something was going on around there. Otherwise, the picture would be devoid of life."

Some of Earl's most striking photographs are portraits of individual mountain people. In these portrait studies, Earl uses pose in a way that corresponds to what Susan Sontag calls the "normal rhetoric" of the portrait. "Facing the camera," Sontag writes, "signifies solemnity, frankness, the disclosure of the subject's essence."[34] Earl's photographic portraits of Newton Hylton and his now nearly classic portrait of the miner, Teach Slone, and his child (71, 72) bear out Sontag's observation. In general, portraits of individuals do not interest Earl, unless they are emblematic of Appalachianness in the way Newton Hylton and the miner and his child are for him. In a clear statement of his taxonomy of significance in photographs, he says, "Thousands of my pictures are people, just people. 'Earl, you've been coming over . . . the baby is two months old, I'd like a picture.' I have those set aside as junk, a whole cabinet. I won't repair to 'em because they won't add anything. The photographs I have then are log cabins, rail fences, apple butter making, walnut cracking, forestry with horses, coal mining, mountain scenery." Unsymbolic poses are just "junk," snapshots as opposed to photographs.

Sontag goes on to say that frontality of pose also suggests the reciprocal bond between photographer and subject. To get the people to pose, the photographer has had to gain their confidence, trust, and friendship.[35] This reading of the photographic pose is perhaps nowhere more apparent than in Earl's portraits of various moonshiners he has known who face the camera unafraid with pistols visible. Earl has won the trusting gaze in front of his camera from a legion of moonshiners over the years because he has been careful not to turn them in to the law (in fact, he provided photographs for the defense in the trials of at least two moonshiners), has kept secret the location of stills, and has given his friends the option of concealing their identities through fictitious names when requested. These photographs bear witness to Earl's firm belief that in moonshining, like anything else, "a mountain man has a right to make a living any way he can."

The third category of signification Barthes identifies, the posing of objects, gives meaning to a photograph because "the objects are accepted inducers of associations of ideas . . . they are veritable symbols."[36] In several still-life compositions, Earl has chosen and arranged objects both for their pleasing pictorial effect and for their symbolic associations with his sense of Appalachianness. In front of weathered boards so characteristic of rural outbuildings in Appalachia, Earl has photographed in one picture (79) a collection of Appalachian baskets to capture their intrinsic qualities of light, shadow, and texture and their symbolic qualities of Appalachian style and "handmadeness" (apparent in their various stages of completion). In another photograph (51), he artfully arranges a basket, two crockery jugs, and a gourd around the threshold of a worn and weathered log building, as if to suggest that someone just came to call and left some gifts of unmistakable Appalachian pioneer origins. These are obviously (and by admission) not "found" scenes of ethnographic significance but created scenes expressive of the photographer's conception of the essence of Appalachia. Intuitively Earl is following the dictum of photographer Minor White, who said, "One should photograph objects, not only for what they are but for what else they are."[37]

Even in naturally occurring scenes, Earl often places posed objects that enhance the "correct" reading of the photograph. He explains that "in photographing a moonshine still, I'll probably take along some fruit jars to make sure I've got some there and I'll also have with me some crocks and little jugs. I'll introduce those into the filming. I want to make sure he's in business. A lot of moonshiners have nothing but a tub there. . . . Well, in order to put him in business, to look like I've got something happening down there, I'll use these." (Earl's store building served as a mini-museum of mountain artifacts he collected over the years, from which he drew objects to enrich the effects of his photographs.) So strong is Earl's inner sense of objects with the right look of Appalachia that he would not photograph the moonshine still of Tom Jeff Cupp, the man whose portrait epitomizes the moonshiner for Earl. Earl says, "He was very elusive of his still. I didn't see it until I nearly left Kentucky. He didn't have a good mountain-made still, more improvised, not a true turnip-bottom still. It was thrown up of oil barrels and things . . . not conducive to my photography."

Barthes concludes that the photographer uses trick effects, pose, and posed objects to control the viewer's interpretation of the photograph. He concludes, "The reading [of a photograph] closely depends on my culture, on my knowledge of the world. If one photographs Agadir [Morrocan port devastated by an earthquake in 1960] in ruins, it is better to have a few signs of 'arabness' at one's disposal, even though 'arabness' has nothing to do with the disaster itself. Connotation drawn from knowledge is always a reassuring force—man likes signs and likes them clear."[38] Earl tries to ensure the right reading of his photographs by including signs of Appalachianness drawn from the romantic mythology about the region so pervasive in American culture. "If a photograph doesn't speak," Earl says, "I work the negative over."

Earl achieves most of his photographic special effects in his basement darkroom where he mixes chemicals, chooses papers and developing techniques, and highlights with delicate sable brushes. He points out how he has highlighted the face of Tom Jeff Cupp to bring out his beard and nose ("I can rebuild a face like an undertaker"), how he "repaired" broken planks on the image of a covered bridge and added a rail fence to hide a pile of debris in front of the bridge (36), where he has added clouds and snow on roofs for dramatic effect ("All those are ploys I use to get what I want"). He uses what photographer Jerry Uelsmann has called "in-process" discovery; rather than previsualizing the completed image at the time the shutter is clicked, he creates much of the image in the darkroom. Uelsmann says that photography created in this way is "alchemy, it is magic" and the darkroom is "a visual research laboratory, a place for discovery, observation and meditation."[39] Earl admits, "it's easy to get lost in the darkroom." Earl may be described as an "image midwife" (Uelsmann's term), helping latent images of his vision of Appalachia come more fully into being. As Earl himself says, "I create life."

Because of his skill in the darkroom, Earl is often called on to restore old photographs for friends or organizations. Some old and rare photographs in his collection he acquired as copies of restorations he has done. One such photograph that he cherishes shows his beloved Newton Hylton fashioning the gristmill wheel for the National Park Service restoration of Mabry Mill on the Blue Ridge Parkway in the 1940s. To Earl this photograph of the small hero behind the scenes of this famous landmark is more authentic of mountain life than the literally millions of photographs made of Mabry Mill annually by tourists. The old photographs he lovingly restores are talismans by which Earl tries to take possession of the past more fully, to recapture his lost Appalachian world.

Like most photographers, Earl rejects photographs that do not meet his exacting standards, discarding many more of his darkroom creations than he keeps. Laughingly he explains that sometimes an image goes awry because of darkroom gremlins: "There's boodles or something in the darkroom. . . . I ran into one yesterday, so I had to reject that picture. My reject pile is three times larger than what I put out."

Adding, subtracting, restoring, and rejecting keep Earl in control of the photographic world of Appalachia he presents to the public, his rhetoric of Appalachia. Lindley, in his analysis of the persuasive intent in Walker Evans's supposedly documentary Farm Security Administration photographs of the 1930s, notes that even Evans used such techniques to help resolve the paradox of photography: "What [photography] does—at least black and white photography does—is to set up a paradox which contains, on the one hand, strict and exact limitations built into film and paper, and, on the other hand, an almost infinite possibility of choice given the photographer about how the finished print shall actually look. The photographer is both controlled and in control. One way for the photographer to keep some degree of control is by careful manipulation of materials and the photographic process."[40]

Photographers have other means of control over their creations outside the chemistry of the darkroom. Sequencing of photographs and adding text (e.g., captions or stories) to accompany the photographs extends the photographer's control over interpretation. In both processes the whole is greater than the sum of the parts; that is, the interpretation is even more tightly controlled than in any individual photograph or groups of words alone. Barthes contends that the implied connections in a sequence of photographs or in the message of a text or caption "loads the image, burdening it with a culture, a moral, an imagination."[41] Earl puts together sequences of photographs and writes elaborate captions or short essays for his photographs largely to suit his imagination and cultural world view and to satisfy the demands of the commercial markets for his material. He is less concerned with historical facts in these efforts than he is with evocation of emotion and preservation of the image of Appalachianness. He voices this concern when he says, "I sometimes put a compilation of pictures I've taken somewhere else [i.e., in different places or times] into a sequence to feed it"; or, in showing a picture of moonshining, "I've written half a dozen captions around that darn thing—every time I change it."

One illustration of Earl's fictional serializing occurs in a feature he wrote in recent years on mountain herbs and their use in folk medicine, one of his favorite topics and one on which he is knowledgeable. (He has a collection of photographs of plants with curative powers, used for what he calls your "ails, feelin' pores, and jest to'ables"). For this story, he arranged a group of photographs made in widely divergent years and at several locales in the mountains and wrote a text suggesting, by its use of present tense, that the photographs represent some contemporary Appalachian reality.

Writing about his photographs has been only slightly less important than photography to Earl. He believes the combination of words and images has made him successful, though he offers disclaimers about his writing ability whenever he discusses his work. "Now, I do a great deal of writing in sometimes lengthy captions on the print as well as added text on such events as apple butter and molasses stir-offs, quilting, moonshining. . . . In fact, editors all across our land acclaim my verbiage, rough feathered though it may be, a valuable adjunct to the prints."[42]

Earl's writing style combines the breeziness of magazine journalism with sentimentality of diction, a penchant for dialect, and older syntatical structures more reminiscent of literature and journalism in his formative years of the early twentieth century. Of someone long dead, Earl will write, "he has departed from the halls of this life, his earthly work over," or he will describe spring as "a season perchance conceived in Eden." He writes of his father-in-law, Robert Bowman, that when he needed a gun stock, he got his wood and "then whittled said gun stock hisself." Earl declares, "I like sentiment, I like to write with feeling."

Earl's sentimental prose is as old-fashioned as the scenes he loves to photograph. His writing gets its old-timey sound in part from word usages that are specific to his culture and often archaic and from his use of formulaic commonplaces, a characteristic of traditional mountain diction that is more akin to epic poetry than to prose. From old-style mountain speech, Earl chooses such traditional words as "rived" (for making shingles), "paling fences," "homemade remedials," and "cobbling" (for shoes). He nearly always uses formulaic diction for description—earthy man, nectar-sweet, fire-hot, flint-hard, all-sufficient. Appalachian scholar Cratis Williams and others have pointed out that the use of such compound words or redundancies is common in mountain speech, reflecting its largely Anglo-Saxon heritage.[43]

Earl's professed fascination with Anglo-Saxon speech and his fondness for poetry and its rhythms, all apparent in his own speech and noncommercial writing (as, for example, in personal letters), account for his reliance on such usages in his captions and essays. They form the metaphorical base for his thinking and have become for him fundamental and second nature, as he explains:

> I've thought all along that a night is storm-tossed or star-blessed, or the morning is dew-pearled. . . . I've never used the words beautiful, awful, or mighty in my writing. I've never reached for superlatives. I've gone along the lines of . . . so spring is here . . . across the meadow the meadowlarks sing . . . boisterously the blue-coated jays and robin-redbreasts express themselves as pleased with the infant season and they sing their cantatas as if there may never be a season so opportune—and if you can't explain spring in such a fashion as that, then you can't write about it. [PSP 8-86A]

As he tries to do in his photographs, Earl uses his writing to preserve in a verbal form those same qualities of Appalachianness he captures in his visual images. He often uses dialogue in captions to give them a sense of immediacy and to preserve the sound of Appalachian dialect as he perceives it. For example, in the caption for his famous miner and child photograph, he reconstructs a conversation he had with the miner: "Name's Teach Slone and this boy is my son . . . with that sawed off shovel of his'n he can load about as much coal as I can in this pencil-stripe mine."

For Earl, photographs embody narratives of experience more than selected moments of experience; they are stories he needs to tell you. His verbal narratives are localized in their particulars, preserving traditional names for places, things, and events. He uses local place names (Turkey Cock Creek, Dead Mare Branch, Runnet Bag Creek) for their poetic qualities and to preserve them as part of the region's linguistic heritage. For the same reasons he writes of double-bitted axes, wood hicks, pencil-stripe mines, coffee pot stills, grit bread, bee coursing, jolt wagons, and trace chains.

In some lengthy captions, Earl gives detailed descriptions of processes or events he thinks have disappeared from the mountains, are disappearing, or have undergone radical change. One of his early photographic subjects—old-time, horse-powered mountain logging—compelled him to write detailed captions about the logging procedures and the men who did the logging because he was watching logging practices change even as he recorded them. Knowing that moonshining is a fascinating subject for the uninitiated and being privy to its secrets, he has tried to preserve in captions some of the lore of likker (73-76) as well as the look of this mountain subject so steeped in mystery and mythology.

His early photograph of Preacher Winton Bolton performing a river baptizing also produced a lengthy caption reflecting Earl's concern that old-time preachers such as Bolton and significant mountain rituals like river baptizing have all but disappeared. He writes, "Winton Bolton was a member of a fast disappearing group of oldtime preachers the likes of which we do not see anymore, now that a modern day time has exacted such a toll of things traceable to our forebearers."

Earl's narratives, like all stories, embody his values and attitudes, particularly the way he views Appalachia in relation to the rest of the world. In his captions, he clearly identifies what he sees as characteristic of mountain people. He describes their "proud and self-sufficient heritage," "the versatility of old-time mountaineers," and sees a tradition-bound culture in which "children learn the old arts early." Earl asserts that mountain people "have an inherent interest in what follows" (after death), their "affairs are not overly pressing," and that the "stingy soil" of mountain farms make it necessary "to run a little likker to jack up a hillside economy." The culture painted by Earl's captions resounds with tradition, isolation, self-sufficiency, deep religious beliefs, close ties to the natural world, seasonal cycles, family, and local community.

Through captioning and the interplay between images and text, Earl gains additional control over the interpretation of meaning in the photographs, especially their meaning as symbols of Appalachianness. Lest the viewer be tempted to read into an image of a deserted cabin the qualities of decay, emptiness, and irrelevance, Earl's words imbue the cabin with warmth, memory, and significance. Turning again to his most widely-known photograph of the miner and his son, the boy's ragged clothes, the primitive mining tools, and the necessity for the father to dig his own coal and use his small son as a laborer could lead the viewer to a multiplicity of interpretations about the cultural context for the photograph. But Earl's caption gives us his interpretation of the photograph's meaning: it is a story of mutual curiosity on the part of the photographer and the miner that drew them into the encounter and a story with a message about Appalachia. When the miner says his boy "can load about as much coal as I can in this pencil-stripe mine," the message is not about poverty but pride, pride in self-sufficiency, hard work with one's own hands, and pride in family across generations—all traits Earl believes are part and parcel of mountain people.

Although Earl takes a clear rhetorical stance in his writing, he only occasionally makes obvious editorial comments. His dislike for what he regards as unnecessary government intrusions into a traditional culture creeps into several captions. Lamenting the loss of Evie Shelton's cured hams, Earl writes that "people in government who know all there is to know about such doins enacted laws that called for both state and federal inspections. This killed Evie's business." Writing about Newton Hylton's work for the National Park Service in rebuilding Mabry Mill, he comments: "It is said he was paid 75 cents per hour for this monumental work." (Earl often says that when government agencies touch something in Appalachia, it loses its authenticity.) Earl's disdain for urbanity and the pace of modern life are as strong in his writing as they are visible in his photographs. In more than one caption he contrasts the lives of people "cooped up in canyons of steel and concrete in far-off cities" with the serenity he sees in mountain life. When he writes of traditional customs and practices that took time and patience, such as taking grain to mill for grinding, Earl bemoans that they have "long ago departed the scene of our mountains, victims of an age when people are too busy to await the slow but sure millstones to grind." This change of life's pace, he concludes, leaves one "to conjur' how busy can earthy man be."

If the acid test for success in photography for Earl is publication and exhibition, his major criterion for successful writing also is accessibility for a popular audience. Earl explains that in his writing "there's never been any attempt to be pedantic or ostentatious, if I might use those words. I've always written on the level of whoever was going to buy my things. I always wrote on the level of the reader, to give him a vicarious adventure that had provided me with a day of pleasure or a week of pleasure."

As he does with his photography, Earl works hard at his writing, reworking each caption or story until it has the right sound and message for him, but being careful he says, "not to write the blood out of it." Earl dislikes writing with "no veins and arteries in it" and big words "you have to twist around your tongue." These body-centered metaphors seem to reflect Earl's unspoken conceptions of writing; that is, that writing must feel organic and alive like vivid speech, that somehow words add the lifeblood to the static images in the photographs.

Historians, folklorists, and other scholars devoted to faithful rendition of culture may criticize Earl for fostering and fortifying romantic stereotypes about the region and for creating local color in photographs and writing. But Earl has felt obliged to beautify and idealize Appalachia because he is an artistic and commercial photographer, not a scholarly observer of the culture. He uses photographs, as Kaufman suggests in his discussion of the sometimes arbitrary relationship between photographs and history, "in a rhetorical mode which shows no allegiance to history."[44] One may wonder about the role of editors, who seldom question the reliability of photographs or photo-stories in the same way they question the reliability of written documents. And some may worry about the image of Appalachianness Earl's photos present in popular publications for an audience unfamiliar with mountain culture and uncritically receptive to the imagery. But critics might keep in mind the caveat that it is a privileged historical and cultural viewpoint that gives some a way of knowing, better than earlier or less schooled observers could, how truthful images are, especially images of earlier times.[45]

AS IF APPALACHIA

> Photography never lies; or rather, it can lie as to the nature of the thing, being by nature tendentious, never as to its existence.
>
> *Roland Barthes*

Earl's approach raises some fascinating questions that are at the crux of the longstanding critical debate about truth and falsity in visual images, a debate discussed by Sontag in *On Photography:* "The consequences of lying have to be more central for photography that they ever can be for painting, because the flat, rectangular images make a claim to be true that paintings can never make. A fake painting (one whose attribution is false) falsifies the history of art. A fake photograph (one that has been retouched or tampered with, or whose caption is false) falsifies reality. The history of photography could be recapitulated as the struggle between two different imperatives: beautification . . . and truth-telling."[46]

Evaluating Earl's photographs as clustering solely at one or the other end of this spectrum, from beautification to truth-telling, misses too much of the rich ambiguity his work presents. To admire or dismiss his photographs only as photographic fictions or artistic creations, or to accept them uncritically as documentary photographs traps us in what Allen Sekula calls "binary folklore"—the interpretation of photographs as art *or* documentary.[47] Sekula chides critics for persisting in these convenient dichotomies and calls for a more sophisticated approach to interpreting photographic ambiguity.

How then are we to read what the Palmer photographs tell us about Appalachia? What sense can we make of their fascinating blend of fact and fiction? Mark Roskill and David Carrier in their recent book, *Truth and Fiction in Visual Images*, provide some effective guidance. Roskill and Carrier say that "visual images cannot be true or false in the sense that the propositions of science or mathematics are true or false, but they can be considered true or false, or come to seem that way, in the varying senses in which we ascribe truth to an account of a significant historical event or of a person's behavior; to a document such as a will with a series of signatures on it; and to a perspective on social and political values held in a particular period or community."[48]

Roskill and Carrier outline three versions of visual truth and identify three types of visual lying. Their schema is useful for examining Earl's photographs. An image is visually true if it (1) conveys a certain truth about the world, the way a map denotes the fact that the earth is round; (2) communicates some accepted or ready-to-be-accepted truth so that it contributes evidence to that effect, a visual marker of what happened on a given day; or (3) sums up and shows forth what is held to be true about people and things in either a general way or specifically for a time or place.[49]

By these criteria, there is no doubt that Earl's photographs give us a great deal of visual truth. They show us faces of people who live or have lived in the mountains; occupational and avocational activities that have engaged at least some mountain people over time; spatial and cultural aspects of the ways in which many rural, mountain people have lived on the landscape. They show us mountain people who have lived hard and others who have lived relatively well; people who are spiritually and culturally rich if sometimes materially poor. The power of the truth of these photographs is explained by James Agee in *Let Us Now Praise Famous Men*: "In a novel, a house or person has his meaning, his existence, entirely through the writer. Here [in photography], a house or person has only the most limited of his meaning through [the photographer]: his true meaning is much huger. It is that he *exists*, in actual being, as you do and as I do and as no character of the imagination can possibly exist. His great weight, mystery, and dignity are in this fact."[50]

Perhaps the most remarkable achievement of Earl's photographs is the rich array of folklife in Appalachia he has preserved on film. With the intuitive appreciation of a native son for his region's traditional expressive culture and with the acumen to realize the commercial market for images of folk culture, Earl, with no training as a folklorist, nonetheless has seen and photographed perceptively many well-known mountain traditions (basketmaking, moonshining, apple-butter making) as well as less known or nearly vanished traditions (buggy making, walnut cracking). At times, he has captured interesting traditions really by chance even in his tightly controlled images. In his photographs of the quilting party, for example, Earl has recorded, not by design, the practice of storing canning jars by inverting them over the palings of a fence. His photographs are a treasure trove for those interested in the region's folk cultural heritage.

Earl's photographs, however, are not true in a documentary sense if one accepts a common definition of the documentary approach: "A straight, simple, realistic technique uncluttered with visual aesthetics and avoidance of manipulation [of the image]."[54] But, if Earl's photographs are not documentary, are they then untrue? Do they constitute "visual lying?" Roskill and Carrier identify three categories of visual lying: (1) fabrication, or the creation of "impossible worlds"; (2) dissembling or shamming, the intentional falsehood of making things appear as they are not; and (3) pretense, which applies to visual images in the form of what can be termed "as if" representations.[52]

Earl's photographs clearly do not fit the first two categories of visual lying. He does not create an "impossible world," and he does not make his alterations on the positives or negatives of his photographs with an intent to deceive. He is forthright, even proud, in describing the photographic techniques he uses to maintain the integrity of his artistic vision of Appalachianness.

Like so much literary and visual art about Appalachia, Earl's photographs do fit the category of an *as if* representation of Appalachia. The concept is already well-known in Appalachian scholarship. Henry Shapiro in "Appalachia and the Idea of America: The Problem of the Persisting Frontier" points out that the local color writers of the late nineteenth and early twentieth centuries created a highly selective, fictional Appalachian world that emphasized the exotic, quaint, picturesque, and folksy aspects of the region. As Shapiro concludes, "Because it was more interesting, the 'as if' was preferred to the 'is' and came eventually to be identified as reality."[53] Echoing Shapiro, Appalachian poet Jim Wayne Miller ends his poem "How America Came to the Mountains":

> They [mountaineers] left the mountains fast
> and lived in Is, Illinois, for a while
> but found it dull country and moved back.
> The Brier has lived in As If, Kentucky, ever since.[54]

The reification rather than the reality of Appalachia has a long history among photographers and literary artists of the region. Doris Ulmann often asked her subjects to wear clothing of an earlier era and pull out spinning wheels no longer in use for her stunning photographs of mountain people. Her work became widely known and popular as illustrations for Allen Eaton's book, *Handicrafts of the Southern Highlands,* published in 1937. In the 1920s when photographs of the region were being used to drum up financial support for religious and social work agencies in Appalachia, Mary Swain Routzahn of the Russell Sage Foundation in New York had this public relations advice for mountain social reformers: "Perhaps in real life Lizzie Ann is no longer barefooted, but if we show a picture of Lizzie Ann wearing shoes and stockings, it is doubtful whether she will appeal so greatly to the hearts of those on whose gifts the work depends."[55]

Charles Alan Watkins, in his excellent critique of the highly successful book *Cabins in the Laurel* (published in 1935), notes that Bayard Wootten's photographs of Appalachia, especially in combination with Muriel Sheppard's text and captions, gave a skewed picture of the Appalachian region to the reading public. He says, "Wootten's photographs reveal that she had a . . . romantic vision of mountain life, but a large number of them, if they were divorced from Sheppard's text, would indicate a tremendous amount of poverty and want among the lowest groups of mountain society. Independently, the photos offered the raw material for a new moral position on mountain poverty, but instead, the pictures were randomly distributed in a text which stated that these people were not poor; they liked to live this way."[56]

In contrast to such photographers as Ulmann and Wootten, several photographers who worked for the Farm Security Administration during the Depression years (who have since become legendary) photographed what seems, at least, to have been the gritty realities of much of mountain life in the 1930s and 1940s. Walker Evans, Ben Shahn, John Vachon, Arthur Rothstein, and Marion Post Wolcott all made documentary photographs of various parts of the mountain region. In general, they focused on images that pointed to dire economic and political inequities in the region. Right after the Depression years, FSA photographer Russell Lee began work for the government to document the working conditions and life style of coal miners. The 4,000 negatives he produced were used in an effort to clean up the coal industry and reduce the number of strikes in the coalfields.[57] His photographs repeat graphically the blackened faces of miners, substandard housing, filthy children, and some of the more exotic pockets of Appalachian life such as snake-handling religious practices.

Only two of the FSA photographers echoed in any depth the more rurally romantic and mythic images of earlier mountain photography. One of Arthur Rothstein's first assignments was to photograph mountain life in the Shenandoah area of Virginia. He was charged with documenting a cultural community that was about to vanish with removal of local residents for the creation of the Shenandoah National Park. Marion Post Wolcott was a skillful landscape photographer who was often requested to shoot pastoral mountain photographs by the FSA director. She regarded such work, however, as "FSA cheesecake."[58] The work of the FSA photographers was about change rather than tradition.

Earl is very much a product of the same cultural forces that shaped earlier romantic writers and photographers. Although he has lived and worked his whole life in the midst of Appalachian realities (and has, in fact, on occasion produced photographs as unflinchingly grim as some of the FSA photographs), he has preferred the metaphorical *as if* representations of the region as a way of structuring and making sense of his world as a whole. Earl has been less concerned with changing Appalachia than with conserving it; he is more interested in continuity than change. His work expresses his concept of the eternal mountaineer rather than the modernized mountaineer.

"As if" representations, according to Roskill and Carrier, are inherently neither good nor bad; they generate a kind of "metatruth" or "metafiction" and must be judged against a more in-depth understanding of what is trivializing and dehumanizing with regard to a specific cultural context.[59] Even judged against the more sophisticated, complex, intellectully grounded picture of Appalachia available to us today, few would judge the Palmer photographs as less than an evocative vision of Appalachia or fail to see that the people of the photographs have been interpreted with admiration and tender regard by the photographer. Few could help but appreciate how fully the native artist has articulated for us his sense of his place and the spirit of his people. Earl has worn his camera like a badge of honor and used it as a tool for stewardship of *his* Appalachia.

In Jim Wayne Miller's poem, "Brier Sermon," a mountain preacher admonishes the people of Appalachia, saying:

> Our foreparents left us a very fine inheritance,
> but we don't believe it.
> I just want to set you down, gather you together,
> and read you the will![60]

Earl does believe it. He believes fervently that Appalachia has given him a rich inheritance and his photographs and stories of that heritage are his own gift to the future.

NOTES

1. Christopher M. Lyman, *The Vanishing Race and Other Illusions: Photographs of Indians by Edward S. Curtis* (Washington, D.C.: Smithsonian, 1982), p. 65. 2. Lyman, *Vanishing Race,* p. 148. 3. Joe Clark, *Tennessee Hill Folk* (Nashville: Vanderbilt Univ. Press, 1972). 4. Mary Breckinridge, *Wide Neighborhoods* (New York: Harper and Brothers, 1952), jacket illustration. 5. See "Traipsin' Photographer," *Dodge News* 20 (1955), pp. 4-5; "City vs. Country-cousin Vacations," *Dodge News Magazine* 26 (May 1961), pp. 3-7; for other published stories about Palmer, see "Meet Earl Palmer: The Traipsin' Photographer," *Appalachian South* 1 (Fall/Winter 1965), 16-17; Timothy Evans, "Earl Palmer," *Program of the Blue Ridge Folklife Festival* (Ferrum, Va.: Ferrum College, 1982), pp. 7-8; "Earl Palmer's Mountain Empire," *Virginia,* July-August 1985, pp. 59-63; and Dale Belcher, "Earl Palmer, The Mountain Photographer," *Mountain Laurel,* April 1987, p. 4.

6. "Traipsin' Photographer," p. 5. 7. Lonnelle Aikman, *Nature's Healing Arts: From Folk Medicine to Modern Drugs* (Washington, D.C.: National Geographic, 1977). 8. William G. Lord,*Blue Ridge Parkway Guide, Book Two* (Asheville: Hexagon, 1976), p. 177. 9. Lord, *Blue Ridge Parkway,* p. 110. 10. Barbara Babcock-Abrahams, " 'A Tolerated Margin of Mess': The Trickster and His Tales Reconsidered," *Journal of the Folklore Institute* 11 (1975), 147-86.

11.See Earl Palmer, "This is Country-Ham Country!" *Dodge News Magazine* 22 (1957), p. 6-7; also, Earl Palmer, "Copper Valley Hams Are Shipped Coast to Coast," *Spout* 13 (1958), pp. 2-5. 12. Earl derives this philosophy and takes his illustrations from a book by Claude M. Bristol, *The Magic of Believing* (New York: Prentice-Hall, 1948). 13. Victor Turner, "Process, System, and Symbol: A New Anthropological Synthesis," *Daedalus* 106 (Winter 1977), 61-80. 14. Jack Temple Kirby, *Rural Worlds Lost: The American South, 1920-1960* (Baton Rouge: Louisiana State Univ. Press, 1987), p. 122. 15. Kirby, *Rural Worlds,* p. 87. See also, Ronald D. Eller, *Miners, Millhands, and Mountaineers: Industrialization of the Appalachian South, 1890-1930* (Knoxville: Univ. of Tennessee Press, 1982).

16. David Whisnant, *All That is Native and Fine: The Politics of Culture in an American Region* (Chapel Hill: Univ. of North Carolina Press, 1983), p. 13. 17. See Henry D. Shapiro, *Appalachia On Our Mind: The Southern Mountains and Mountaineers in the American Consciousness, 1870-1920* (Chapel Hill: Univ. of North Carolina Press, 1978). 18. For a discussion of the educational and cultural activity in the mountains during Earl's youth, see Whisnant, *All That Is Native and Fine.* 19. See, for example, Charles Alan Watkins, "Merchandising the Mountaineer: Photography, the Great Depression, and *Cabins in the Laurel,*" *Appalachian Journal* 12 (Spring 1985), 215-38; and David Featherstone, *Doris Ulmann, American Portraits* (Albuquerque: Univ. of New Mexico Press, 1985). 20. See Jesse Stuart, "It's Still 'Stick to your Bush," ' *Mountain Life and Work* 46 (May 1970), 8-11.

21. J.R. LeMaster, Introduction, *The World of Jesse Stuart: Selected Poems,* by Jesse Stuart (New York: McGraw-Hill, 1975), p. xxi. 22. Jesse Stuart, *Man With a Bull-Tongue Plow* (New York: E.P. Dutton, 1934), p. 147. 23. LeMaster in *World of Jesse Stuart,* p. xx. 24. A.D. Coleman, "The Directorial Mode," in *Photography in Print,* ed. Vicki Goldberg (New York: Simon and Schuster, 1981), p. 489. 25. Daniel A. Lindley, Jr., "Walker Evans, Rhetoric, and Photography," in *Reading into Photography,* ed. Thomas F.

Barrow, Shelley Armitage, William E. Tydeman (Albuquerque: Univ. of New Mexico Press, 1982), p. 169.

26. Adolf Fassbender, *Pictorial Artistry: The Dramatization of the Beautiful in Photography* (New York: B. Westerman, 1937). 27. Arthur Rothstein, *Documentary Photography* (Boston: Focal Press, 1986), p. 3. 28. Fassbender has photographs of farmers working in fields using traditional agricultural methods, women engaged in craft work, and types of vernacular architecture. 29. Lyman, *Vanishing Race,* p. 70. 30. Roland Barthes, "The Photographic Message," in *Photography in Print,* p. 526.

31. Ibid. 32. Lyman, *Vanishing Race,* p. 65. 33. Ibid., p. 137. 34. Susan Sontag, *On Photography* (New York: Delta, 1973), p. 37. 35. Ibid., p. 38.

36. Barthes, "Photographic Message," p. 526. 37. Jerry N. Uelsmann, "Some Humanistic Considerations of Photography," in *Photography in Print,* p. 443. 38. Barthes, "Photographic Message," p. 531. 39. Uelsmann, "Humanistic Considerations," p. 447. 40. Lindley, "Walker Evans," p. 175.

41. Barthes, "Photographic Message," p. 528. 42. Personal correspondence, December 28, 1985. 43. Cratis Williams, "Subtlety in Mountain Speech XI," *Mountain Life and Work* 43 (Spring 1967), 14. 44. James C. A. Kaufman, "Photographs and History," in *Reading into Photography,* p. 198. 45. Mark Roskill and David Carrier, *Truth and Falsehood in Visual Images* (Amherst: Univ. of Massachusetts Press, 1983), p. xiii.

46. Sontag, *On Photography,* p. 86. 47. Allan Sekula, "On the Invention of Photographic Meaning," *Artforum,* January 1975, p. 45. 48. Roskill and Carrier, *Truth and Falsehood,* p. viii. 49. Ibid., ix. 50. James Agee, as quoted in *American Photographs of the Depression* (New York: Pantheon Books, 1985), p. 11.

51. Rothstein, *Documentary Photography,* p. 18. 52. Roskill and Carrier, *Truth and Falsehood,* pp. 81-86. 53. Shapiro, "Appalachia and the Idea of America: The Problem of the Persisting Frontier," *An Appalachian Symposium,* ed. J.W. Williamson (Boone, N.C.: Appalachian State Univ. Press, 1977), p. 45. 54. Jim Wayne Miller, *The Mountains Have Come Closer* (Boone: Appalachian Consortium Press, 1980), p. 48. 55. Mary Swain Routzahn, "Presenting Mountain Work to the Public," *Mountain Life and Work* 4 (1982), 29.

56. Watkins, *Merchandising,* p. 233. 57. Jack Hurley, *Russell Lee, Photographer* (Dobbs Ferry, NY: Morgan & Morgan, 1978), p. 122. 58. Sally Stein, "Marion Post Wolcott: Thoughts on Some Lesser Known FSA Photographs," in Marion Post Wolcott, *FSA Photographs* (Carmel: Friends of Photography, 1983), p. 9. 59. Roskill and Carrier, *Truth and Falsehood,* p. 88. 60. Miller, *Mountains,* p. 53.

The Appalachian Photographs of EARL PALMER

Captions are by the photographer except where enclosed in brackets.

Oldtime mountaineers were inherently proud and self-sufficient. The late Newton Hylton was of this breed, a tireless worker, good at anything he turned his strong hands and willing heart to. What a heritage he left for posterity! [Hylton died in 1958.]

Eternal Mountaineer

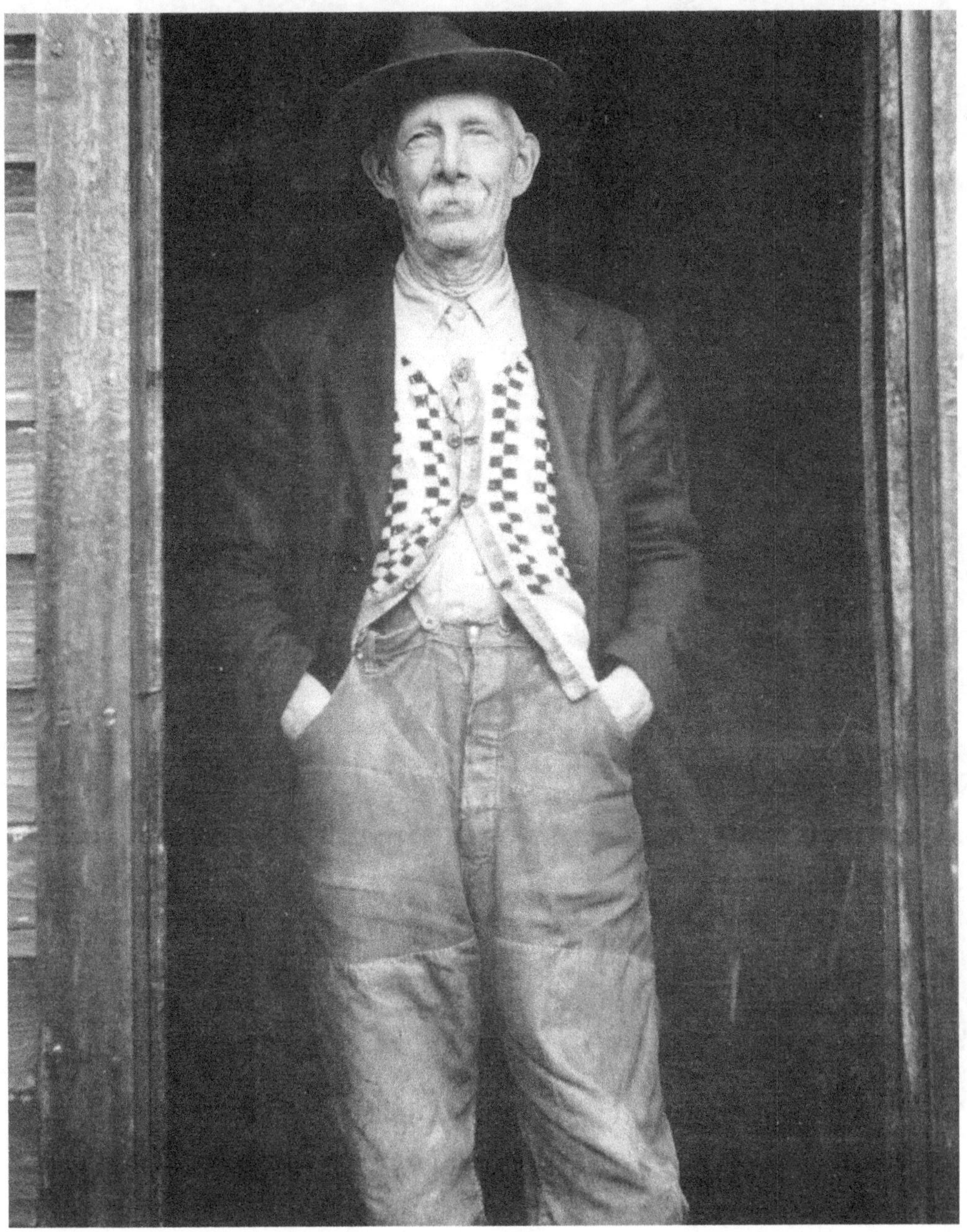

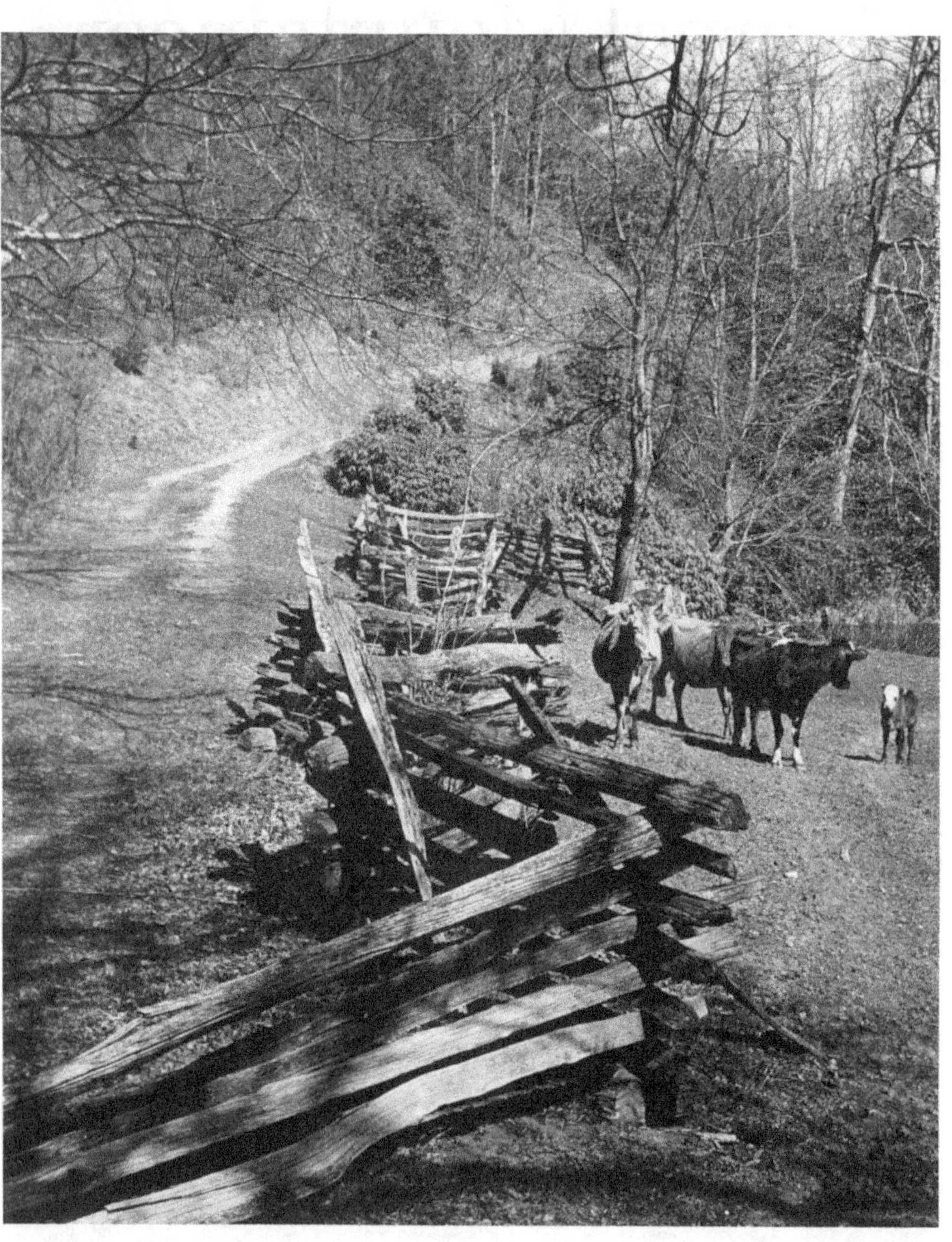

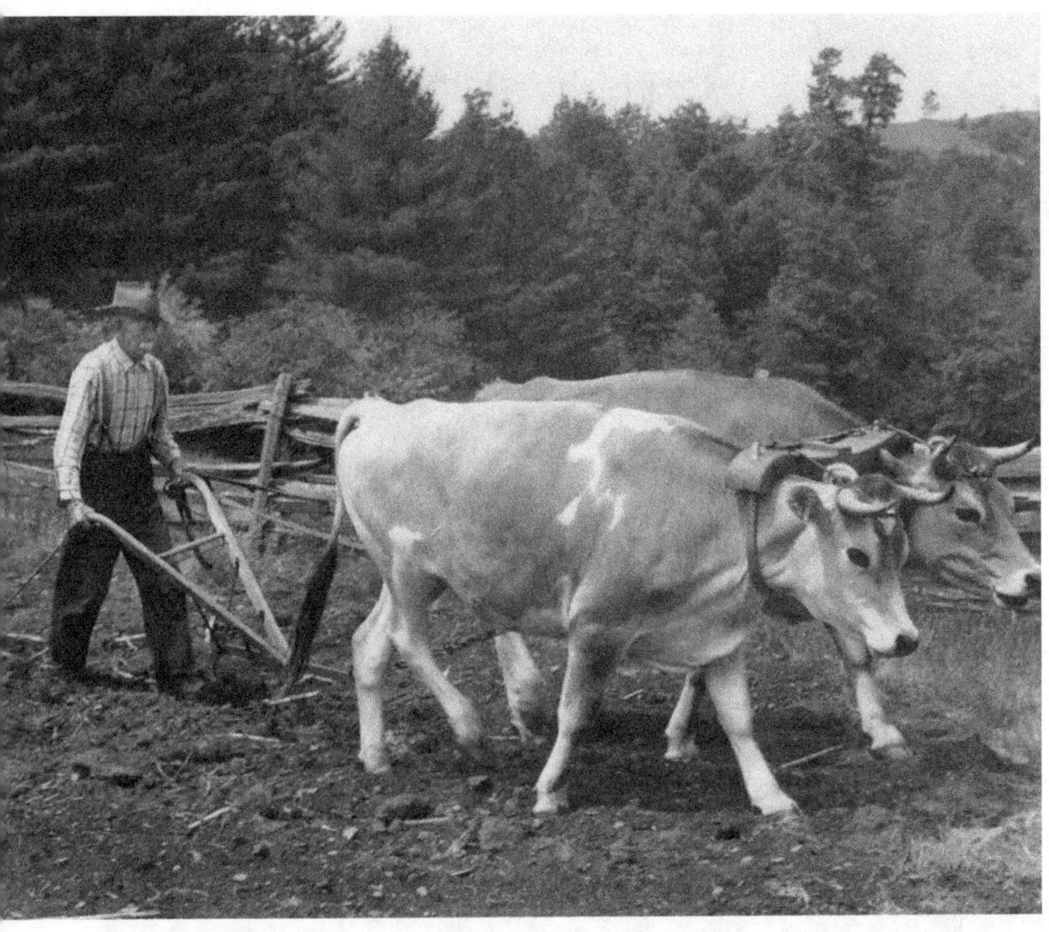

"Give me oxen any day for my plowin'," said Hylton. "Oxen are stronger and more steady than mules and not as cantankerous and honery. A mule will work for just so long, then kick the pants right off a feller first chance he gets." [*Opposite,* entrance to Newton Hylton's farm, Laurel Fork Creek, Virginia, 1944.] Although built in generations past, fences split from chestnut trees still worm their way uphill and down from high to lofty ridge and into the deepest coves to keep cattle from going astray.

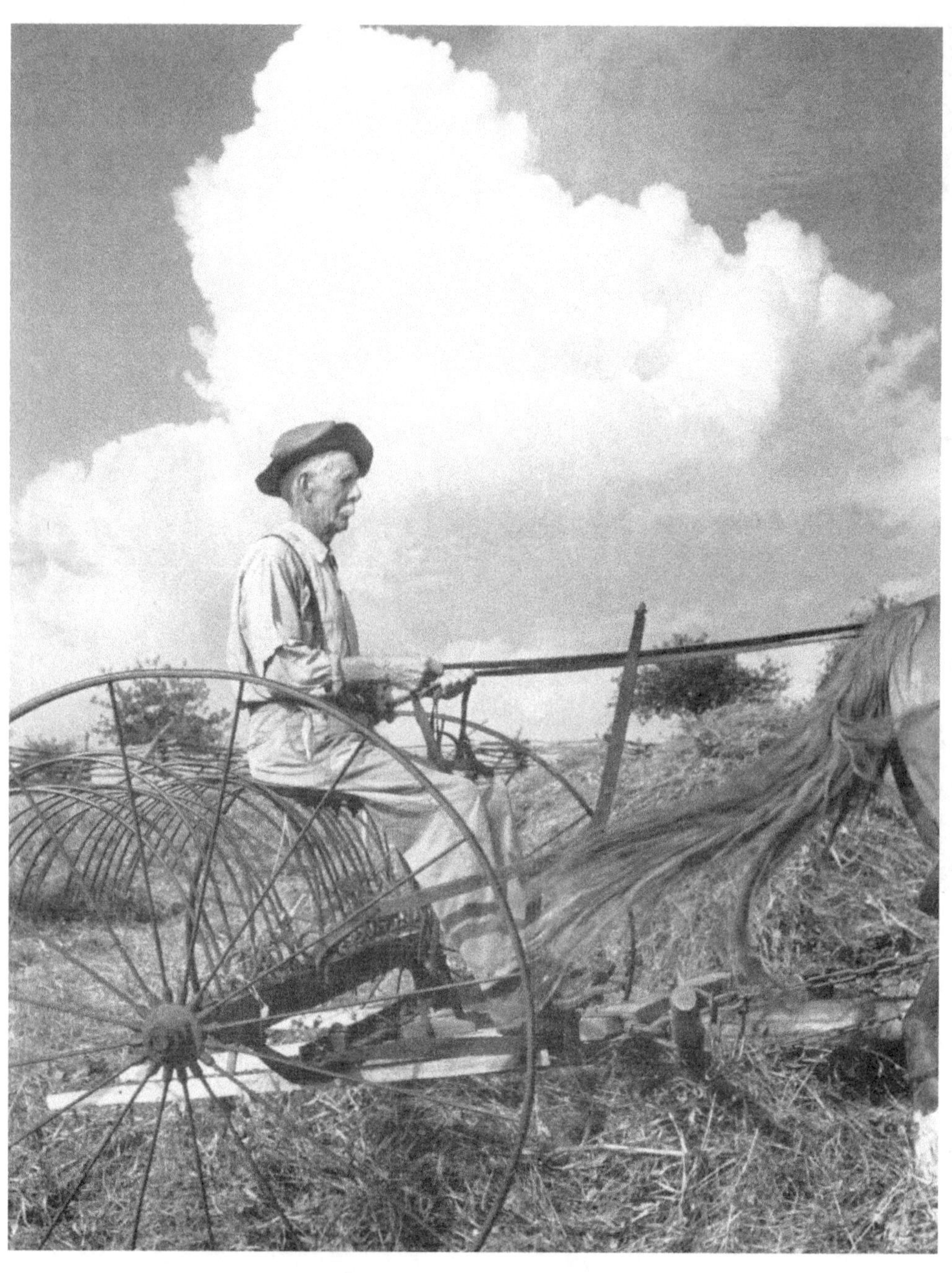

Though past eighty, Newton Hylton worked in his hayfield.

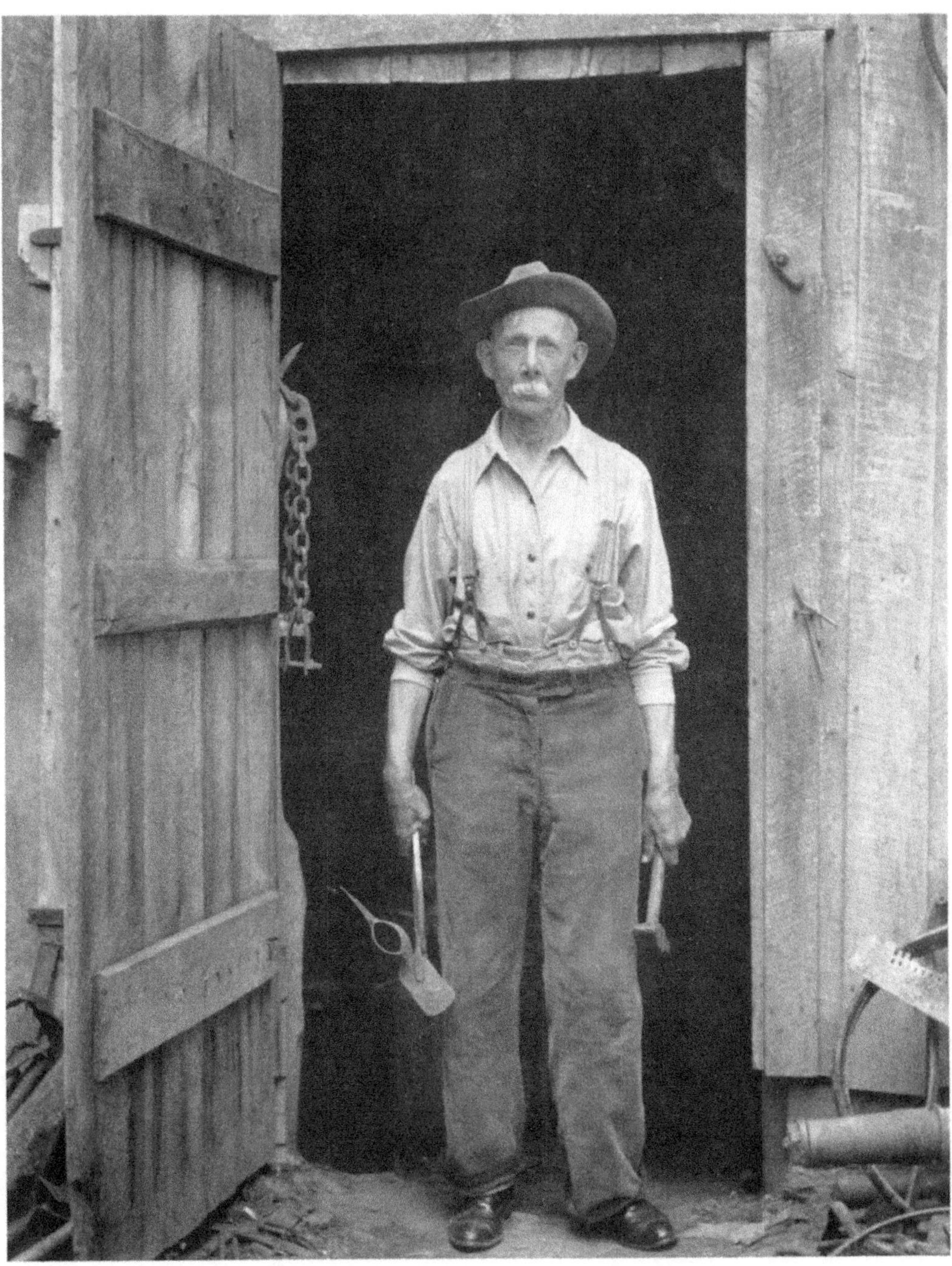

Hylton at the door of his blacksmith shop, on a cliff overlooking Laurel Fork Creek.

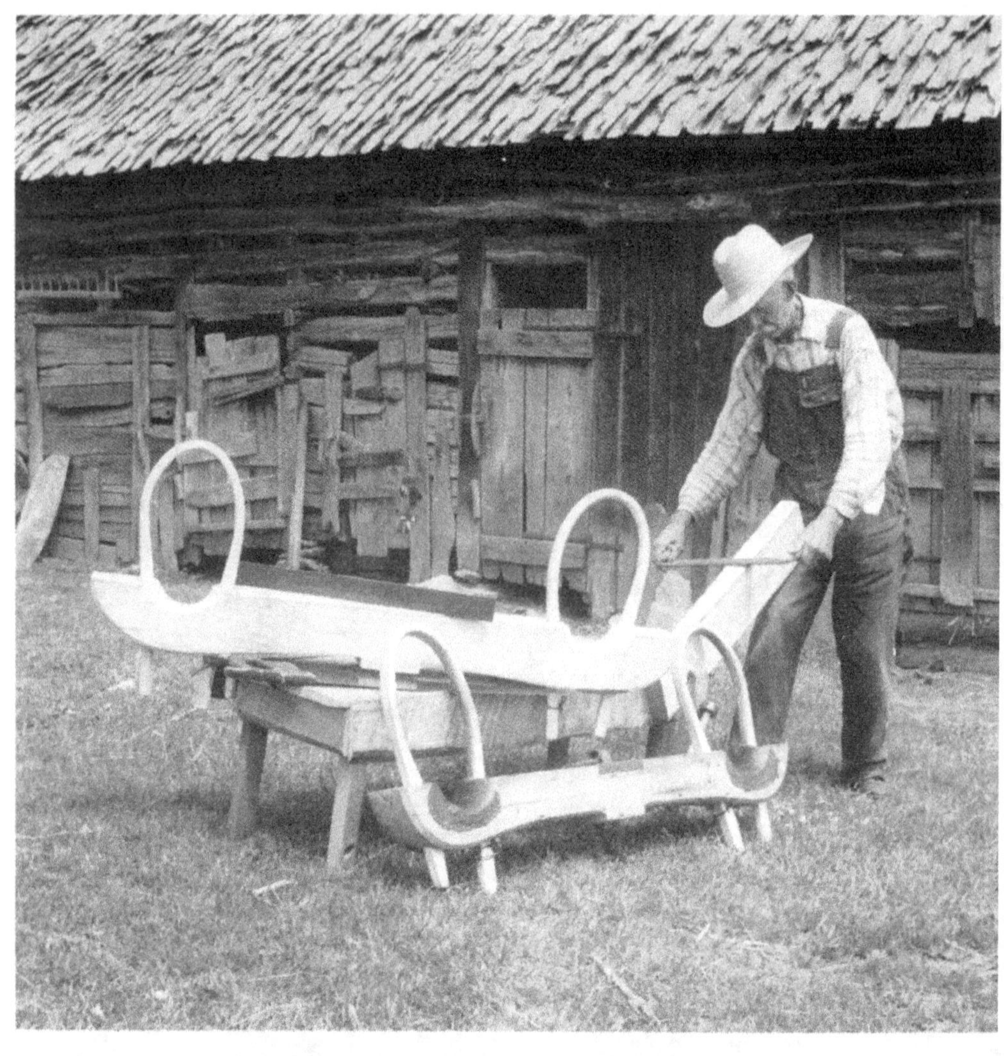

Whatever Newton Hylton needed on his place he made hisself or done without. Here he smooths an ox yoke of cucumber tree wood with a drawing knife.

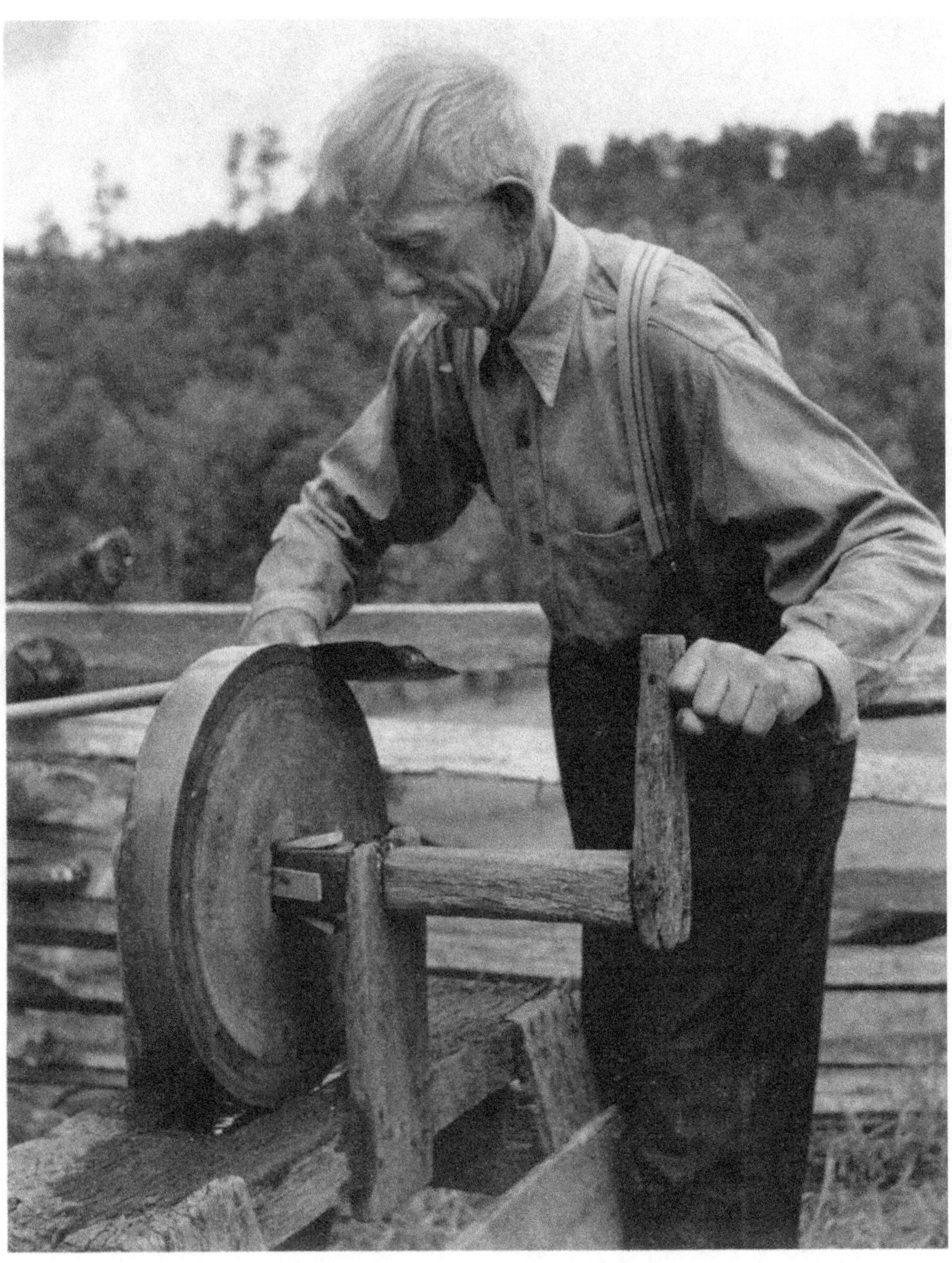

Hylton grinds an edge on a double-bitted woodman's axe.

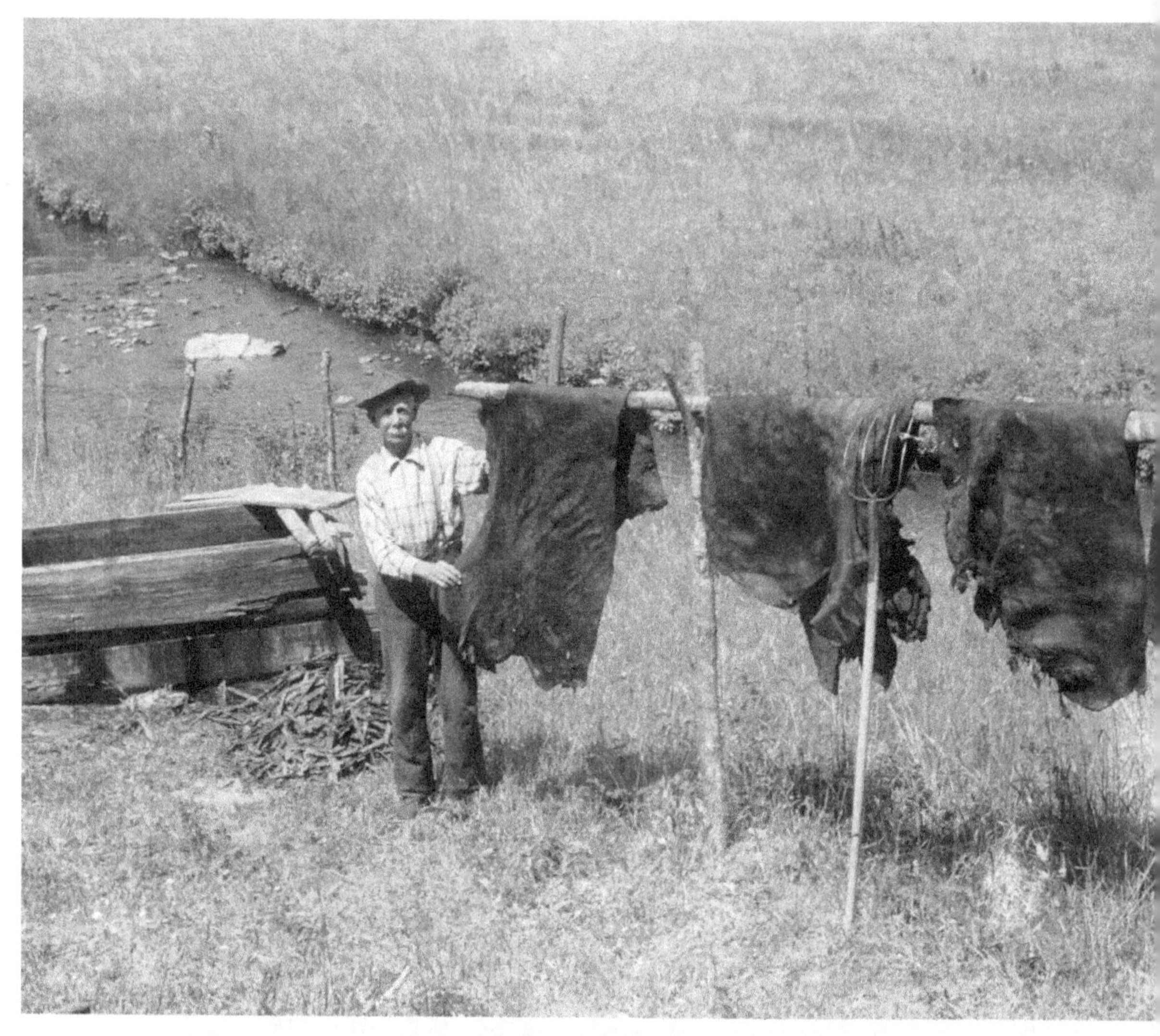

Hylton hangs out a cowhide he tanned to make his own shoe leather.

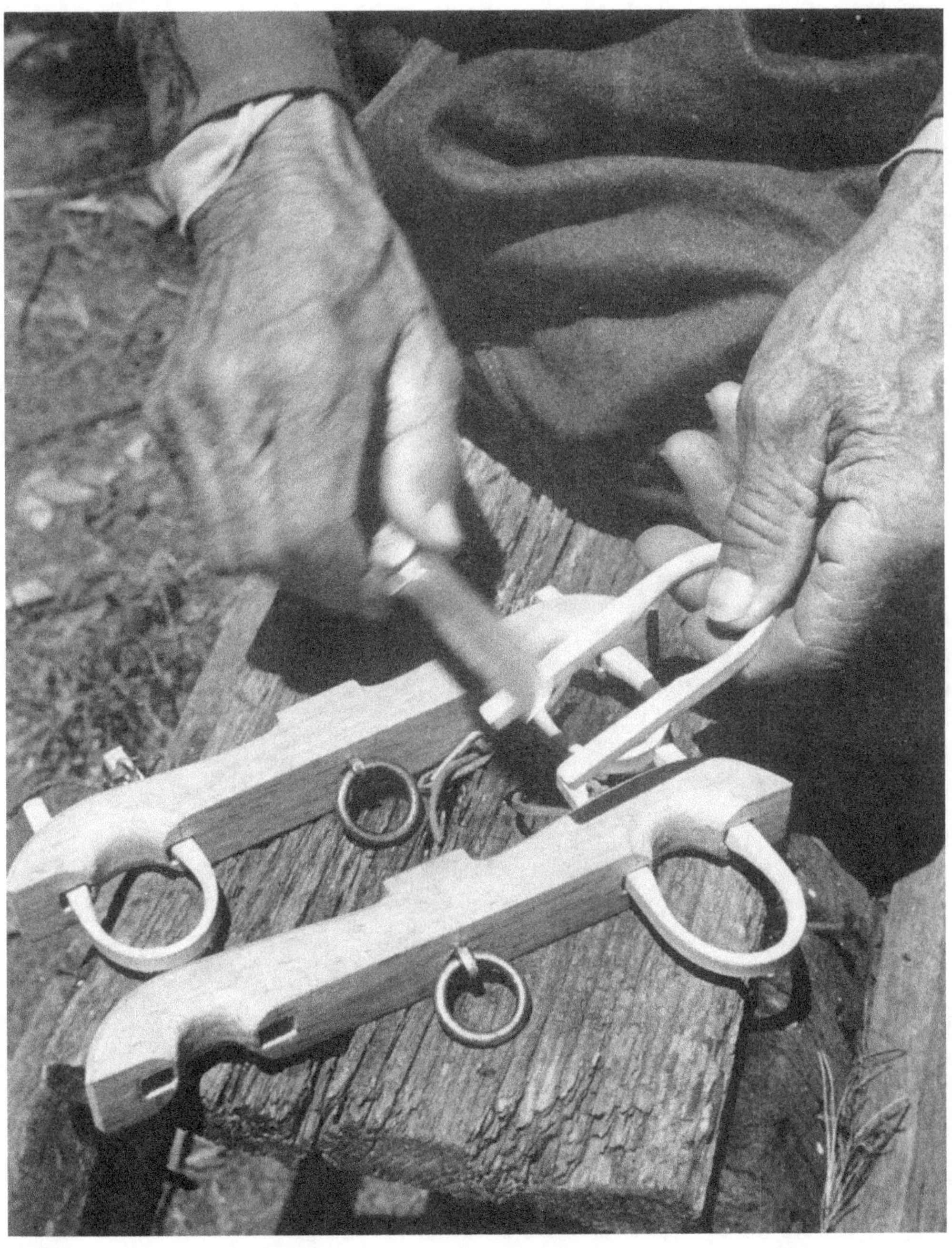

Mountaineers invariably are expert whittlers. Hylton carved this set of miniature ox yokes from white pine and hickory.

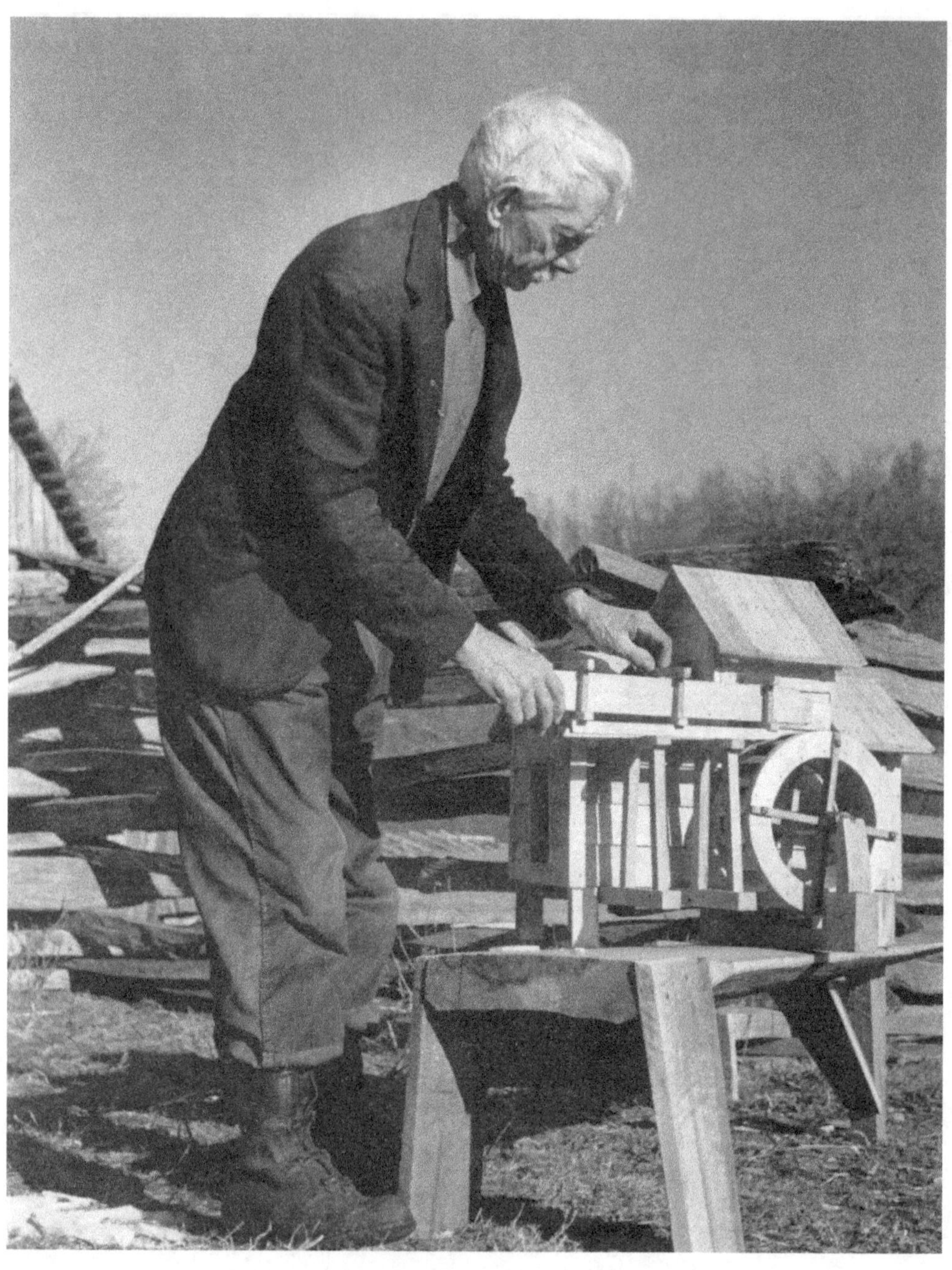

Newton Hylton made this white-pine replica of the world-famed Mabry Mill. When the National Park Service created the Blue Ridge Parkway, Hylton directed the restoration of the old mill, actually building the water wheel without aid. It was said he was paid 75 cents per hour for this monumental work.

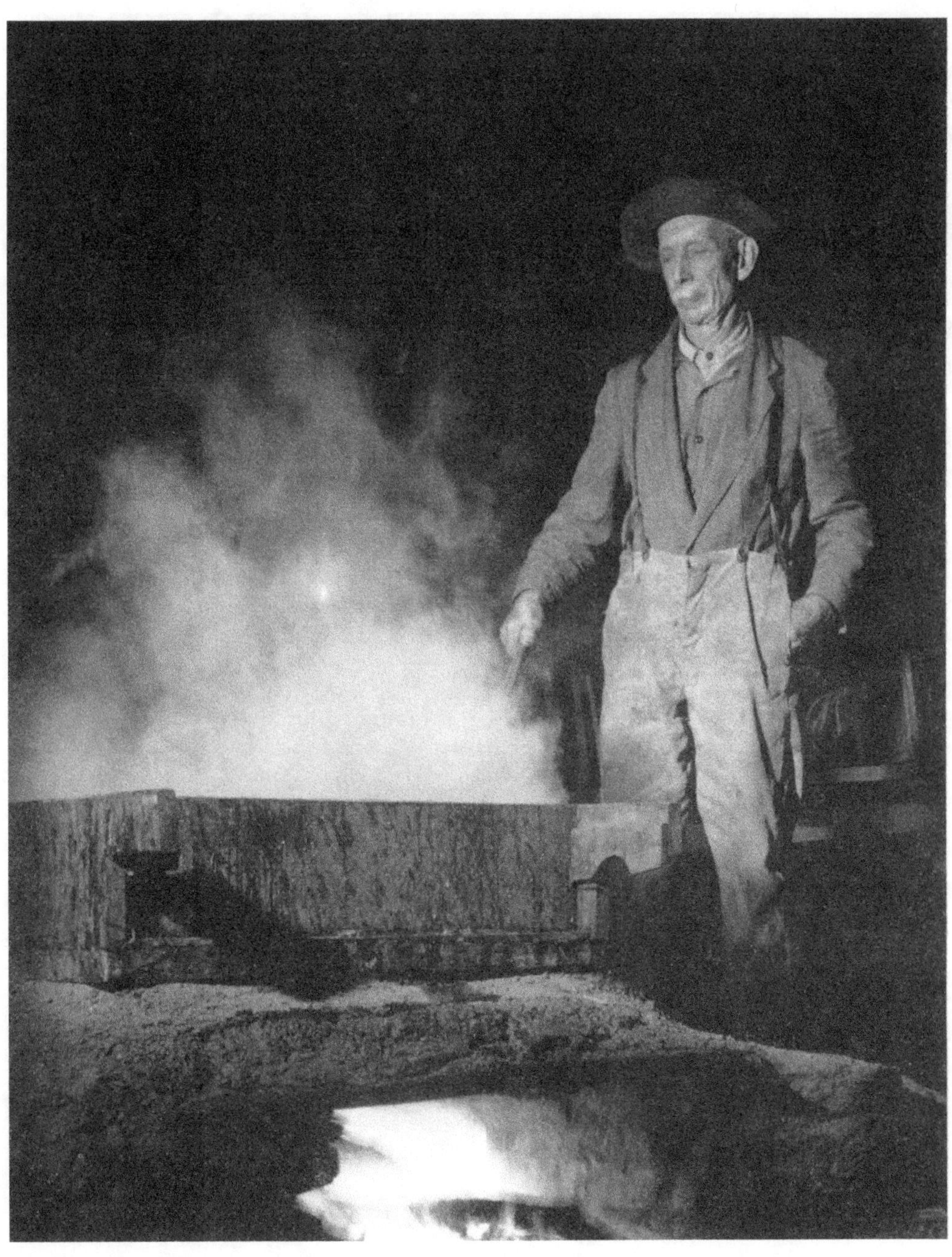

Molasses boiling-down time at Newt Hylton's place.

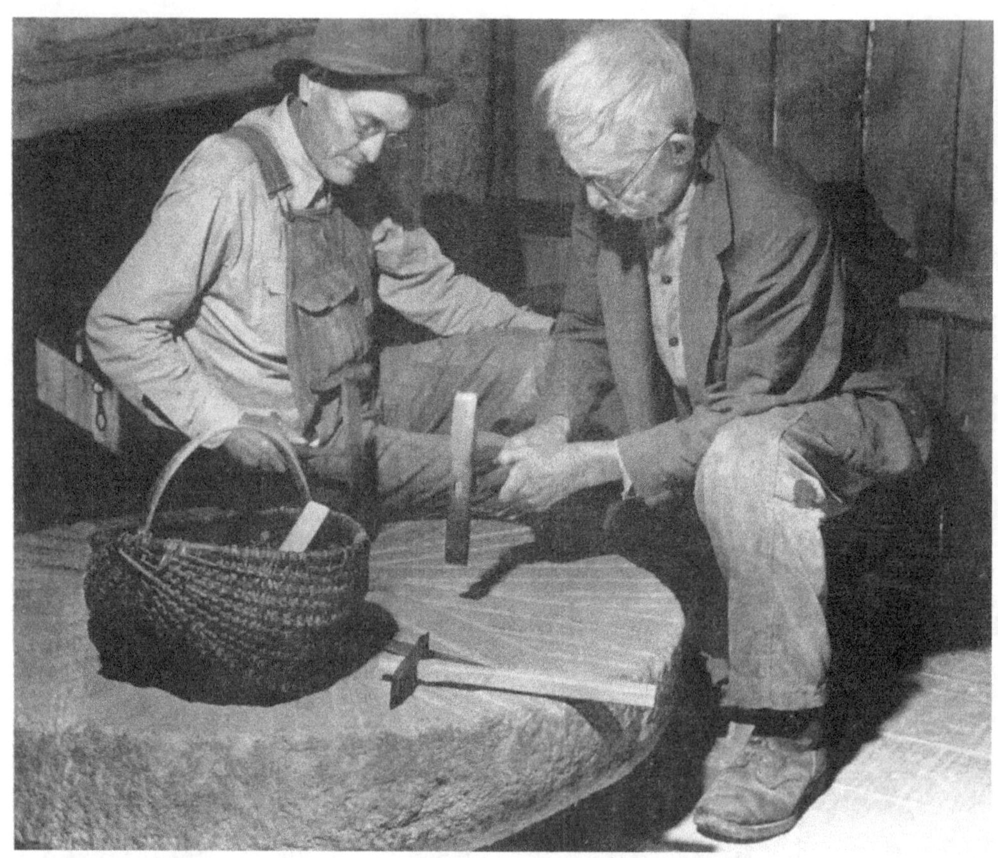

Lost art: Newton Hylton and Jesus Christ Alexander chisel grooves on the face of a flint-hard French-burr millstone. The water-powered gristmills our forebears used to grind corn, wheat, and rye have long departed the scene of our mountains.

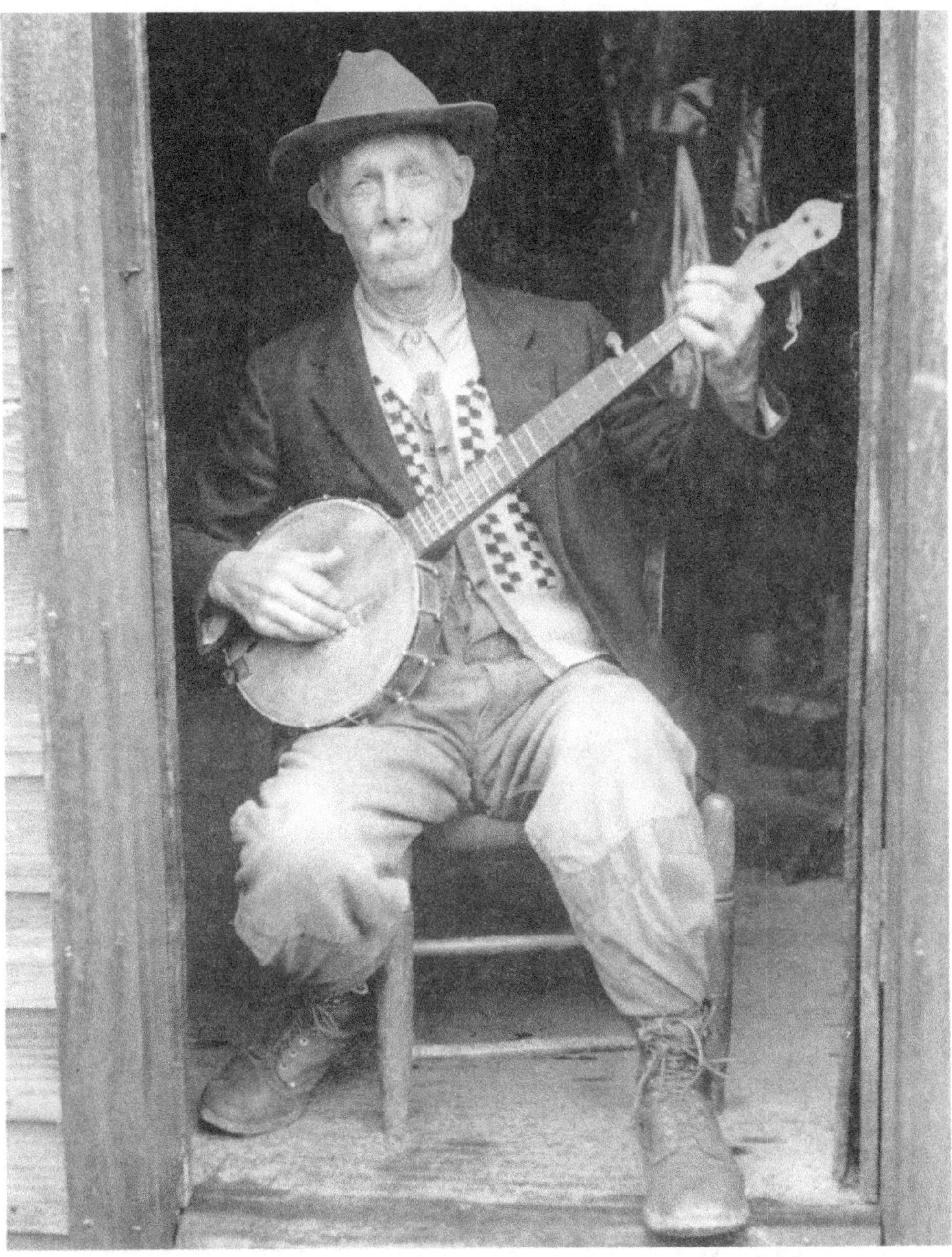

Speaking of the versatility of old-time mountaineers, Newton Hylton made the banjo pictured, using curly maple for the wood part, groundhog skin for the banjo's head.

The late and beloved Mary Breckinridge, founder of the renowned Frontier Nursing Service in Kentucky's Cumberland Mountains, feeds her horse, Calico, from her apron.

Portraits

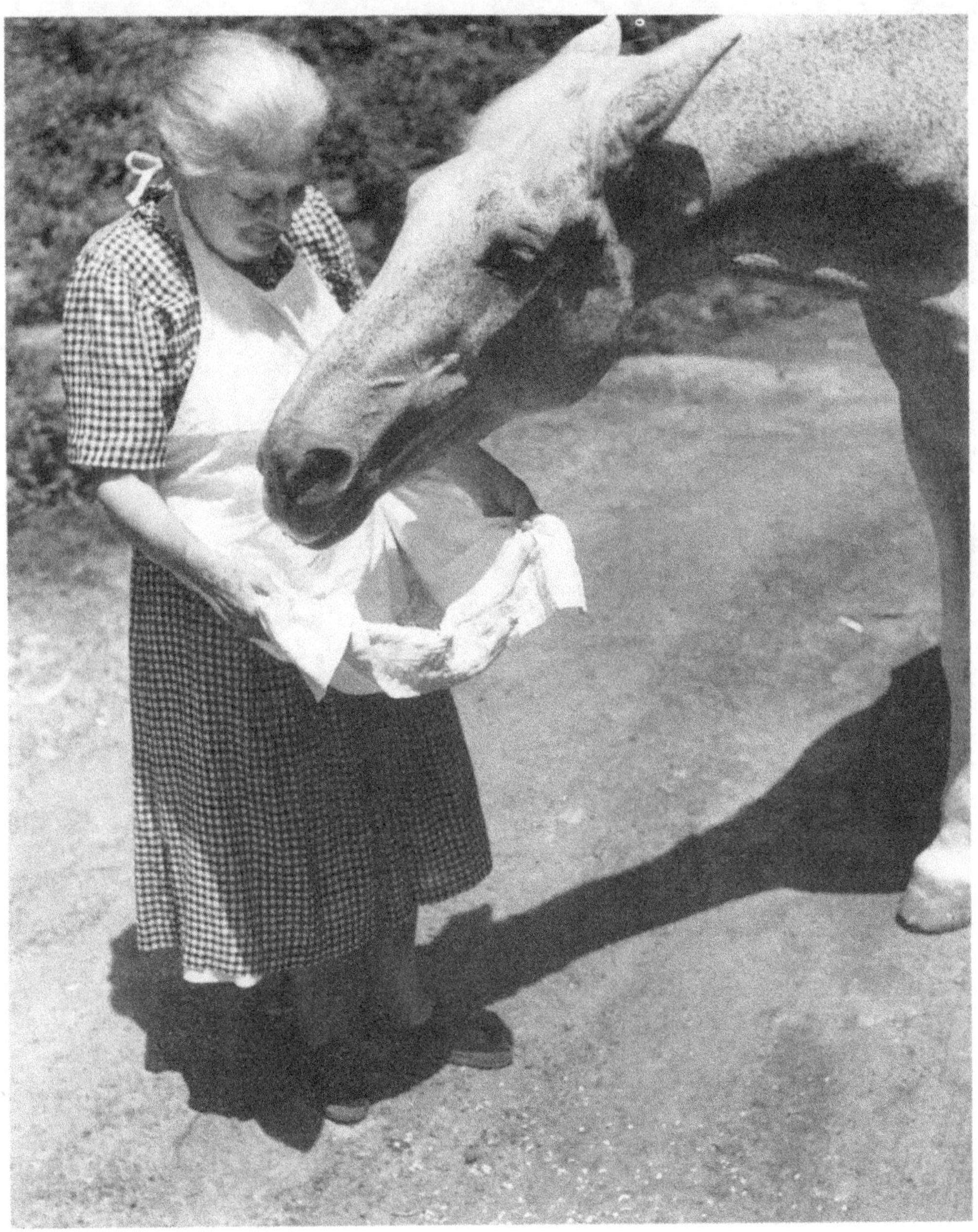

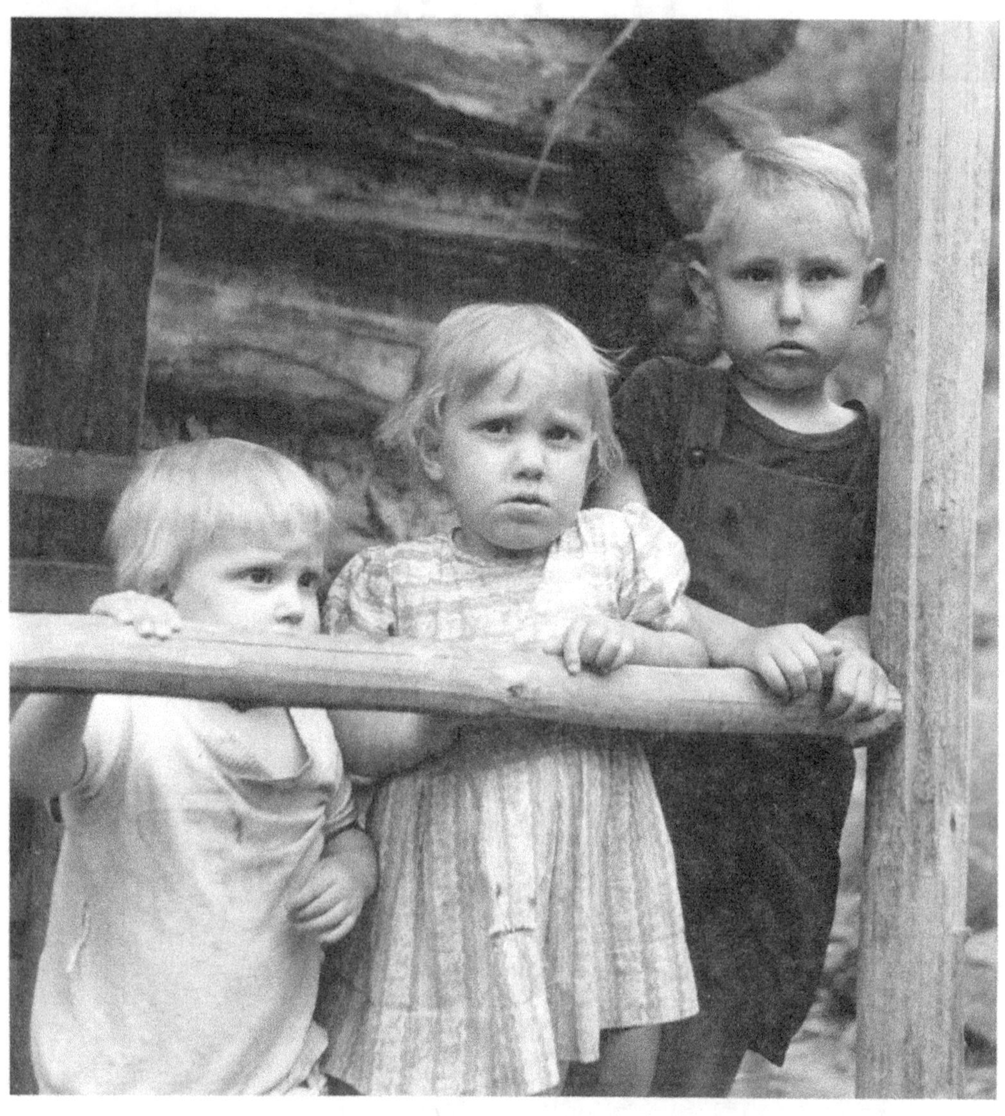

Born in a one-room log cabin on Muncy Creek, near Hyden, Kentucky, these children were delivered by the late Anna May January, a pioneer nurse of the Frontier Nursing Service [1941.] *Opposite,* the late Jethro Amburgey fashions still another dulcimer in his shop on the forks of Troublesome Creek at Hindman, Kentucky [1955].

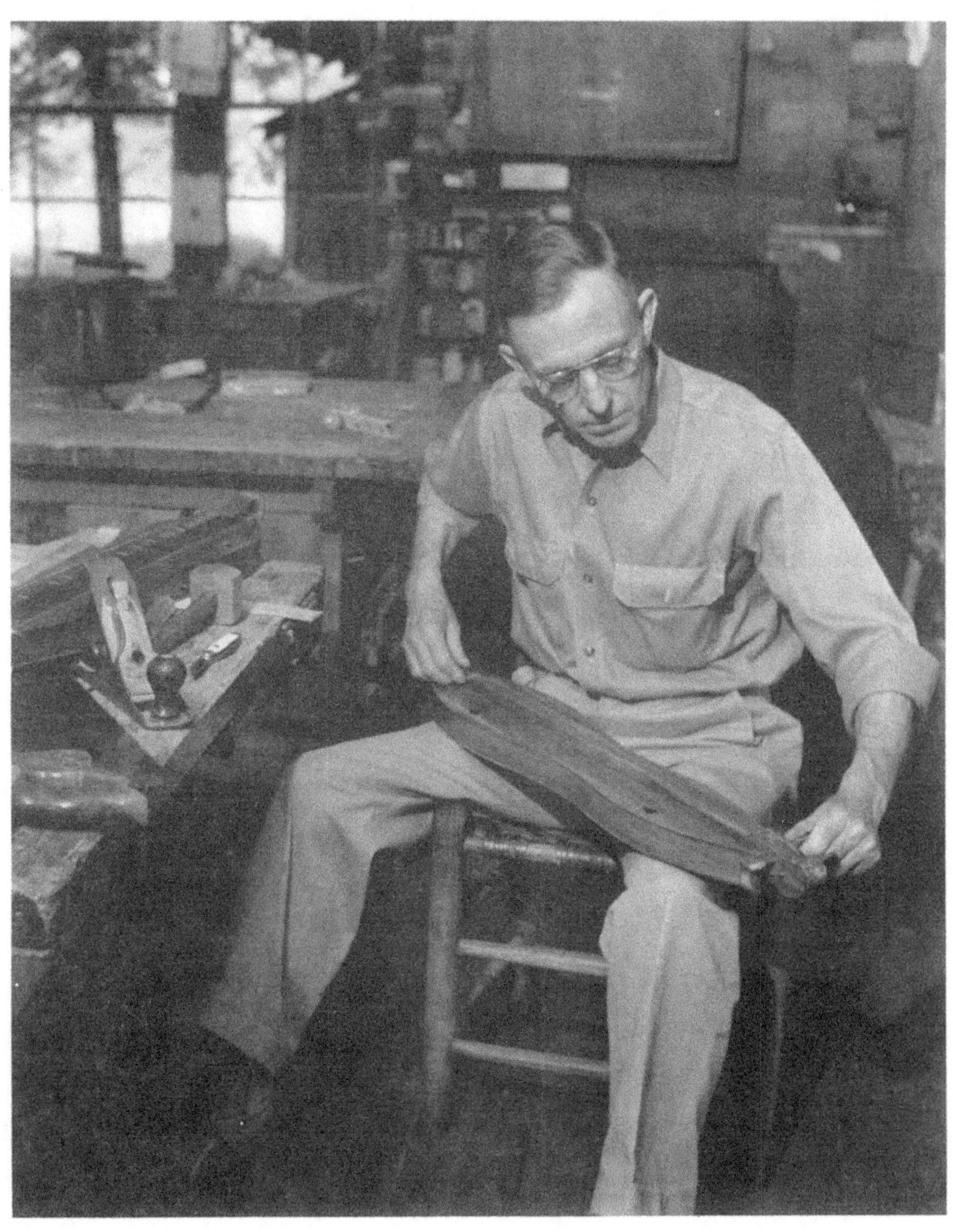

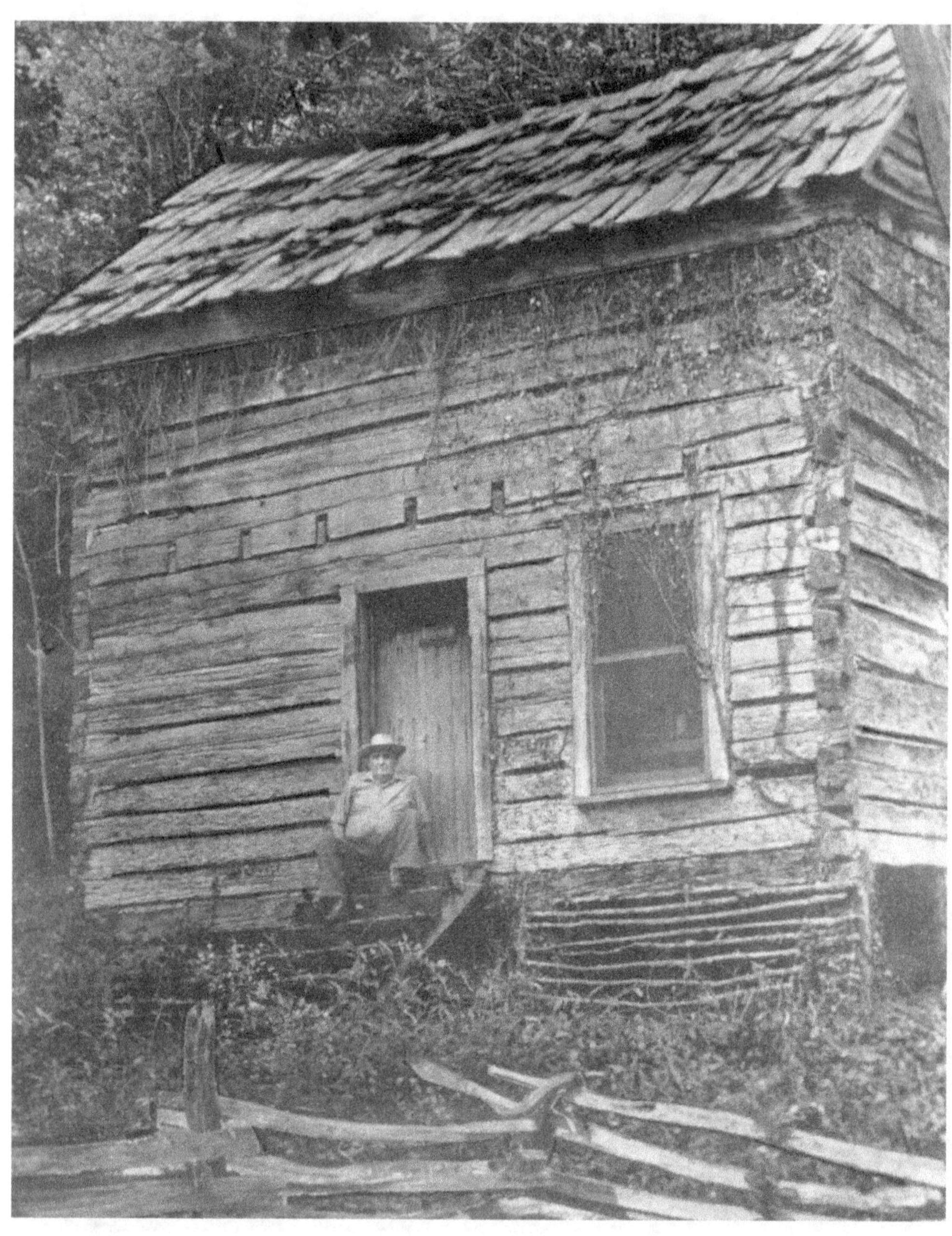

[James Still at the Amburgey cabin, 1983.] This log cabin on Dead Mare Branch near Hindman, Kentucky, was once the home of dulcimer maker Jethro Amburgey. In his will he bequeathed a lifetime habitation of the cabin to his lifelong friend, author James Still.

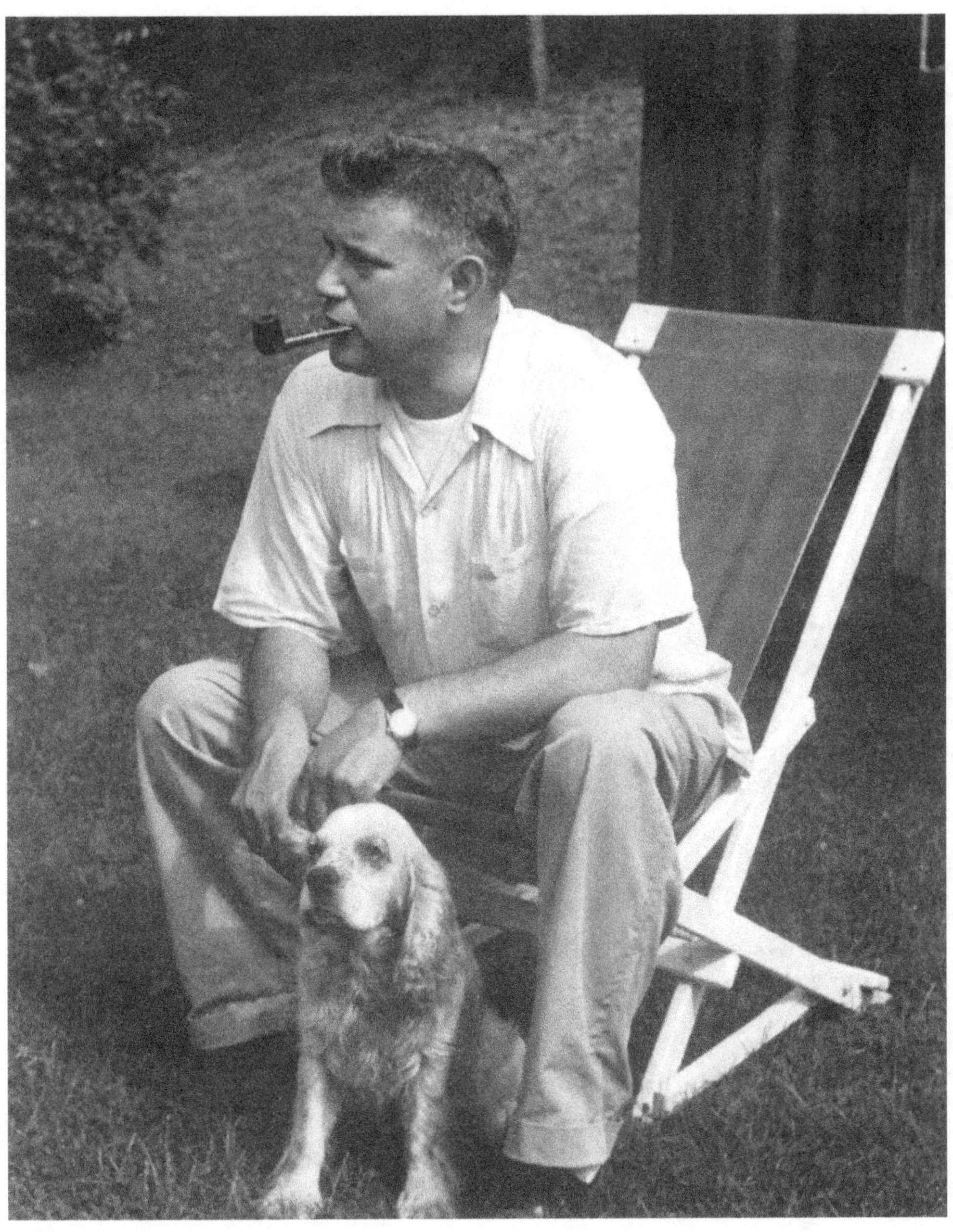

[Jesse Stuart at his W-Hollow farm in Kentucky with his dog, Breakfield, 1954.]

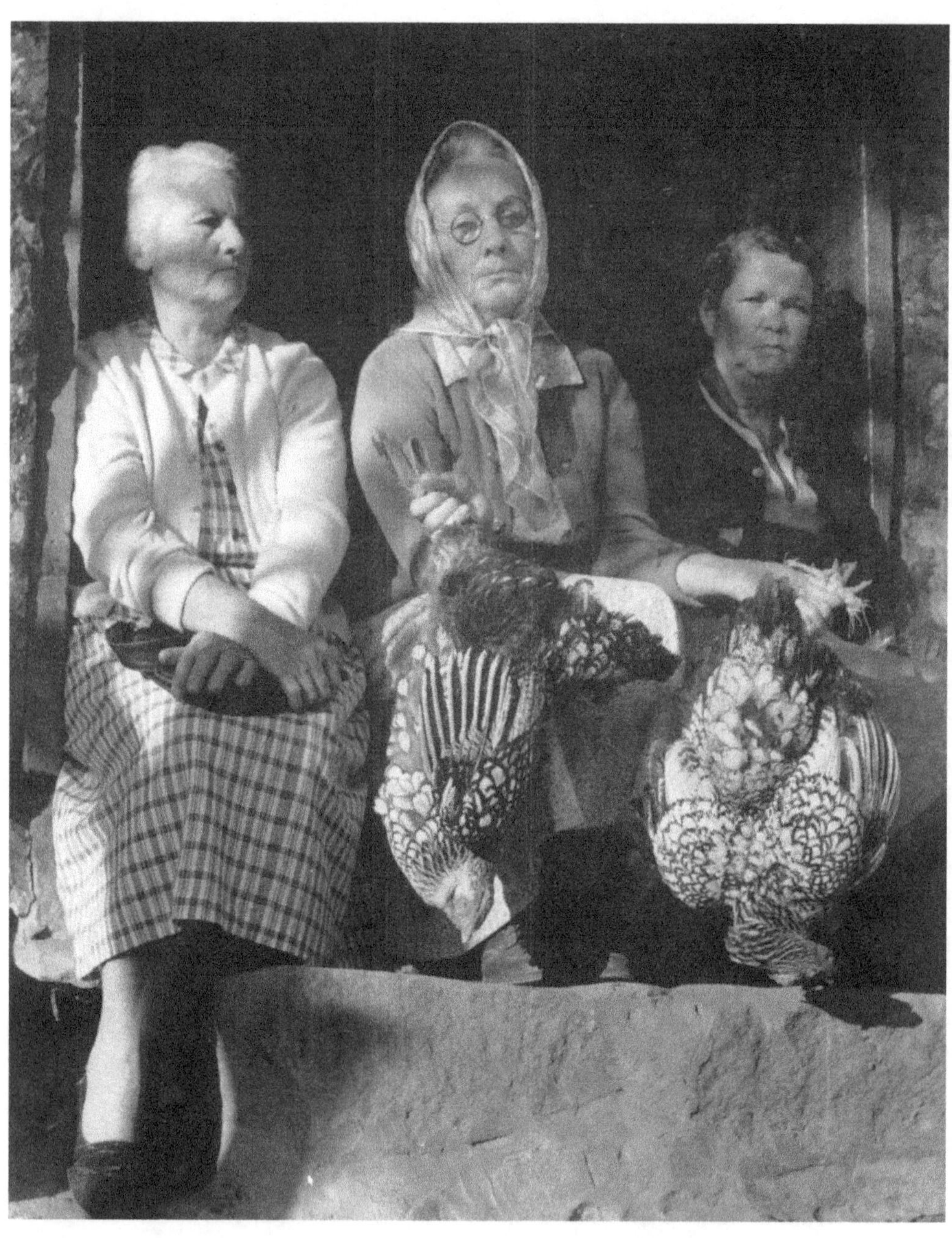

Women with dominecker hens they will swap for clothing at a trading post in southeastern Kentucky. [Pippa Passes, 1940.]

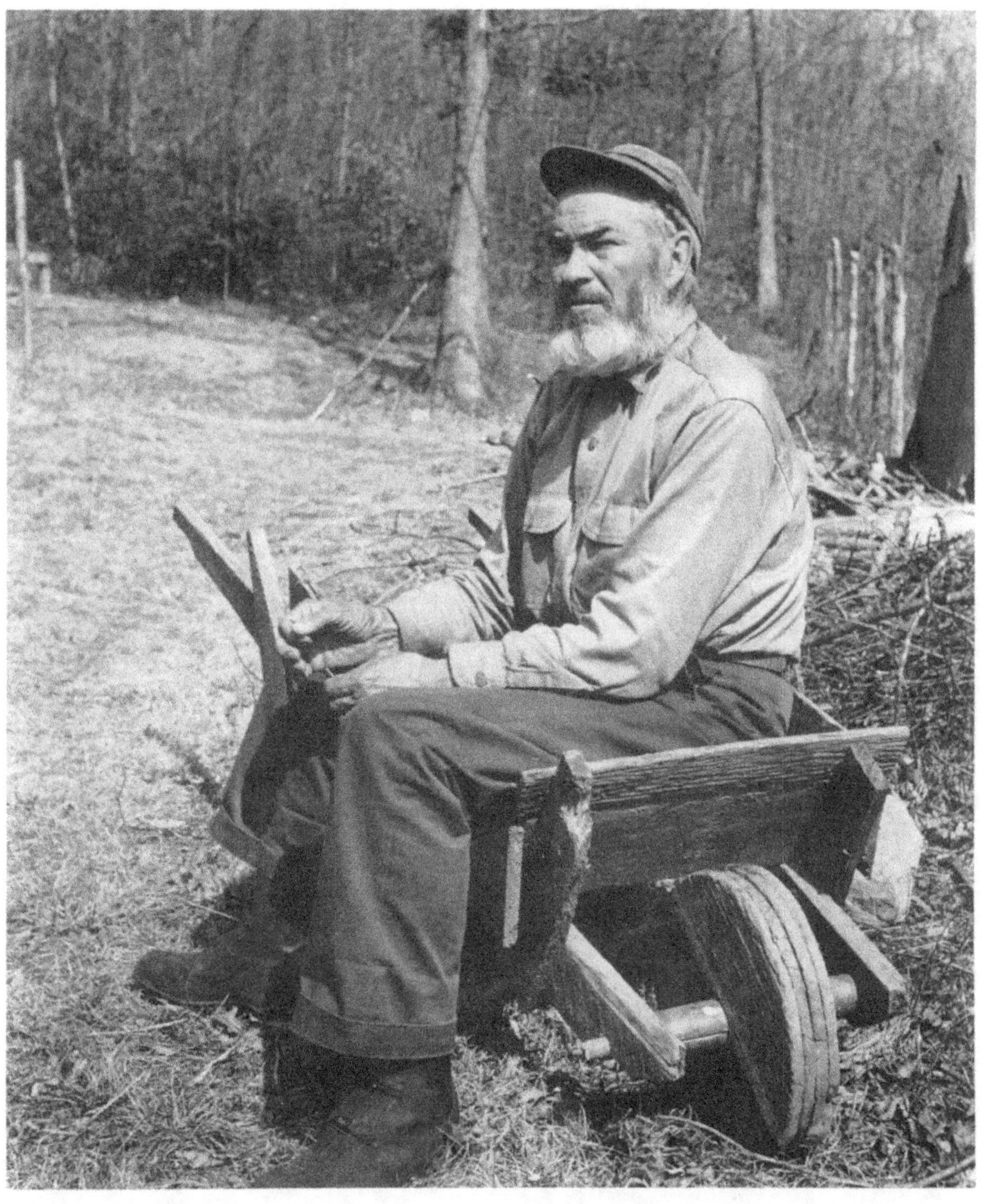

With a generous-giving milk cow, a pen full of fattening hogs, and a flock of Plymouth Rock hens of high laying qualities, Blaine Sartain lives the good life apart from the hustle and worries of a main street world. [Near John's Creek in Craig County, Virginia, 1960.]

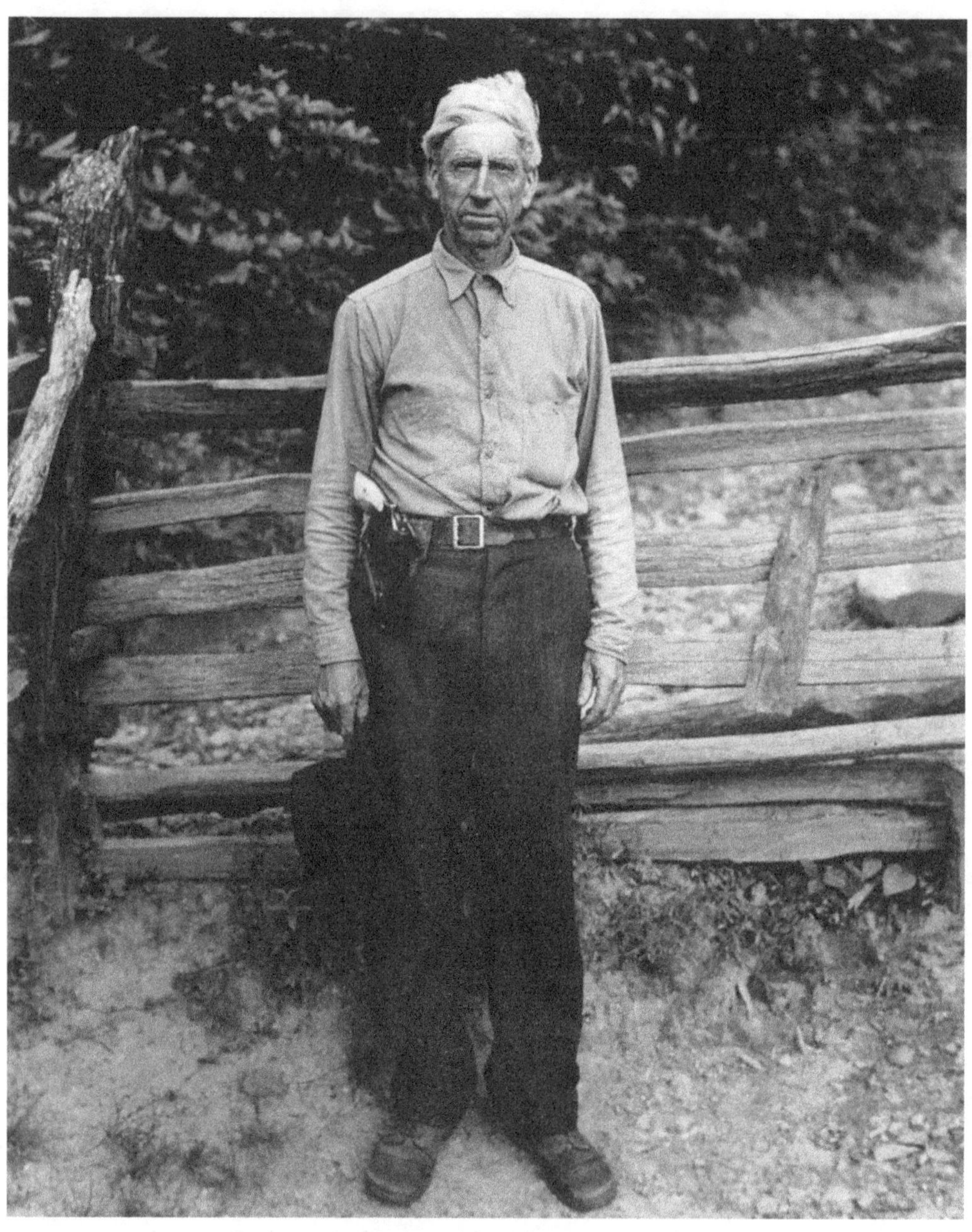

The faces of mountain-born and fetched-up men speak of a life of hard work and frustration on stingy hillside land more suited to growing jack pine and sawbriars than corn, beans, and 'taters. Some, like Thomas Jefferson Cupp here, run a little likker. Tom Jeff has departed the hills and valleys of this life, perhaps to dwell where moonshiners who brew good drinking likker are supposed to go. [1942.]

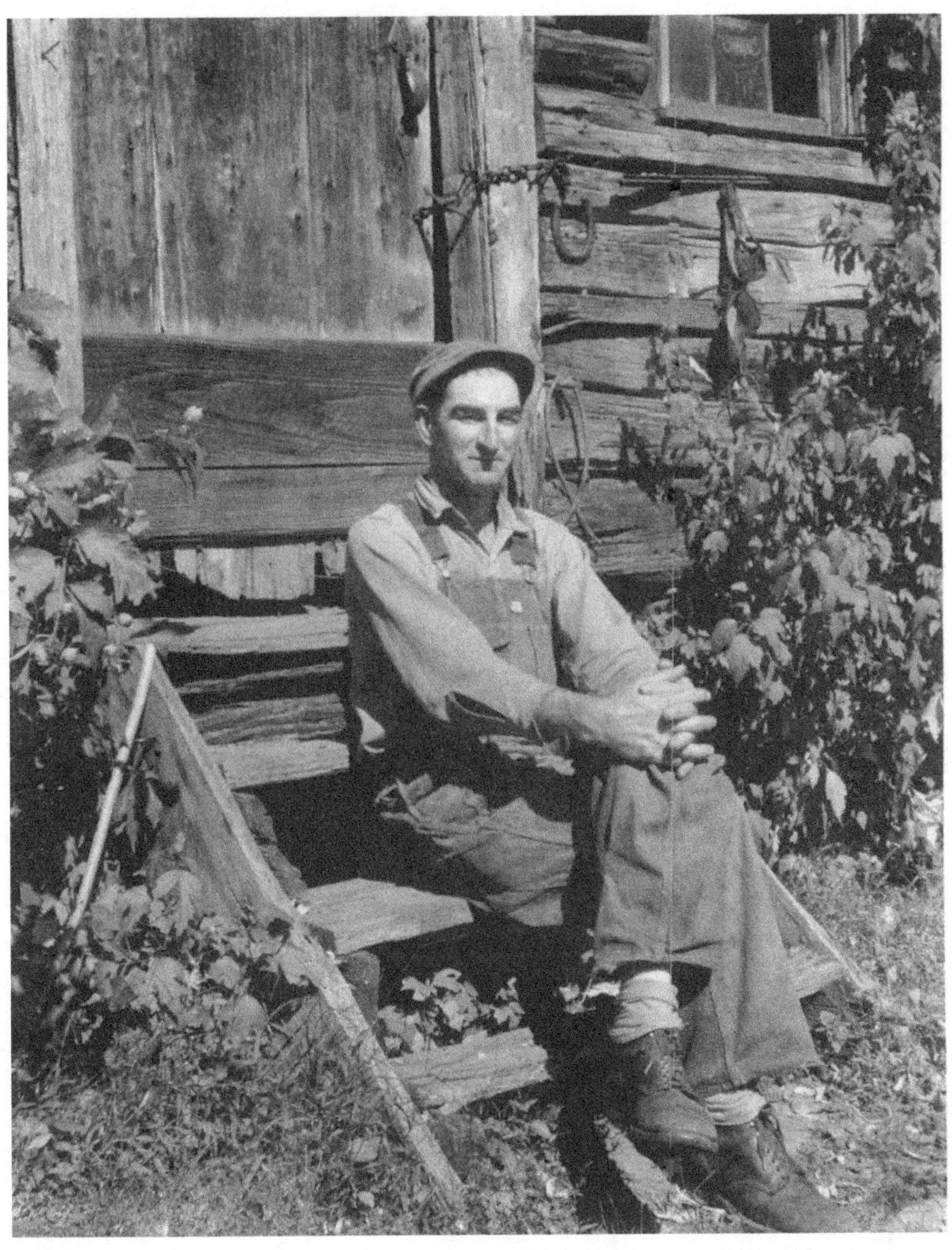

Lincoln Cockram once lived in a deep cove north of the Blue Ridge where Raven's Creek had its birth. He was at home in the woods with a double-bitted woodman's axe in his strong hands. [Rock Castle Creek, Virginia, 1956.]

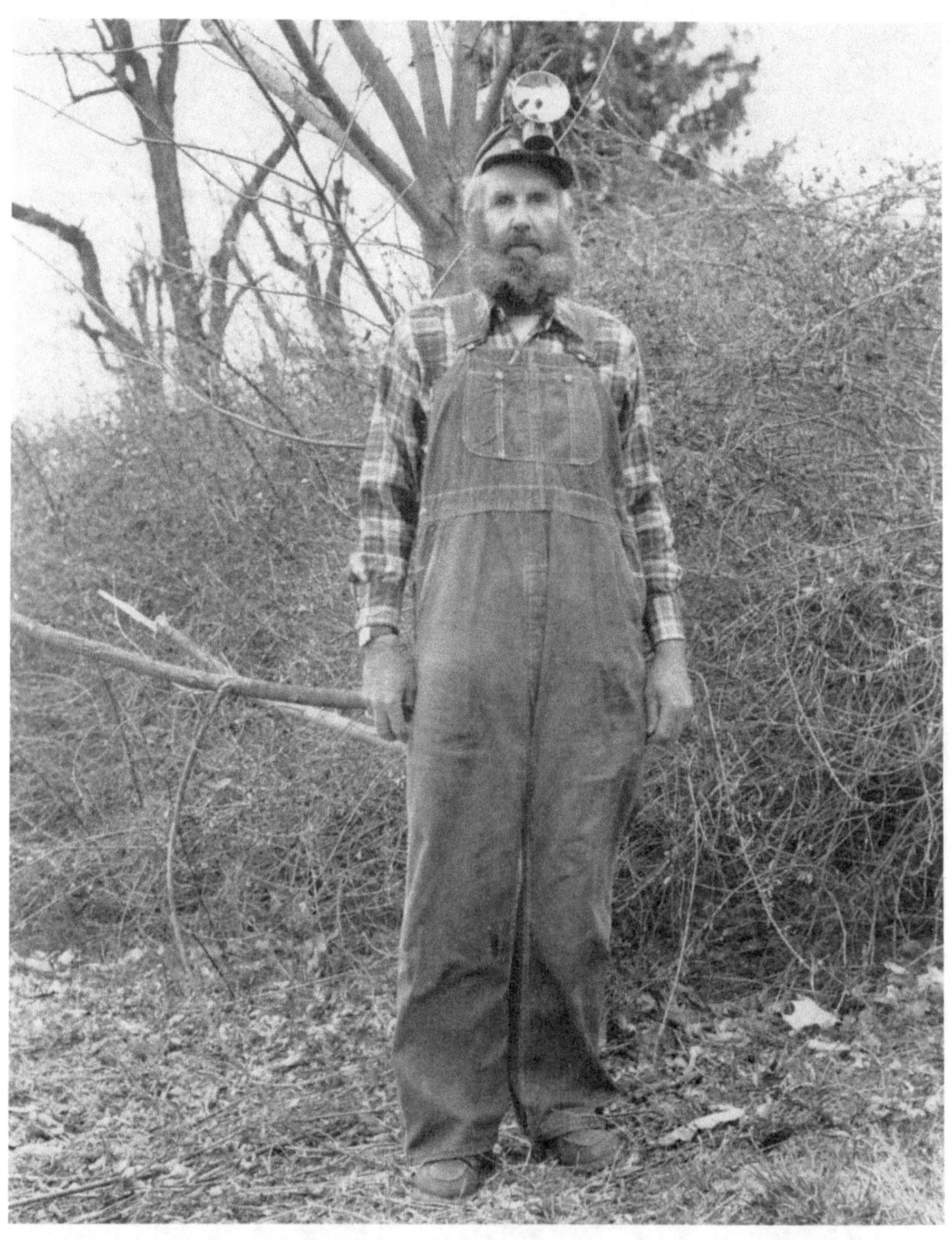

Walter Dobbins, retired coal miner, loaded coal in the Merrimac Mine until the mine closed down for good during a labor strike. "My tools are still down thar in the 'room' where I worked . . . guess they'll be thar forever," he said one day. [Merrimac, Virginia, 1985.]

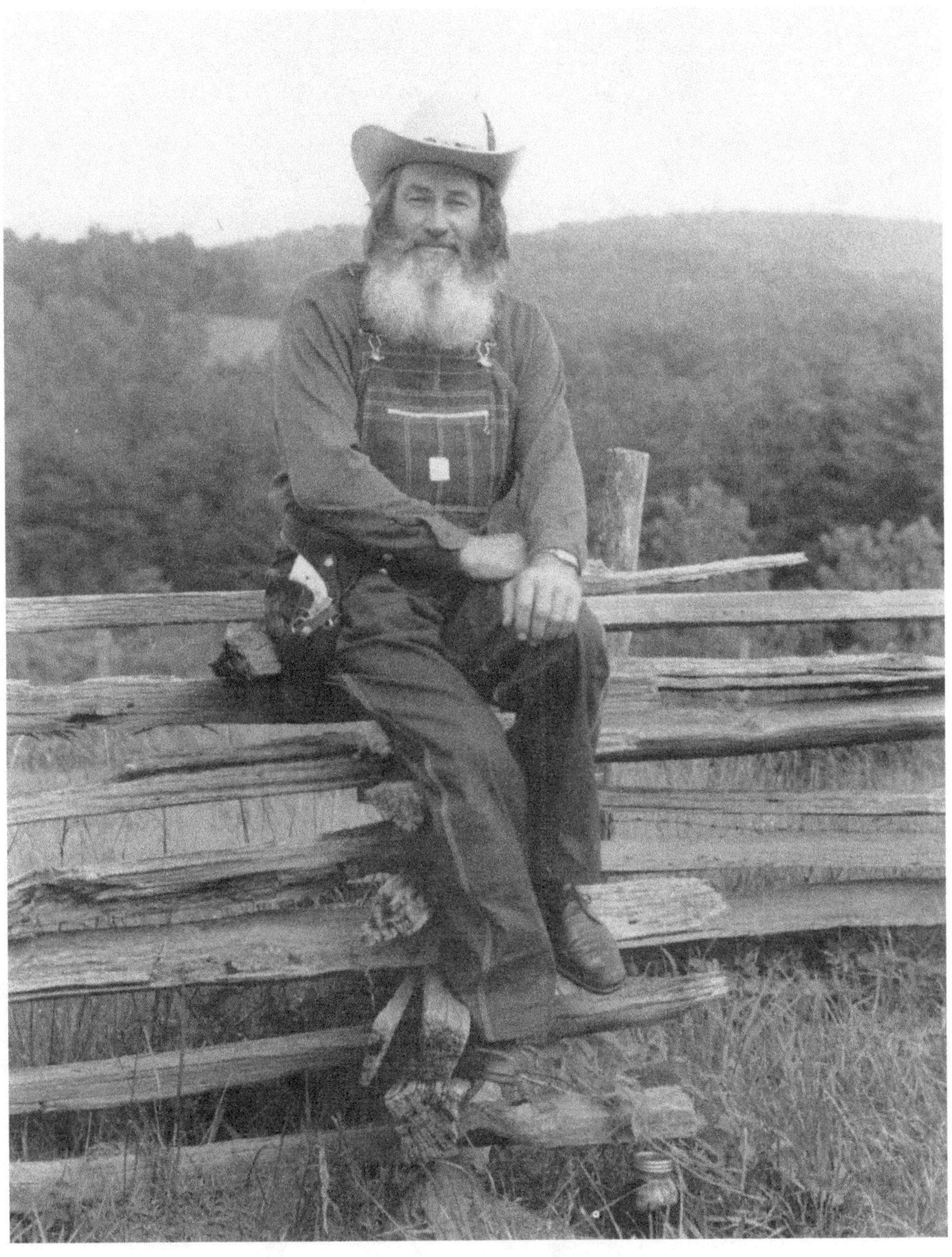

Now and then Sam "Thumpkeg" Dehart likes to show off as pictured here in 1986. This true friend of mine exemplifies the oldtime mountaineer.

A snake-rail fence made of rived chestnut yielded this Christmas card scene. [Near the Blue Ridge Parkway in Virginia, 1960.]

Country Roads

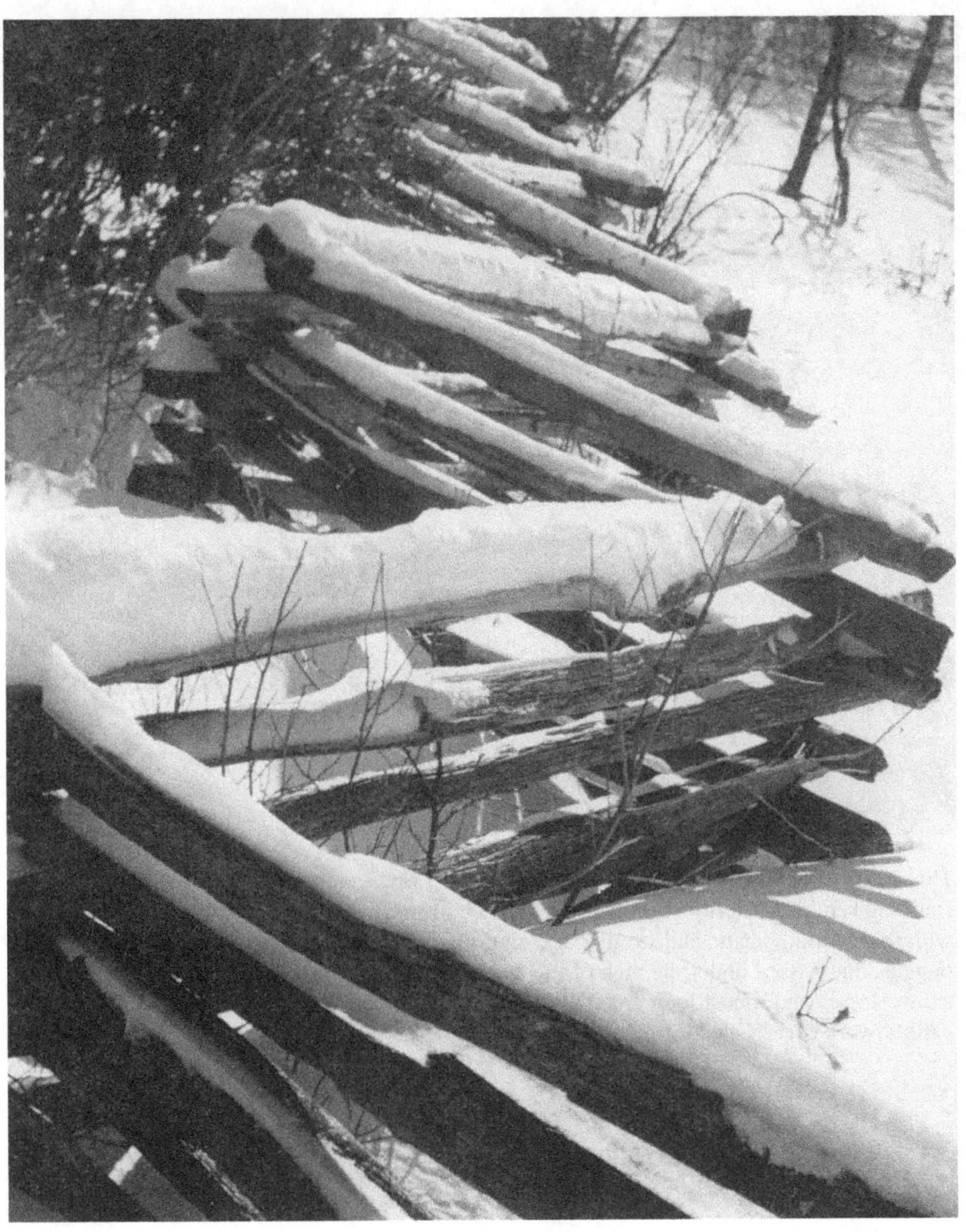

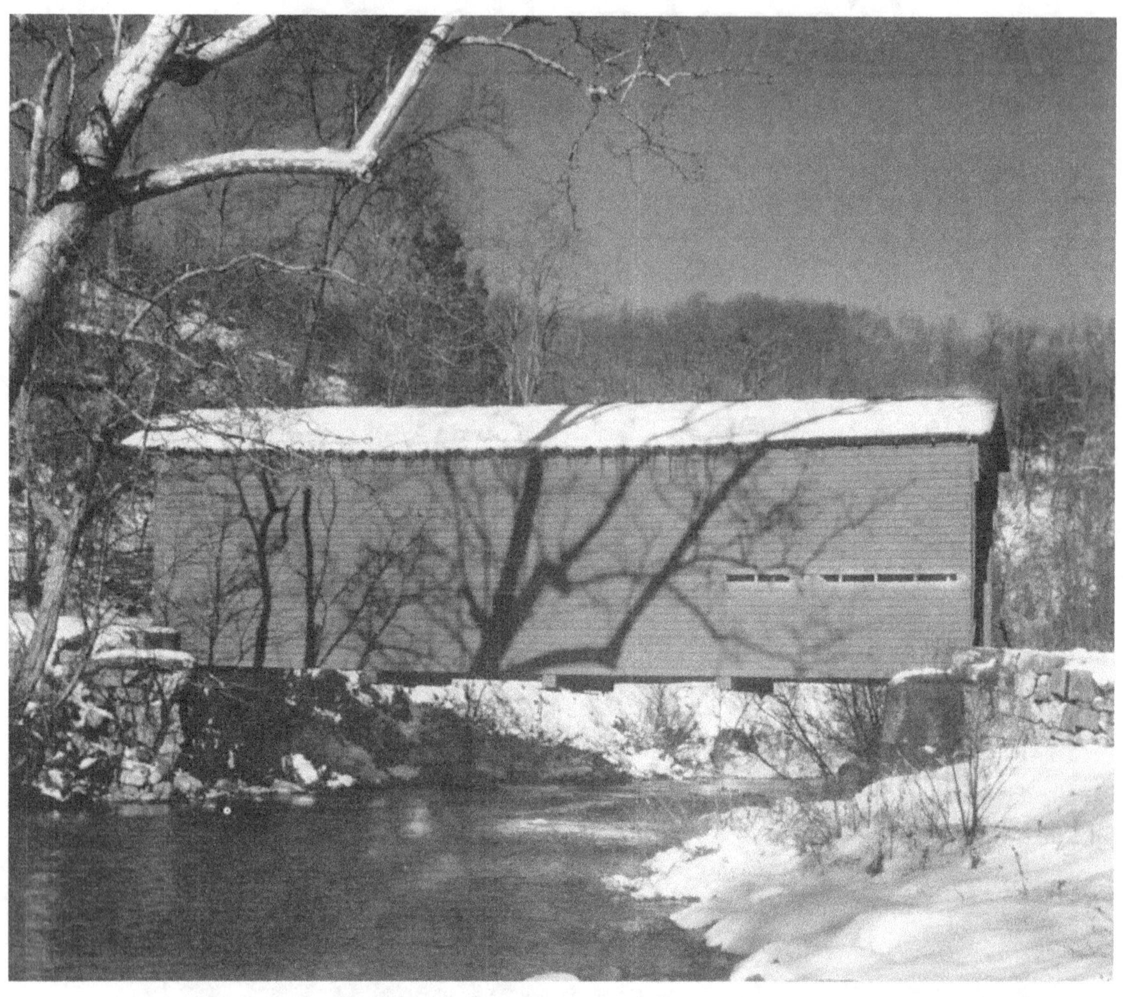

This white oak and poplar bridge spanning Sinking Creek, though erected in 1916, still stands to remind posterity of pioneer folk who built so many things rustic and useful with their willing hearts and strong backs and hands. The rugged wagons and gay-painted buggies that passed under the arch of this bridge have long ago rotted away and the sturdy horses and robust long-eared mules that pulled them sleep forevermore, their earthly work over. [Giles County, Virginia, 1978.]

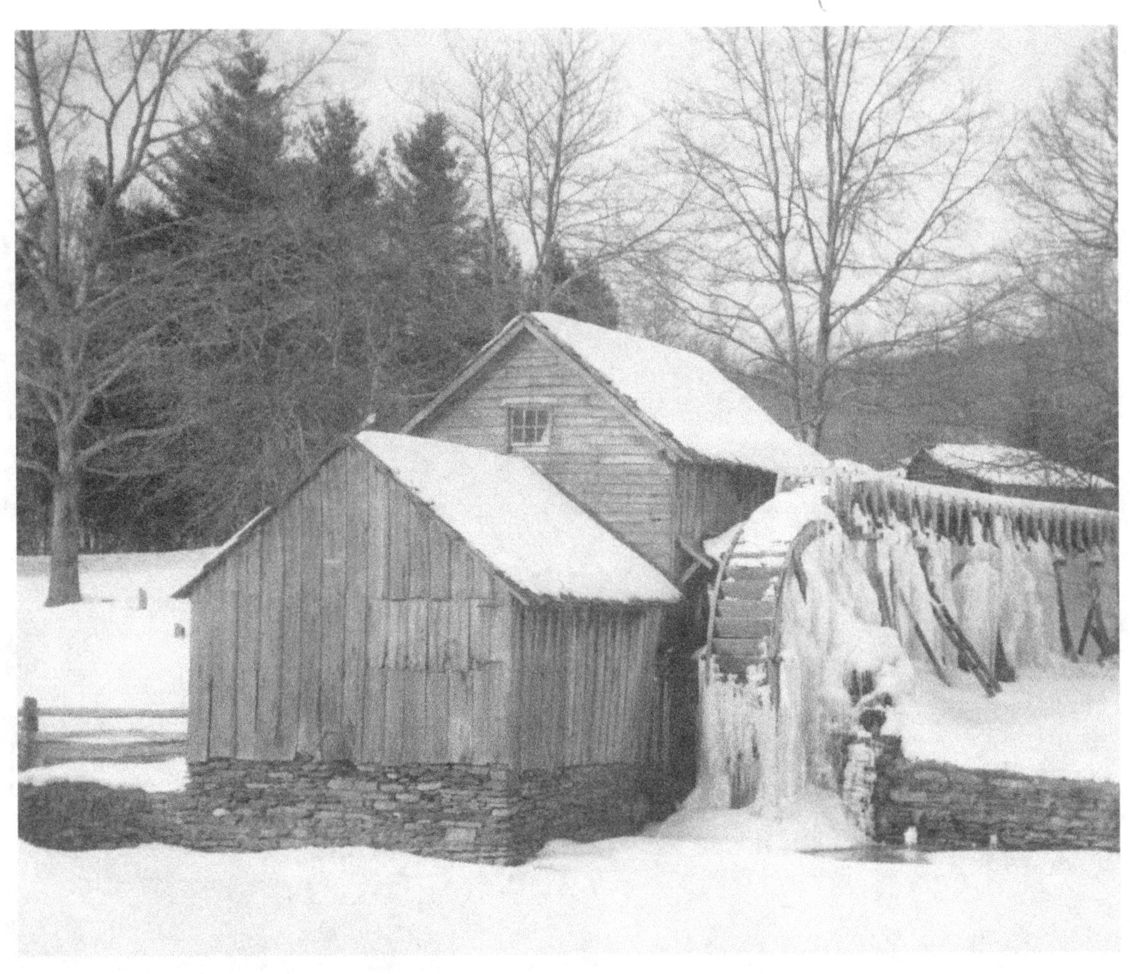

[Mabry Mill on the Blue Ridge Parkway after a midwinter snowfall. Patrick-Carroll Counties, Virginia, 1970.]

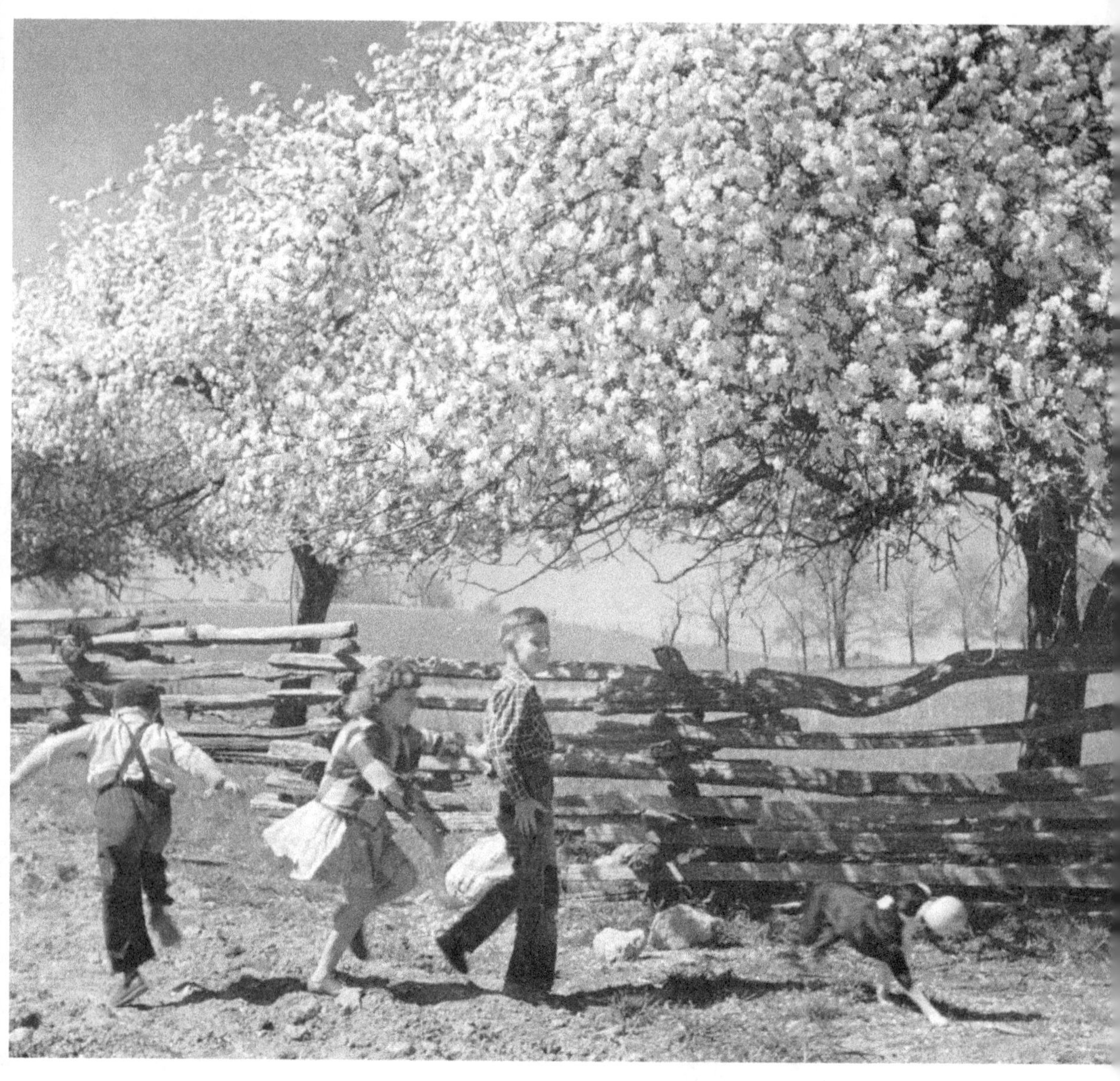

If there are roads that lead from earth to Heaven, may they be back country lanes in mixed sunshine and shade, ever twisting and winding up hill and down, bordered by apple, peach, and cherry under whose blossom canopies the children have their gleeful play. [Near Willis, Virginia, 1960.]

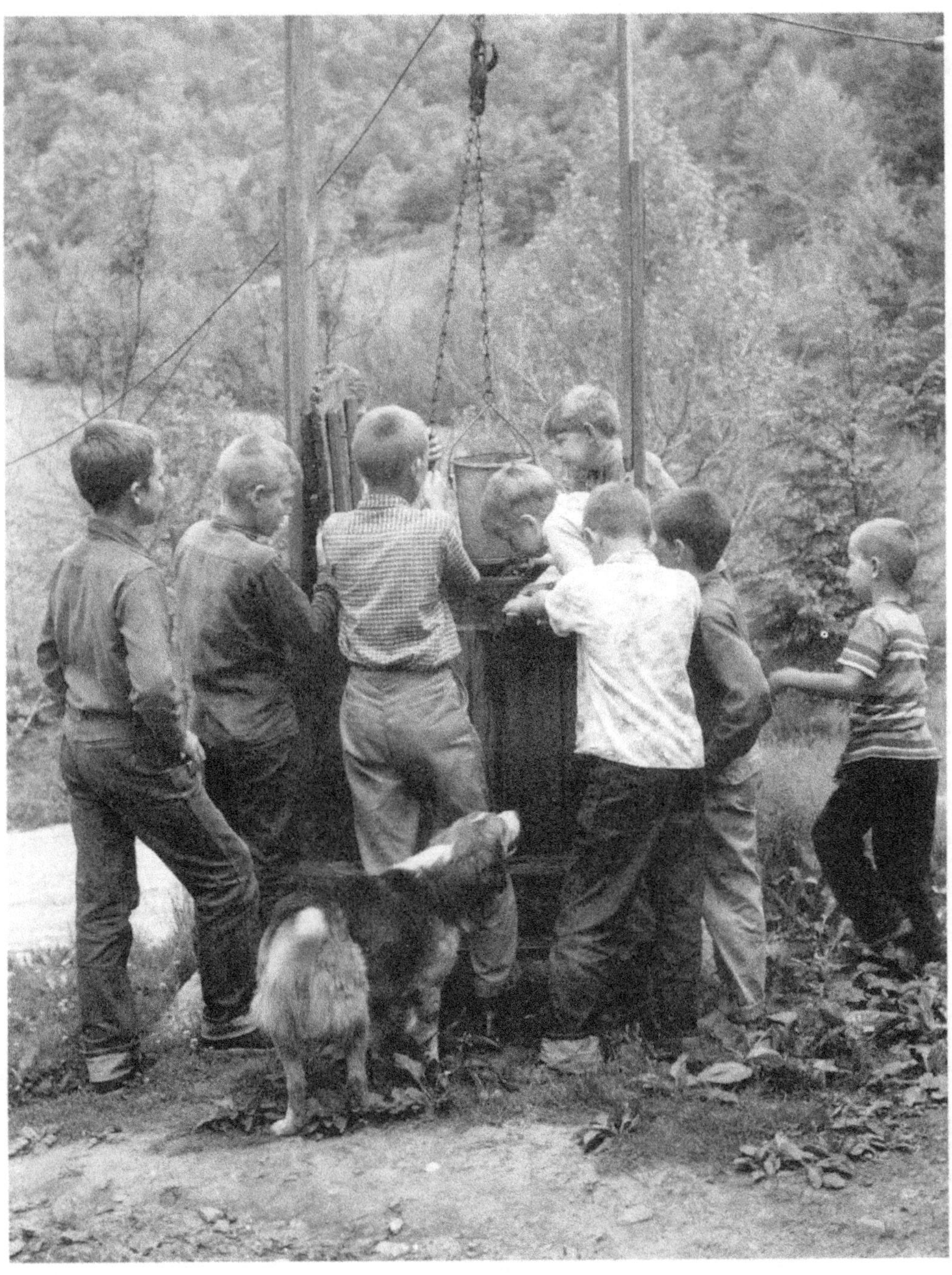

Recess time at Hindman Settlement School finds an eager group of youngsters at a well on the campus. [Hindman, Kentucky, 1959.]

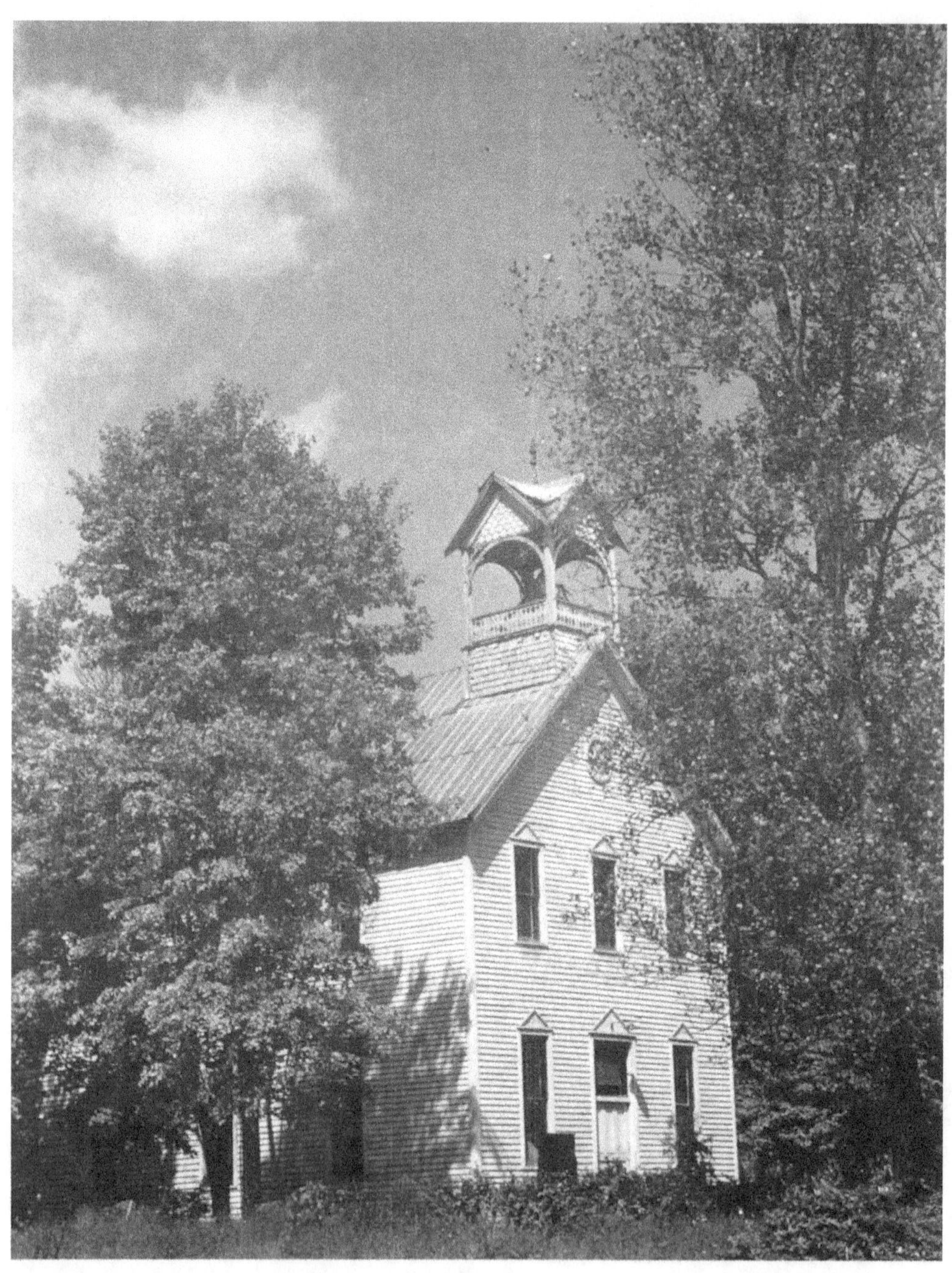

The tiny one-room white churches in the back country, with their hand-carved belfries and well-kept yards and cemeteries, have long held a fascination for my cameras. Earthy man was never so blessed as when he worked hand in hand with the Master to create these wayside places of worship. [Near Cumberland Gap, Tennessee, 1936.]

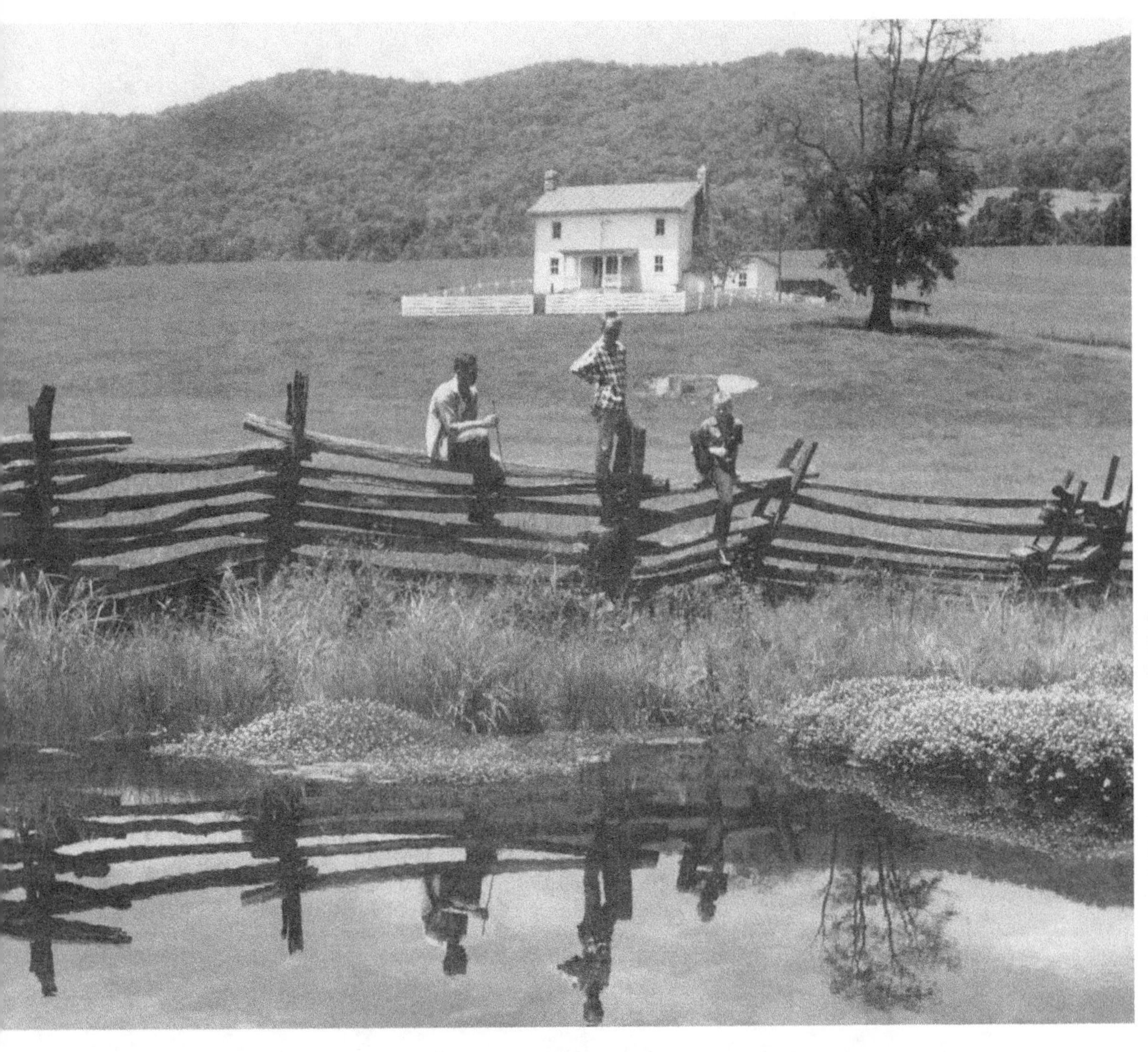

America's river of destiny and history has its birth in this pasture in Blue Grass Valley near Monterey, Virginia. [Headwaters of the north fork of the south branch of the Potomac River, 1962.]

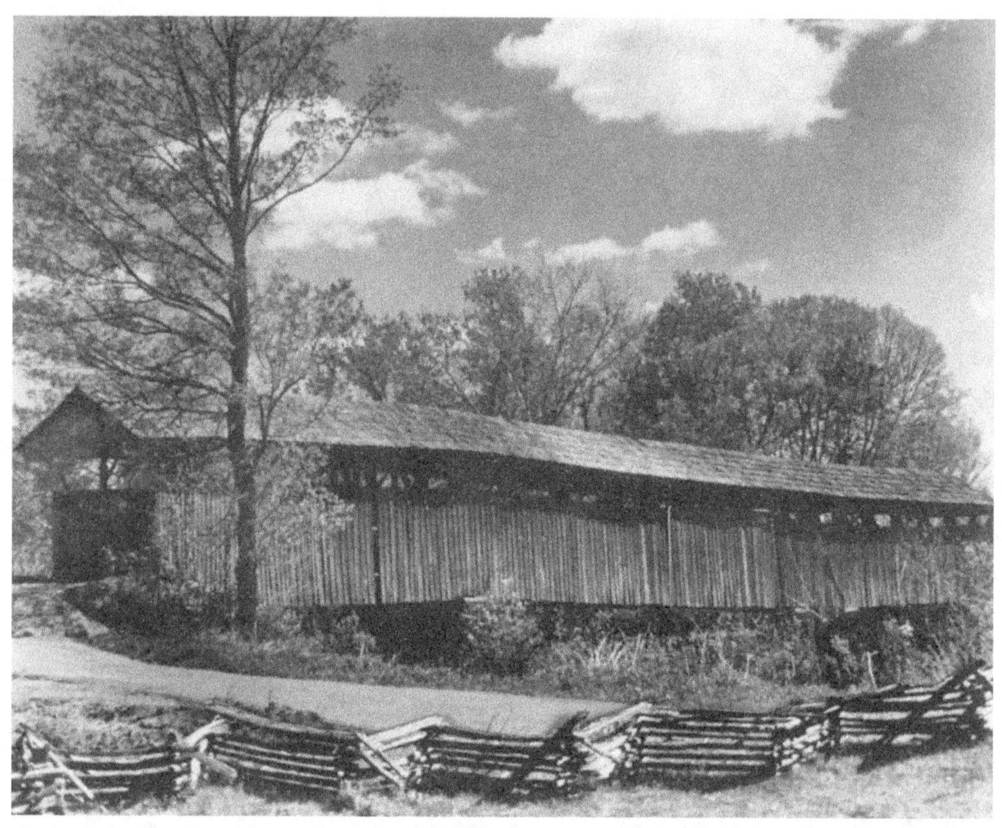

The Oldtown covered bridge [near Jesse Stuart's home in Greenup, Kentucky], 1986. At one time there were over four hundred covered bridges in Kentucky. Many were destroyed during the Civil War, others fell victim to floods, fires, and lack of upkeep as mule-, horse-, and ox-drawn wagons and buggies were supplanted by automobiles and people in a hurry to get from hither to yon.

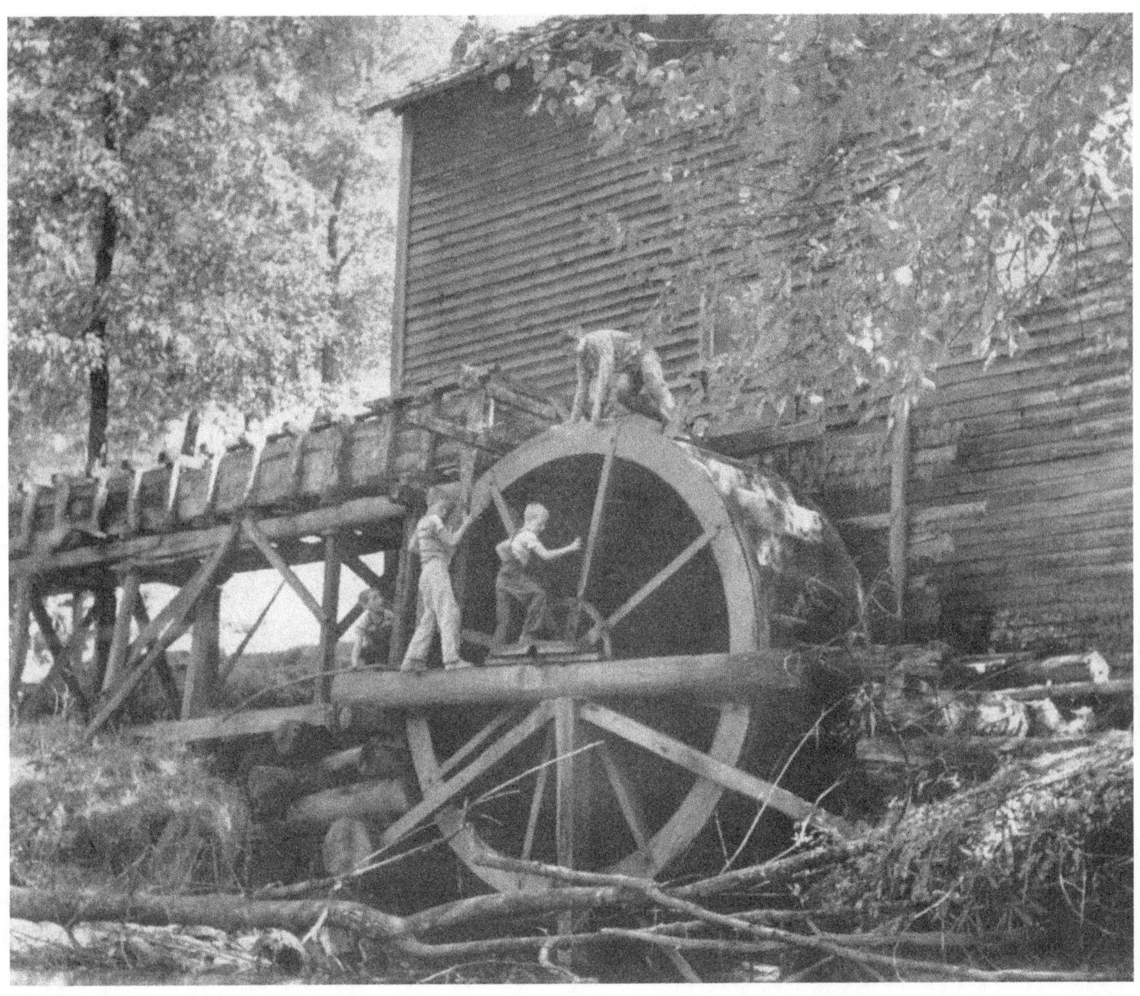

The idle gristmill of Mont Marshall on Stone Mountain Creek [Virginia] makes a fit place for a band of frolicsome children to play. I remember my own youth, and the feeling that I could go on playing forever, outlast the ages, the earth, and all men. The mill pictured here has departed the scene, victim of a time when earthy man has little time for a "turn" of corn to pass slowly but surely through the French-burr millstones.

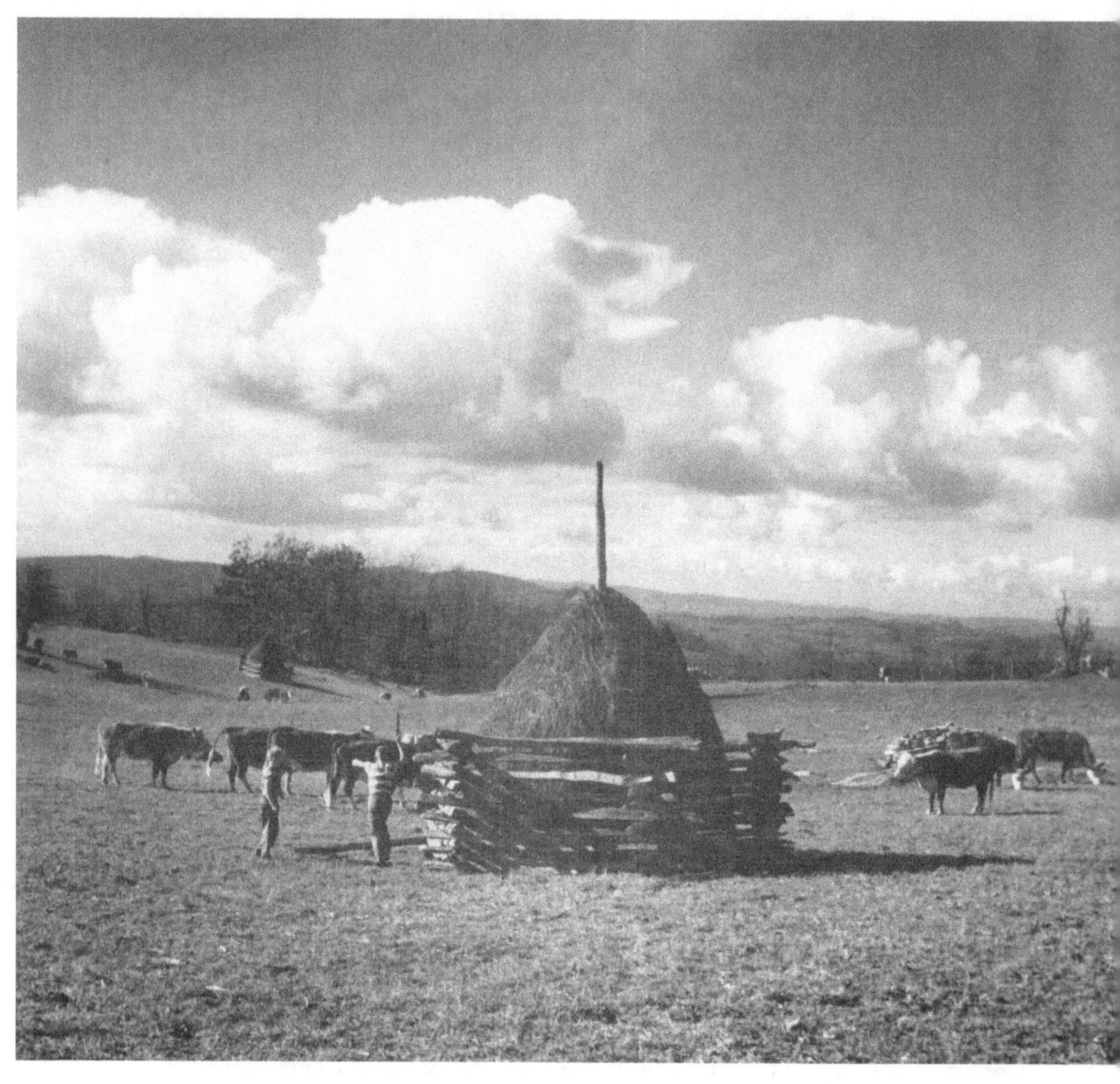

This land is fair for any eyes to see. This is my land and the land is part of me and I am part of the land while my habitation is here. [Floyd County, Virginia, 1980.]

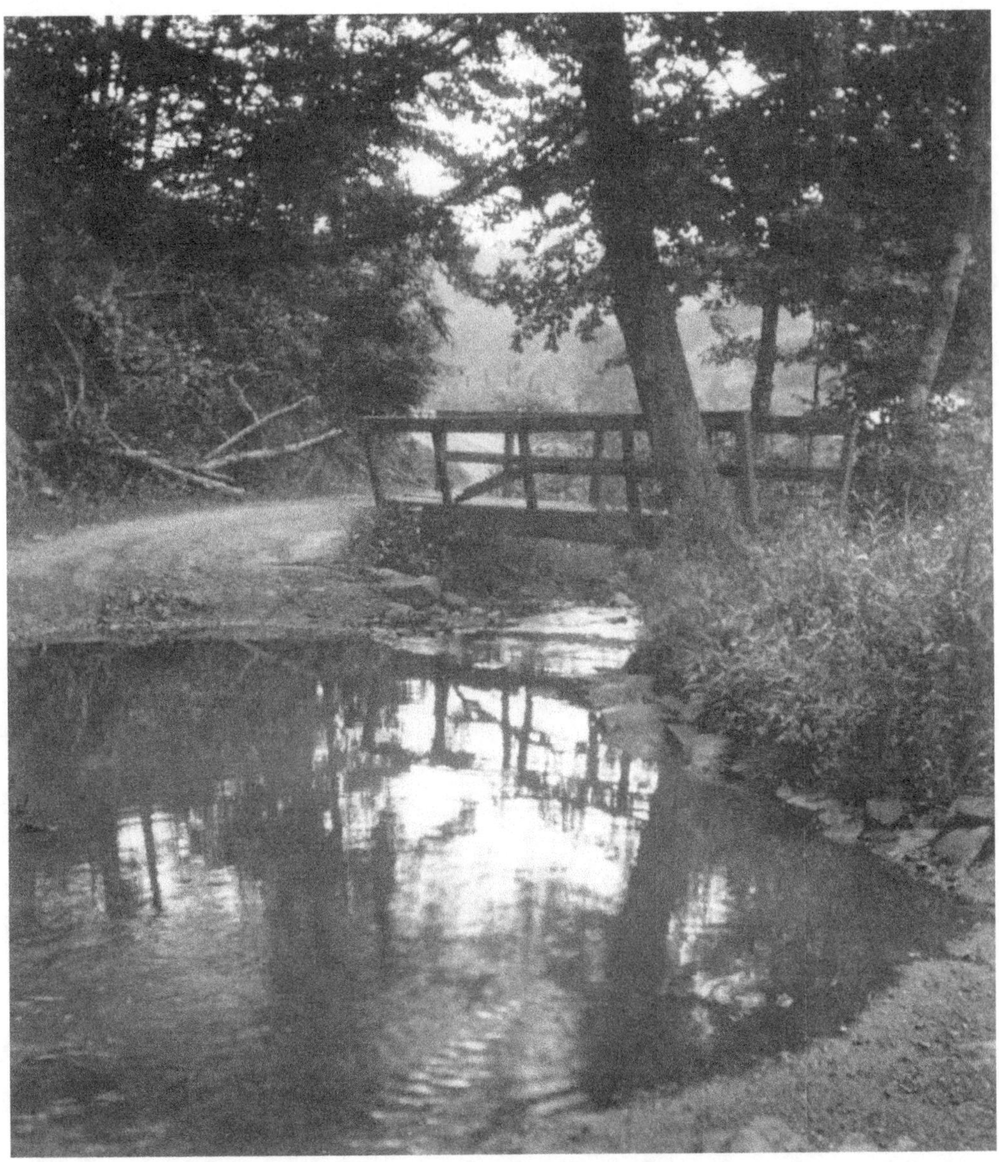

At eventide I watched a valley creek lose itself in the shadow of a day's end. Lingering there, I tried to understand its whispering, fading song, then saw it dance its way into the nearing dark to tell its secret to some distant sea. [One of Palmer's favorite photographs, made in the Great Smoky Mountains National Park in 1936.]

[Farmhouse with split-rail fence. Southwest Virginia, 1960.]

Making a Home in the Mountains

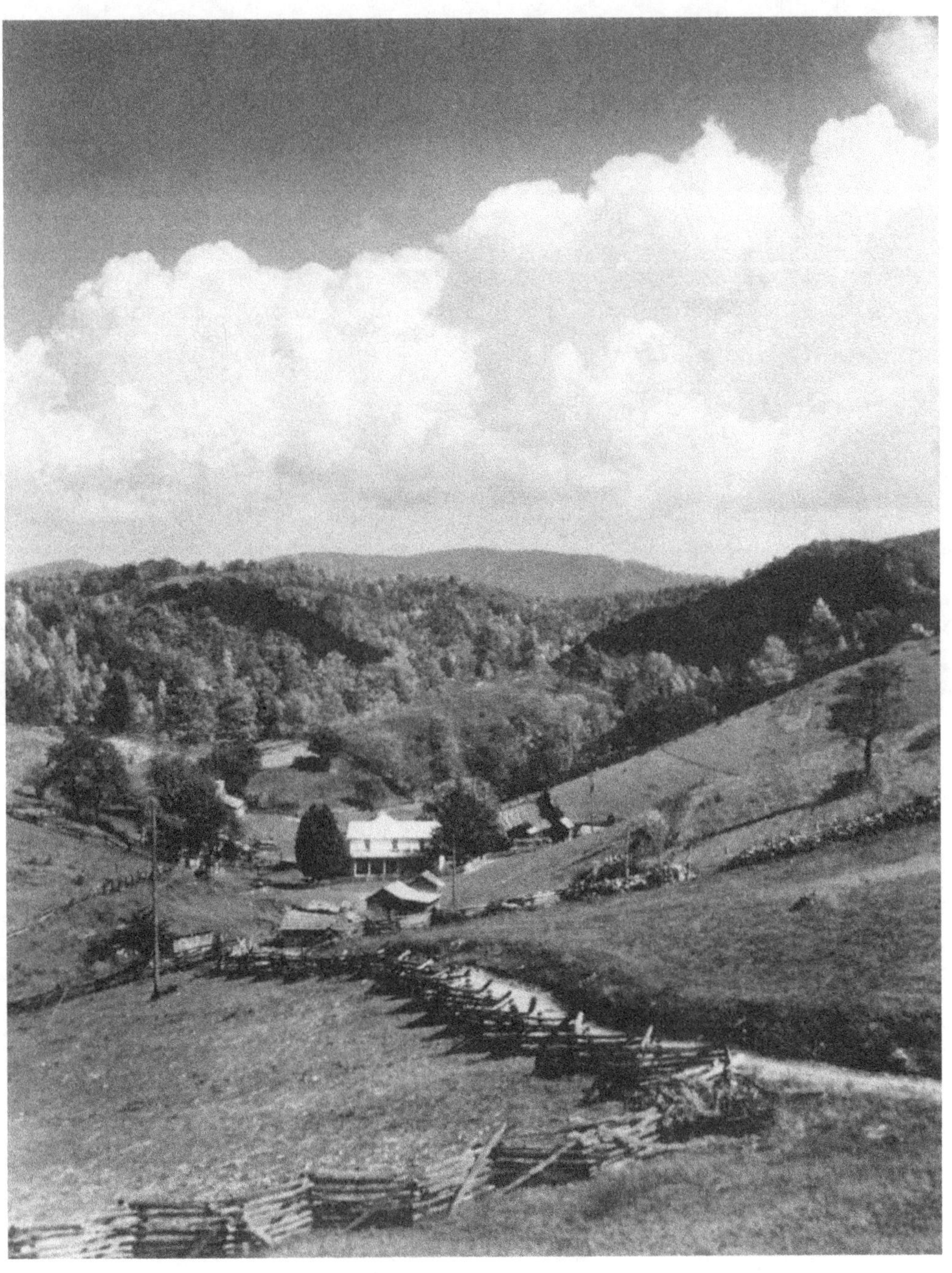

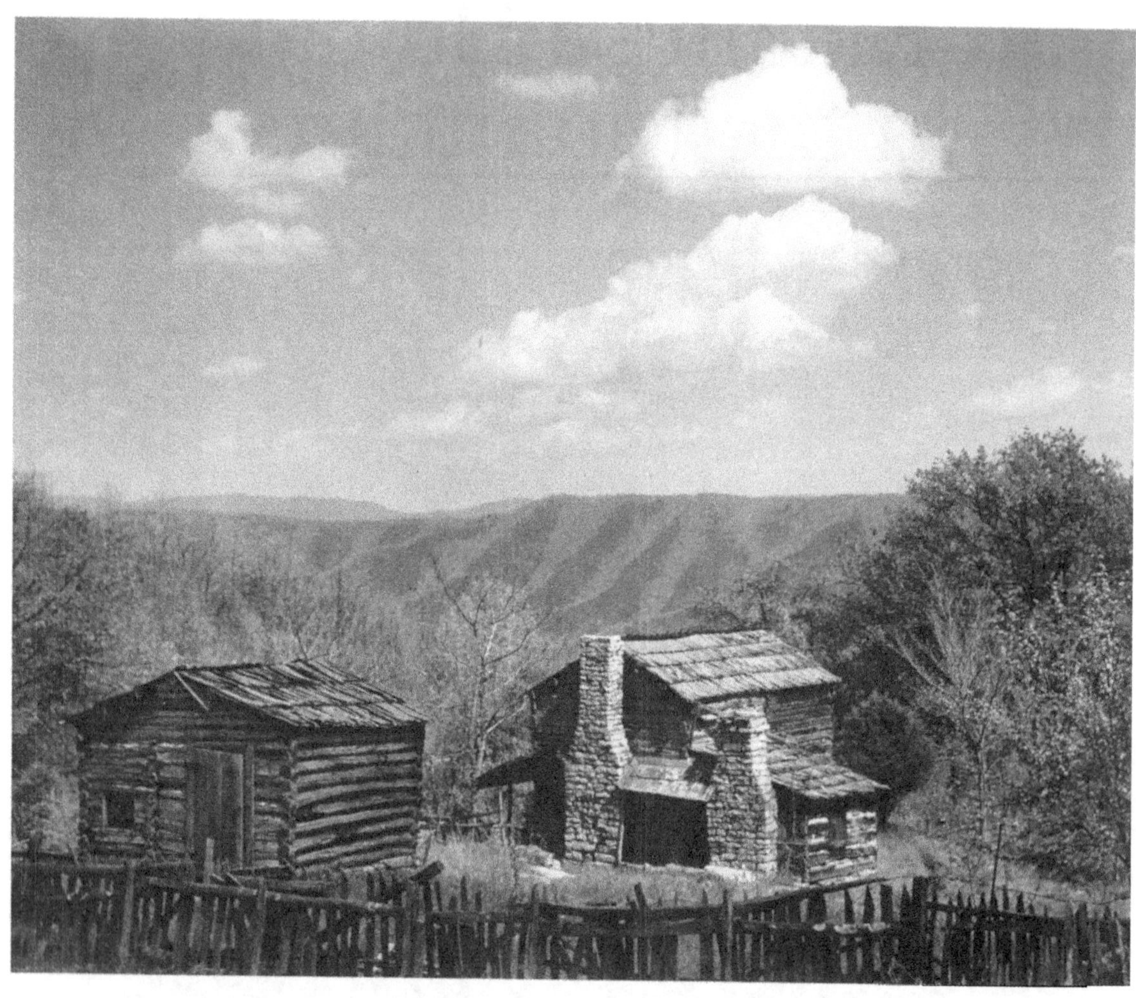

[Sarver cabin on the south face of Gap Mountain, Giles County, Virginia, 1960. Palmer calls this "the prettiest mountain cabin I've ever photographed"; he likes to point out the four-tiered board roof. The cabin is now in ruins.]

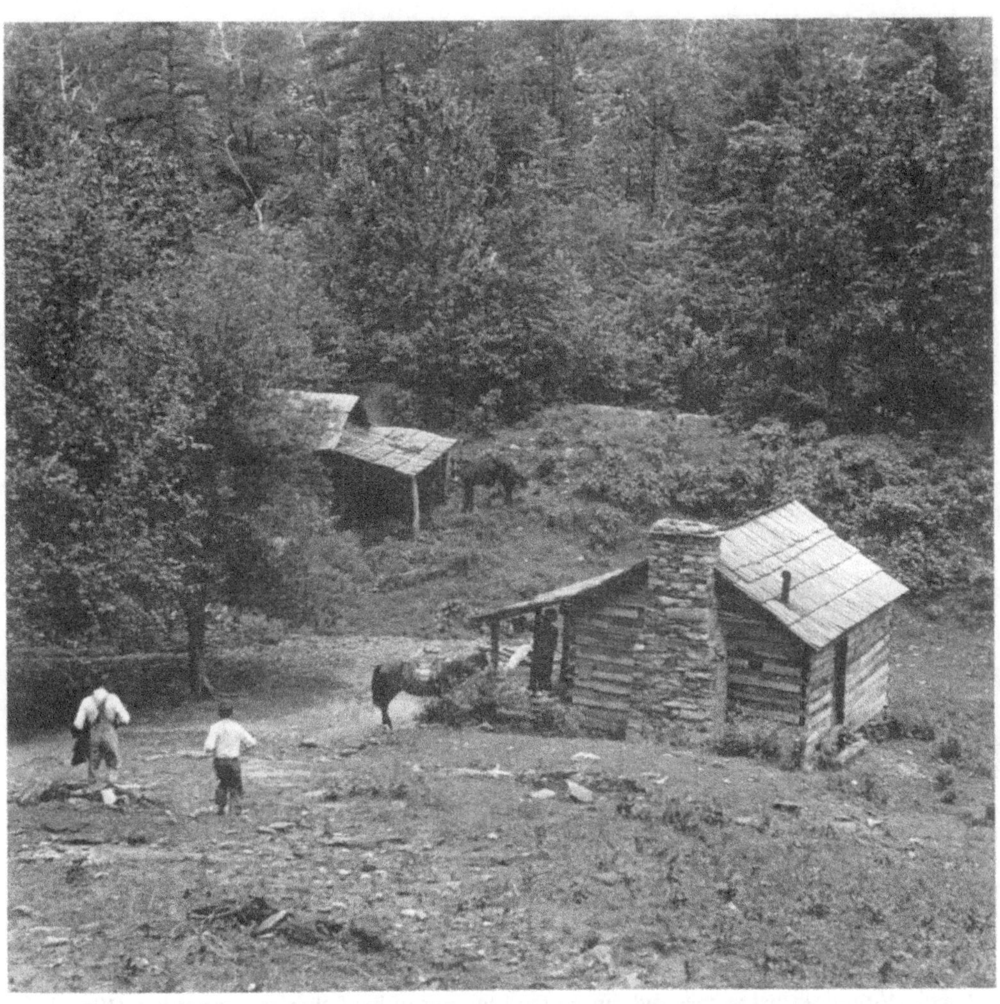

Tom Cupp's cabin, north of Chadwell's Gap, has been restored and serves as an overnight shelter for hikers on the Mischa Mokwa Trail. [Near Ewing, Virginia, 1942.]

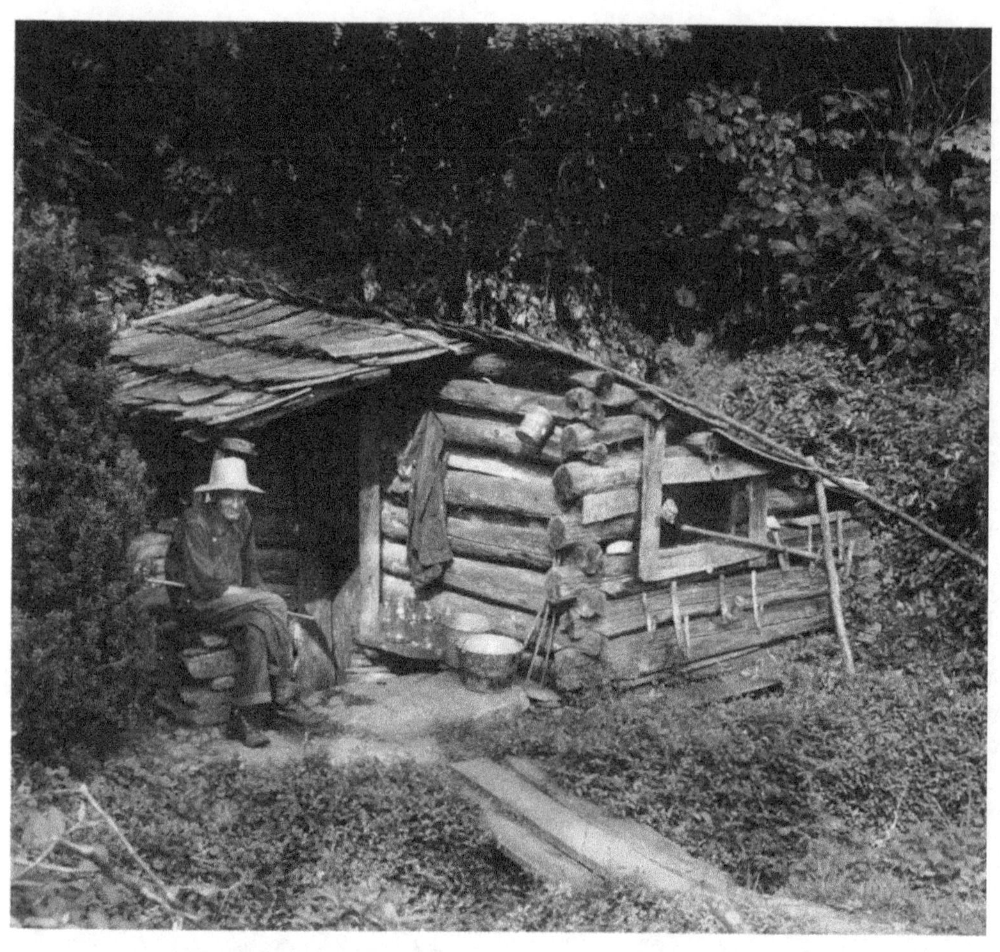

The waters still run cold and clear in Buren Cockram's springhouse on Raven's Den Creek [Virginia], just as they did during the lifetimes of his father and granddad. [1958.]

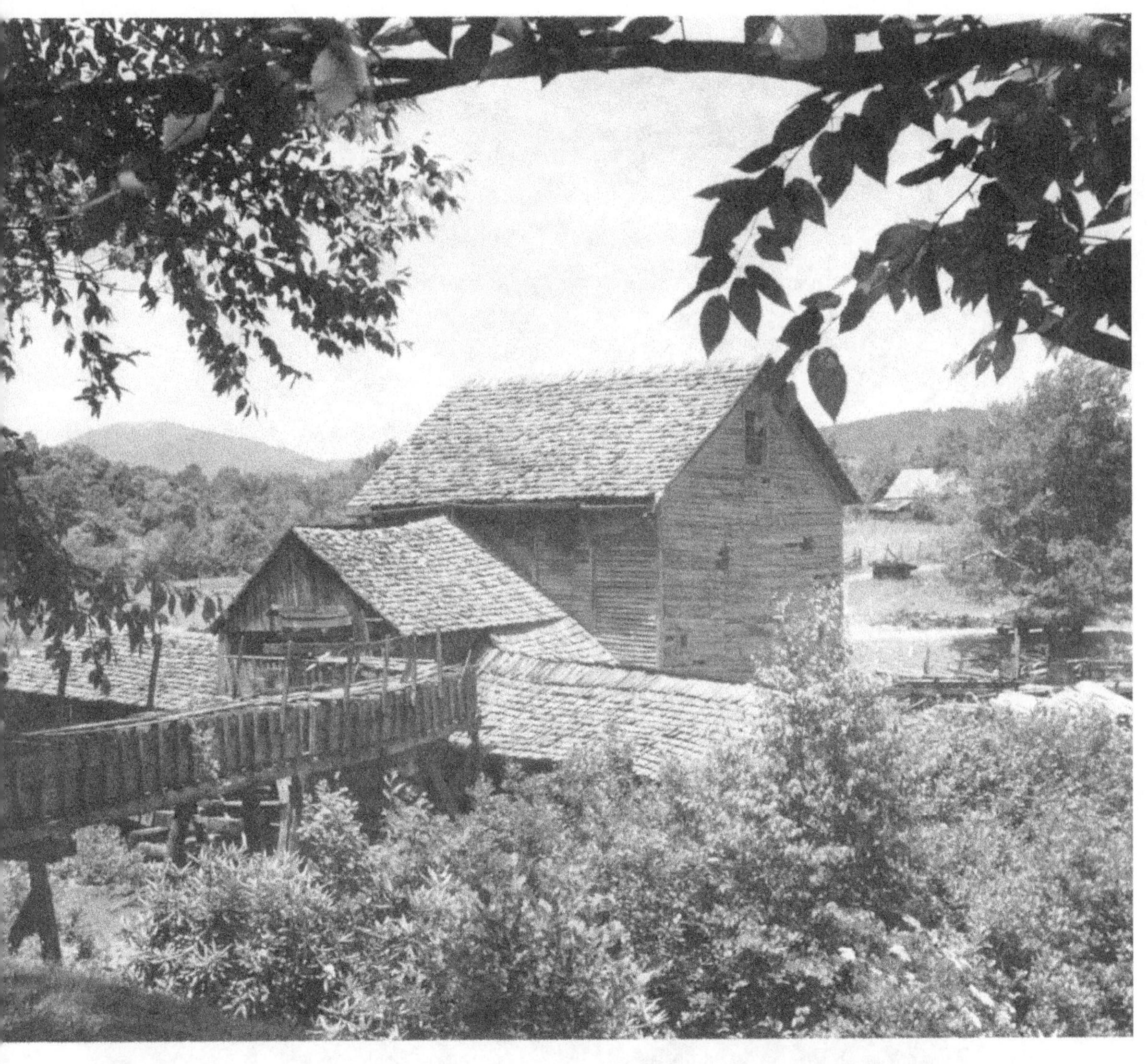

Tom Agee's water-powered gristmill, on Laurel Fork Creek north of the Blue Ridge, ground corn, rye, and wheat for mountain families for over a century until its millrace was destroyed by a flood in 1956. [Patrick County, Virginia, 1956.]

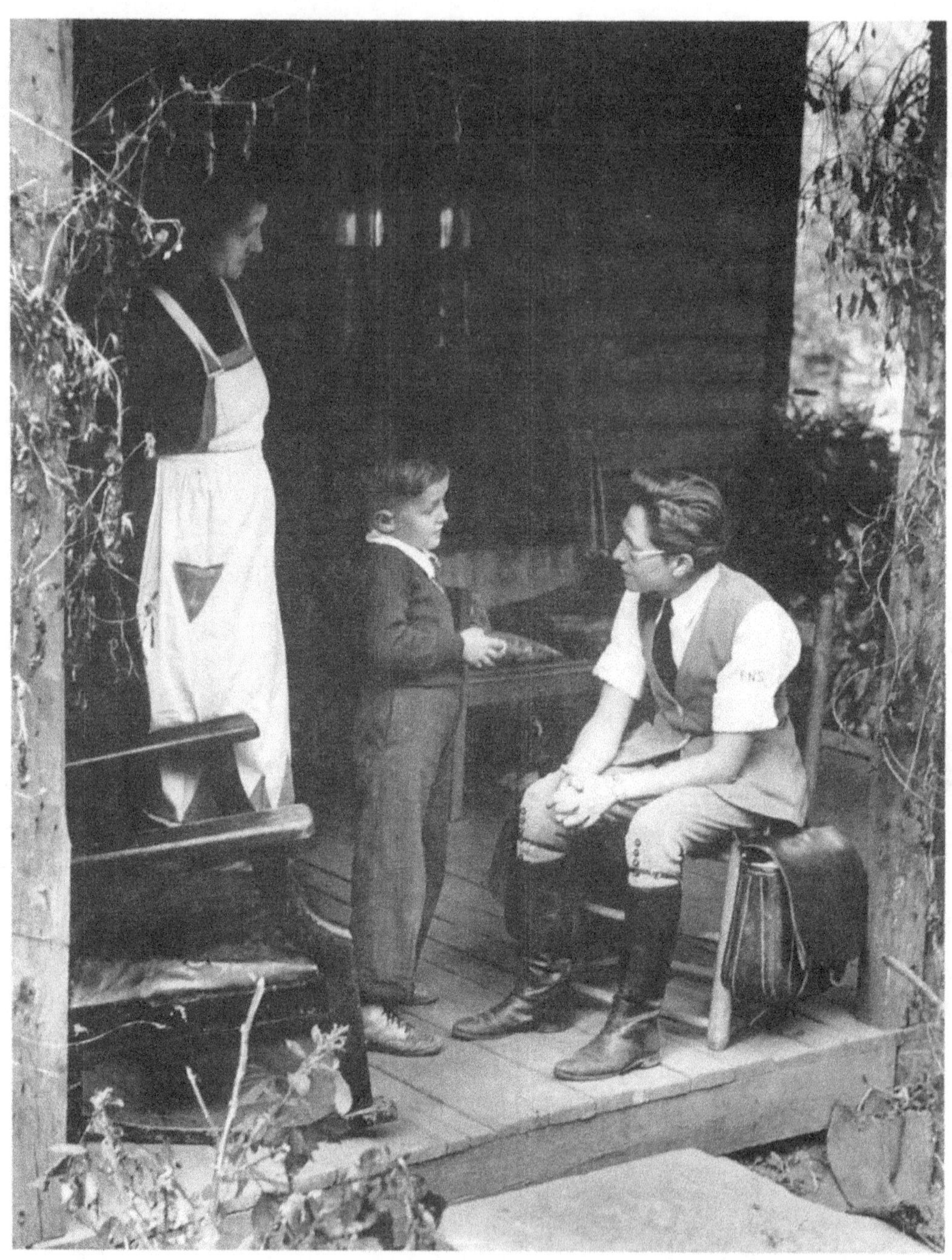

Nola Blair, a nurse of the Frontier Nursing Service, talks to a child she delivered on Munch Creek on the headwaters of the Kentucky River near Hyden, Kentucky [1941]. In the early days of the FNS, the nurses served an eight-hundred-square-mile area on horseback.

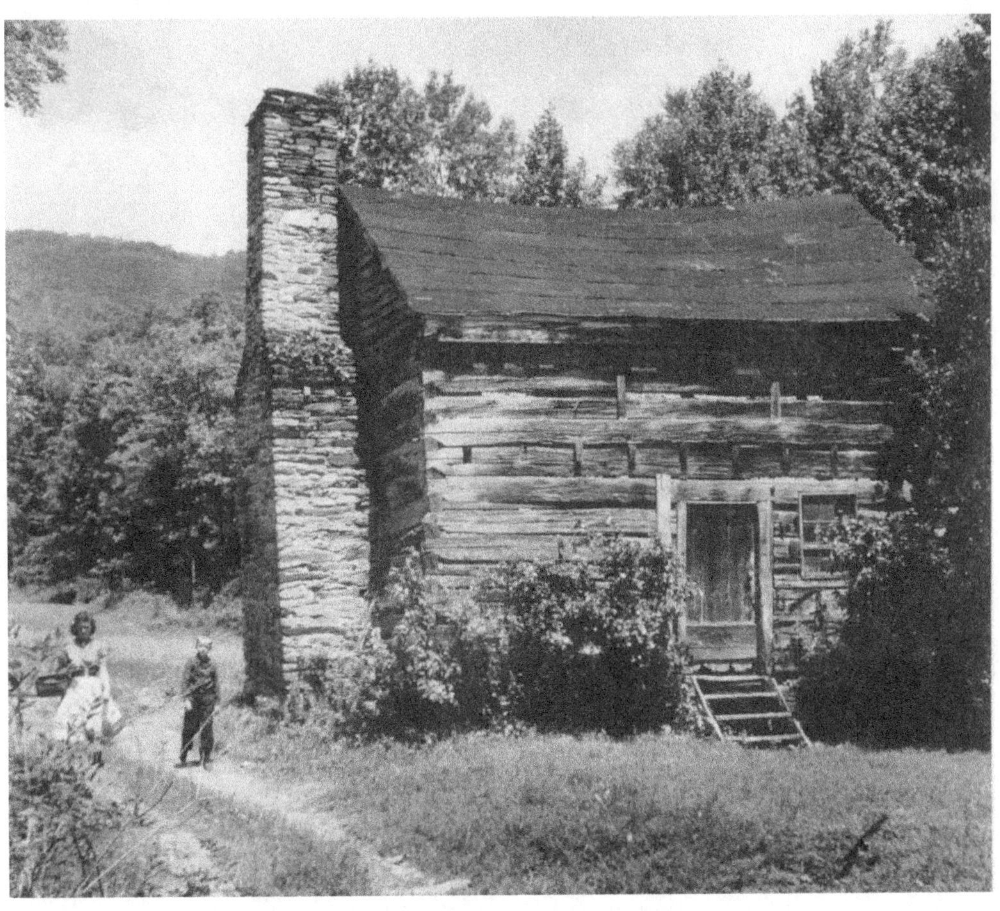

The mountain cabin home of Roy DeHart's boyhood is similar to many still in existence off the beaten path, away from the race of main street living. [Rock Castle Creek, Patrick County, Virginia, 1958.]

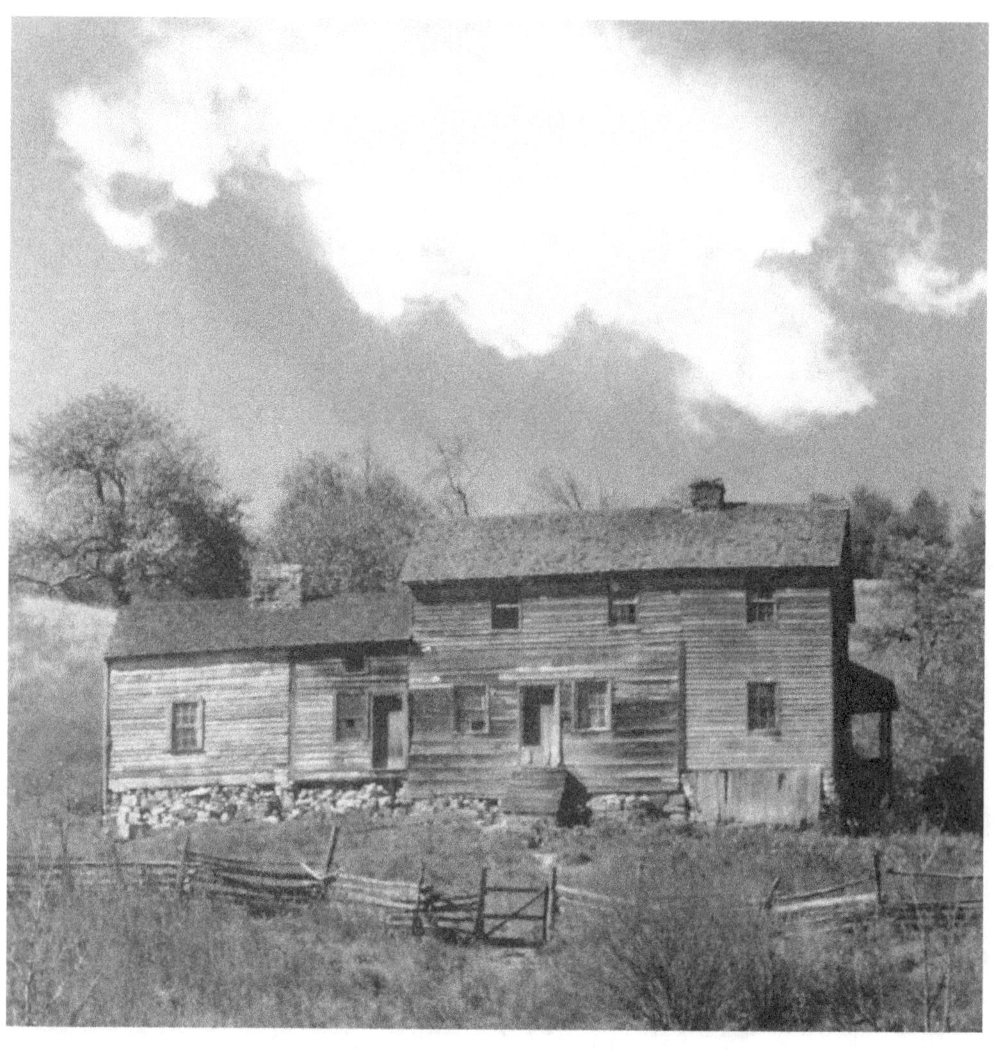

This abandoned farmhouse, still standing in Monongahela National Forest, was once the home of some mountain family who knew joy, hope, and pain within its walls. [1960]

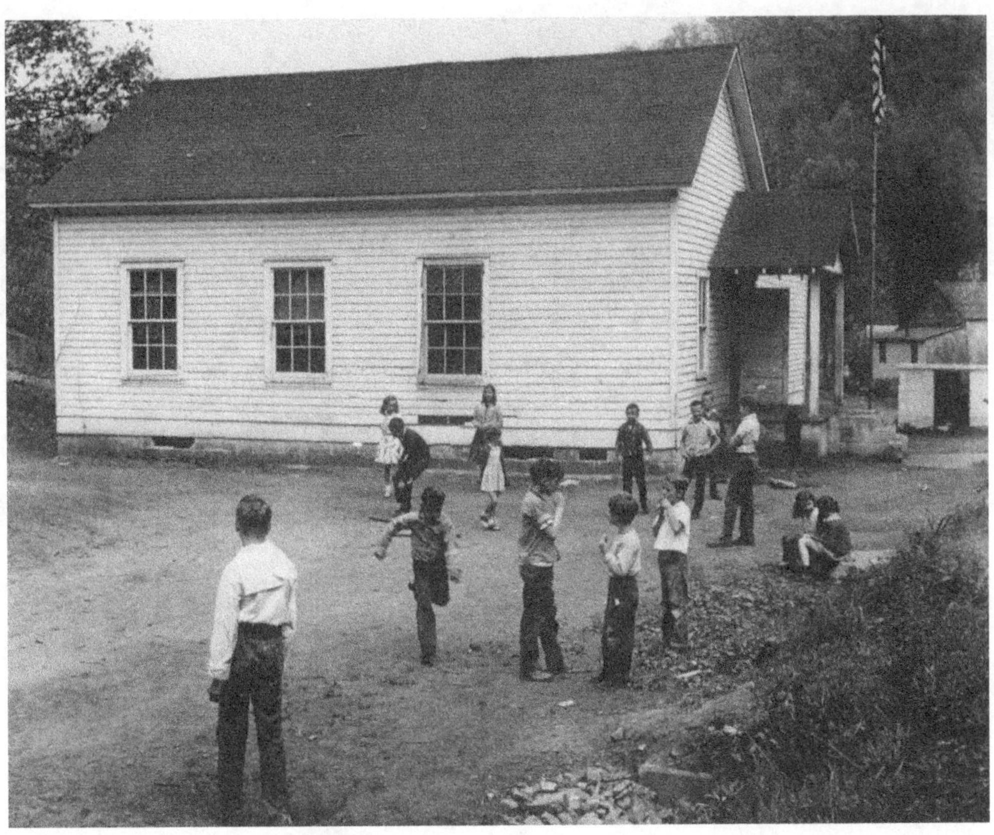

The Wolfe Pen school near Pineville, West Virginia, was one of the few one-room schools left in the state [in 1960].

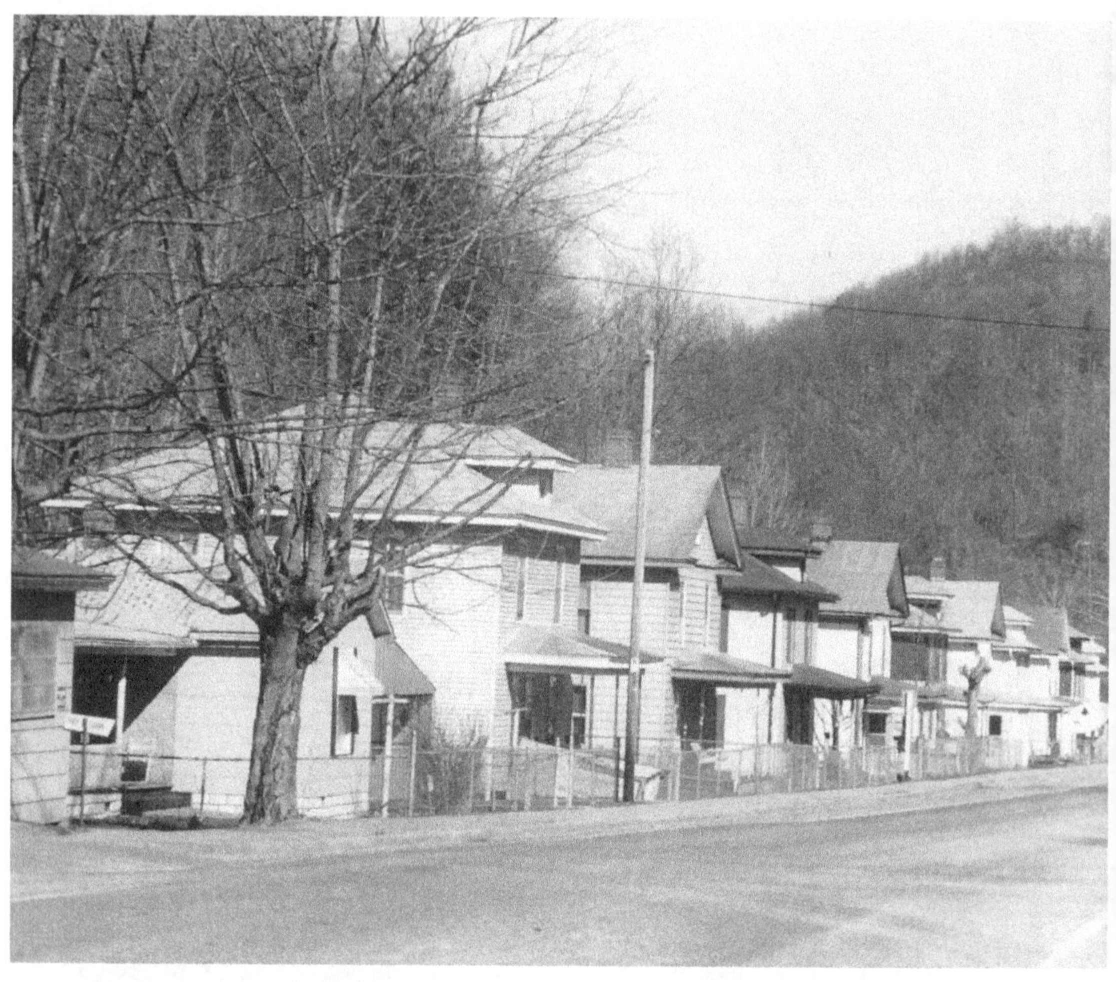

These houses are occupied by former miners who bought them from Pocahontas Fuel Company when the company "freed" its camps. [Bishop, Virginia, 1985. Note the satellite dish, lower right, unusual in a Palmer photo.]

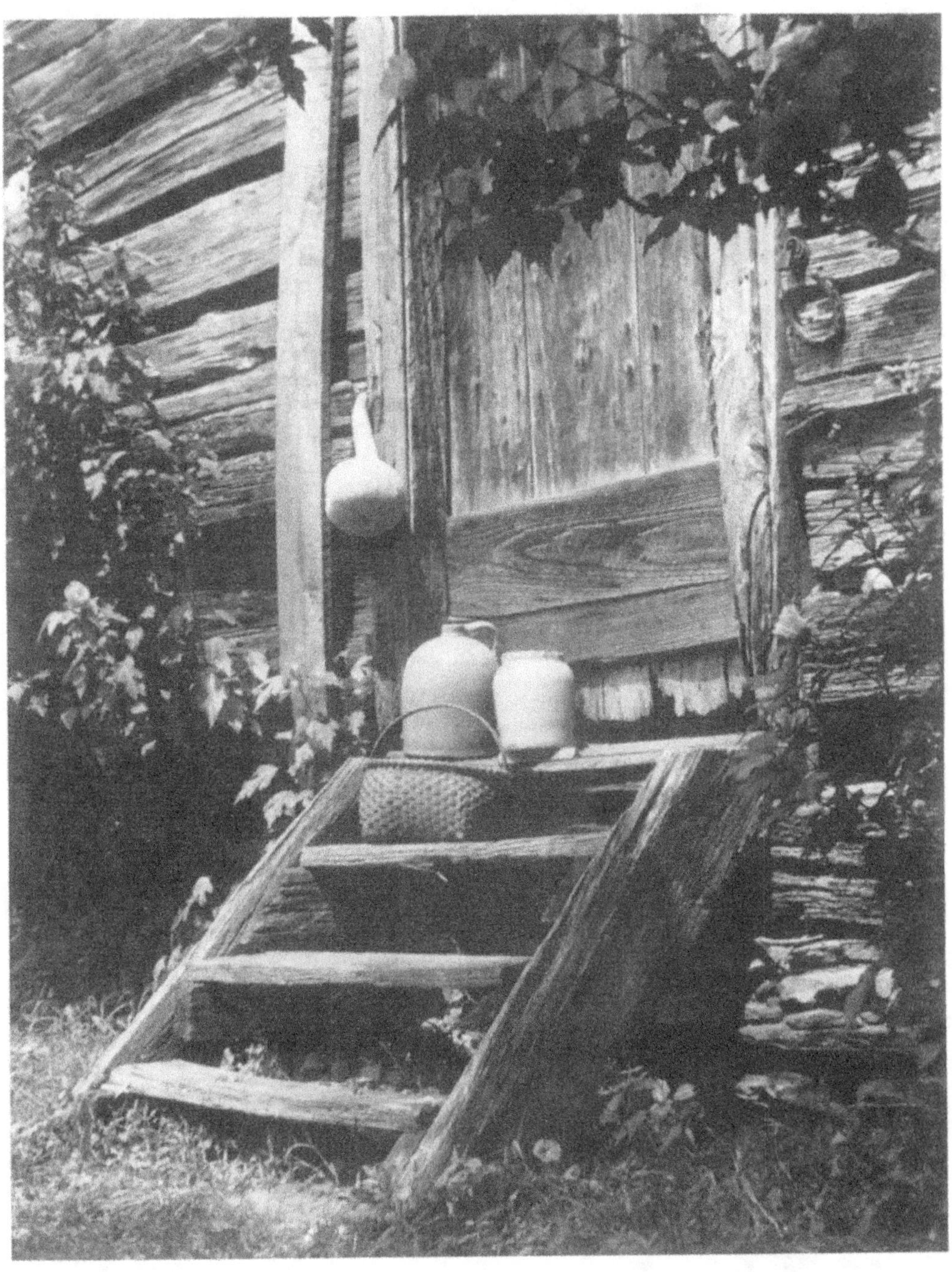

Doorway of a remote cabin. [Patrick County, Virginia, 1956. This is the same cabin pictured on page 47.]

"The sheep roaming a thousand hills are Thine, oh Lord." [Montgomery County, Virginia, 1960.]

Making a Living

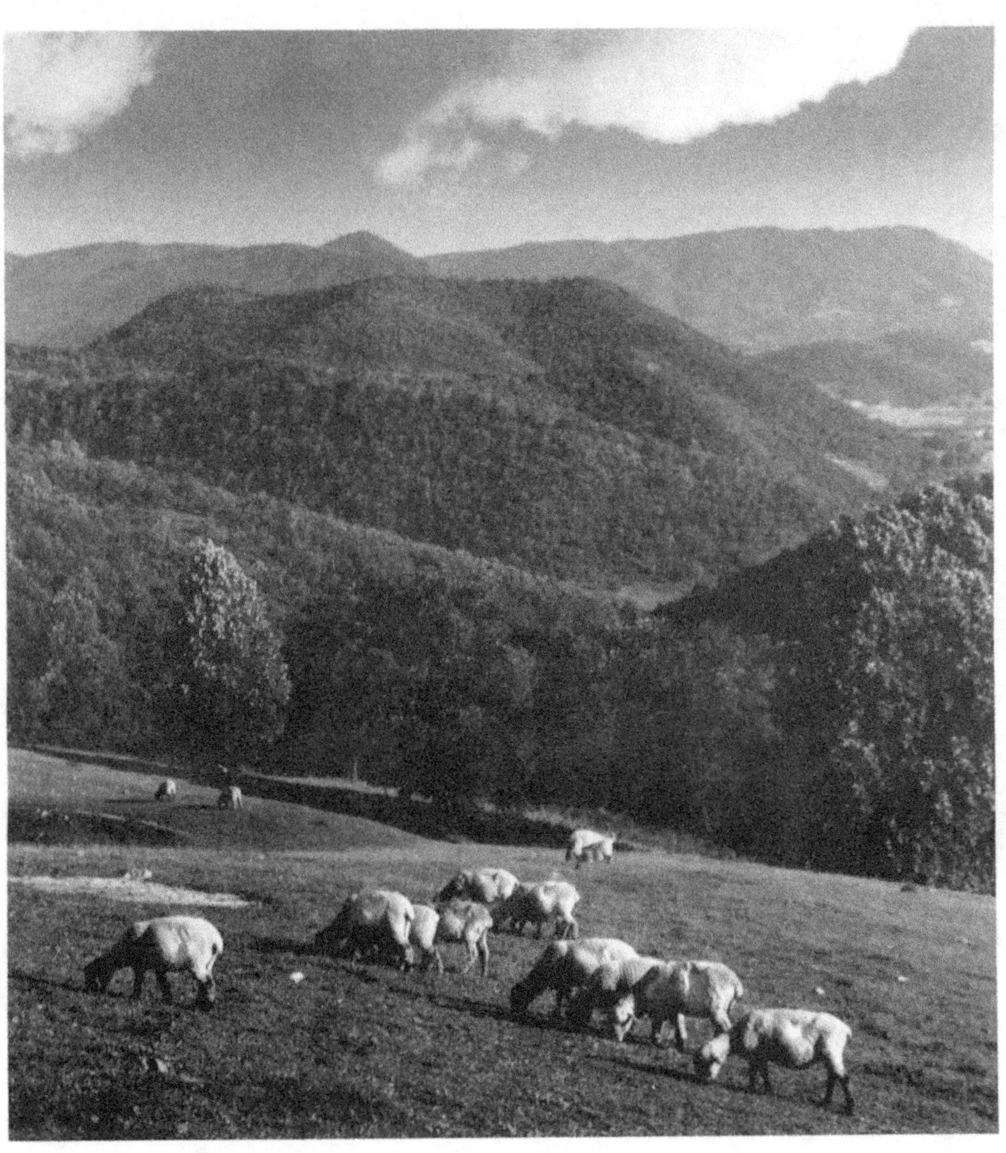

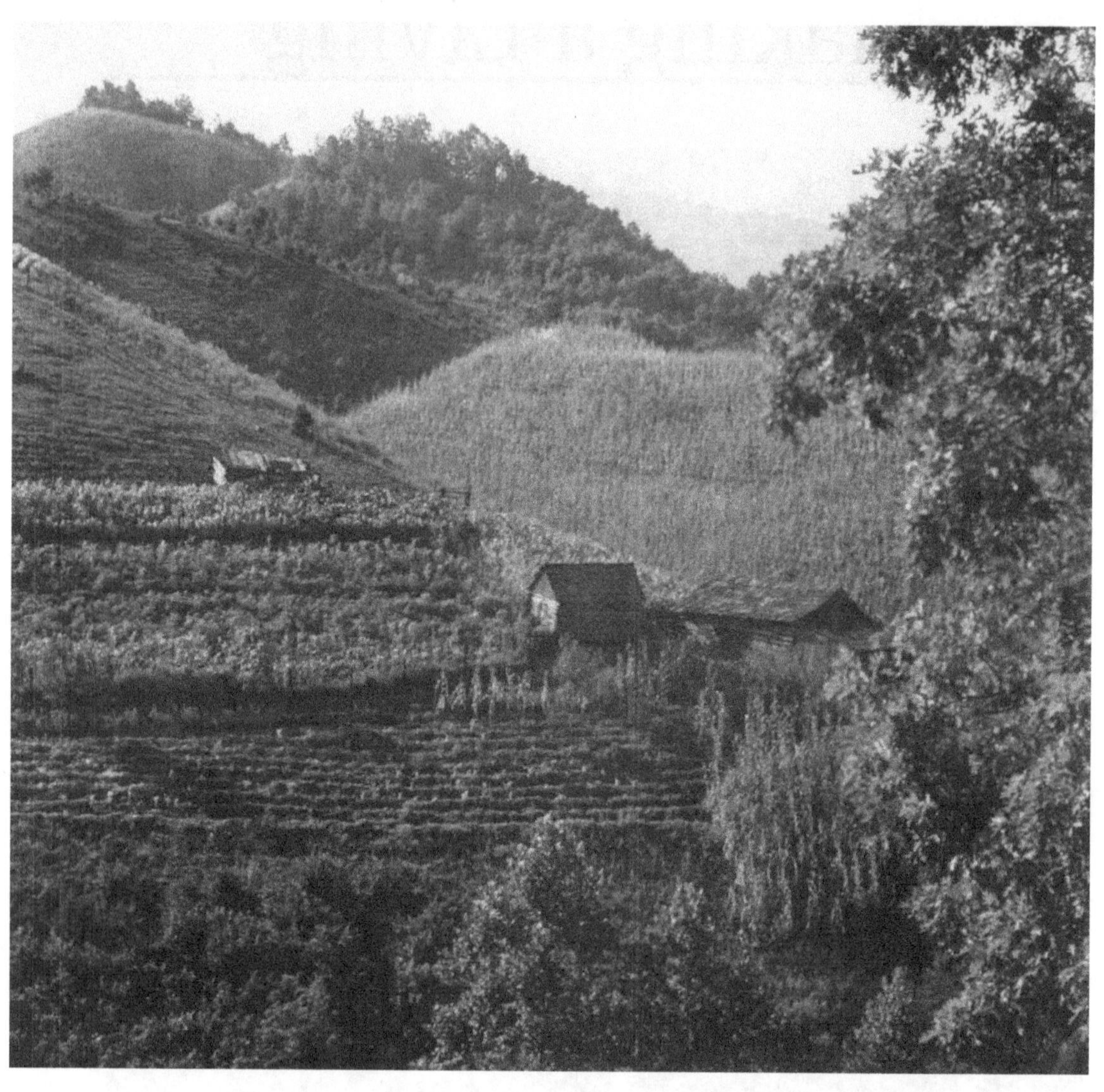

Today I saw the sun come up, like Neptune from the sea. I watched him light the cliffs with gold, and wake a distant tree. I watched him shake his shaggy head, and laugh the night away, then toss to a sleeping world another golden day. [Near the Great Smoky Mountains National Park, 1936.]

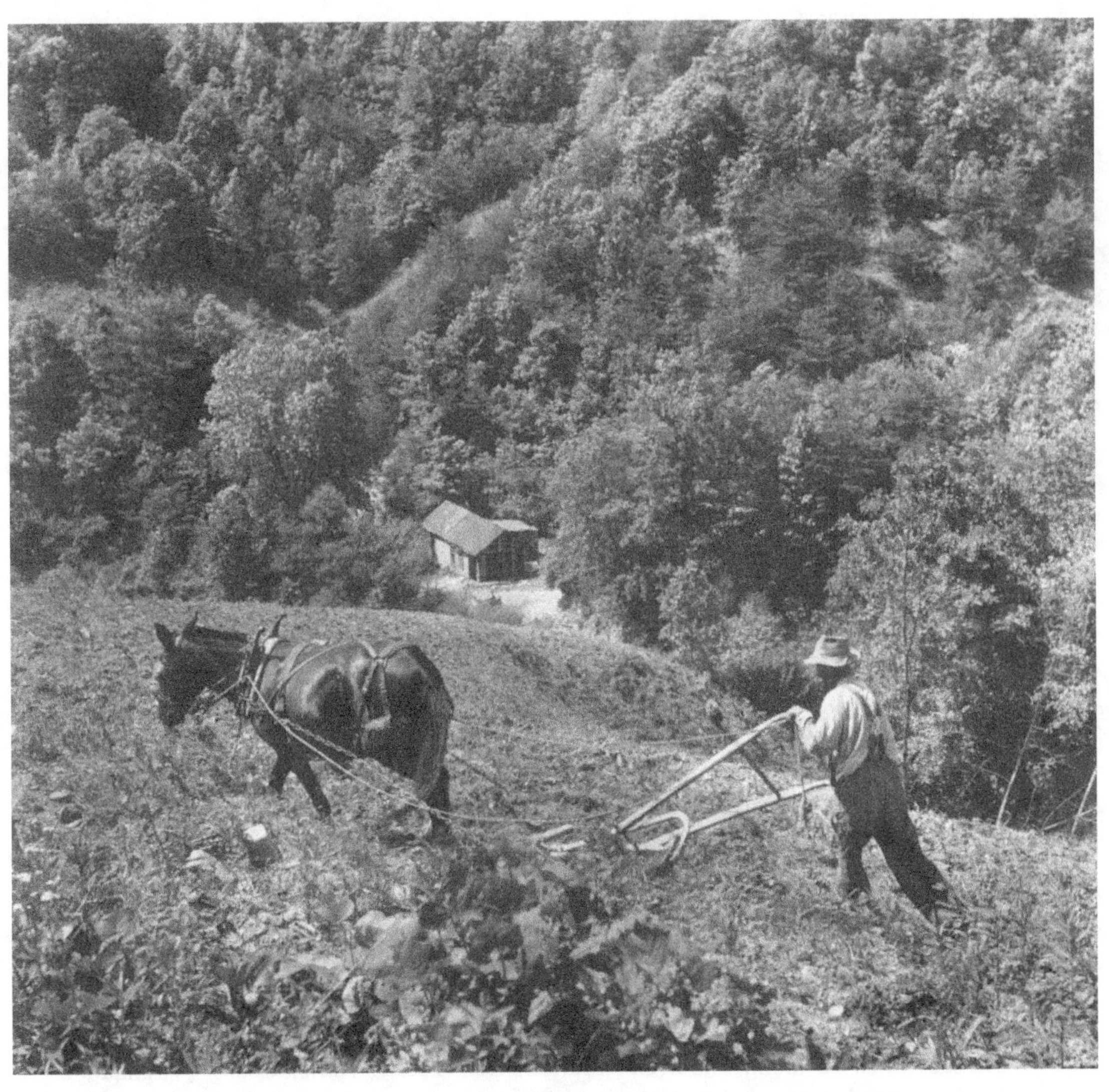

In early spring a mountain man and his long-eared mule plow the sleepy soil that will be planted to corn, 'taters, and beans. [Breathitt County, Kentucky, 1942.]

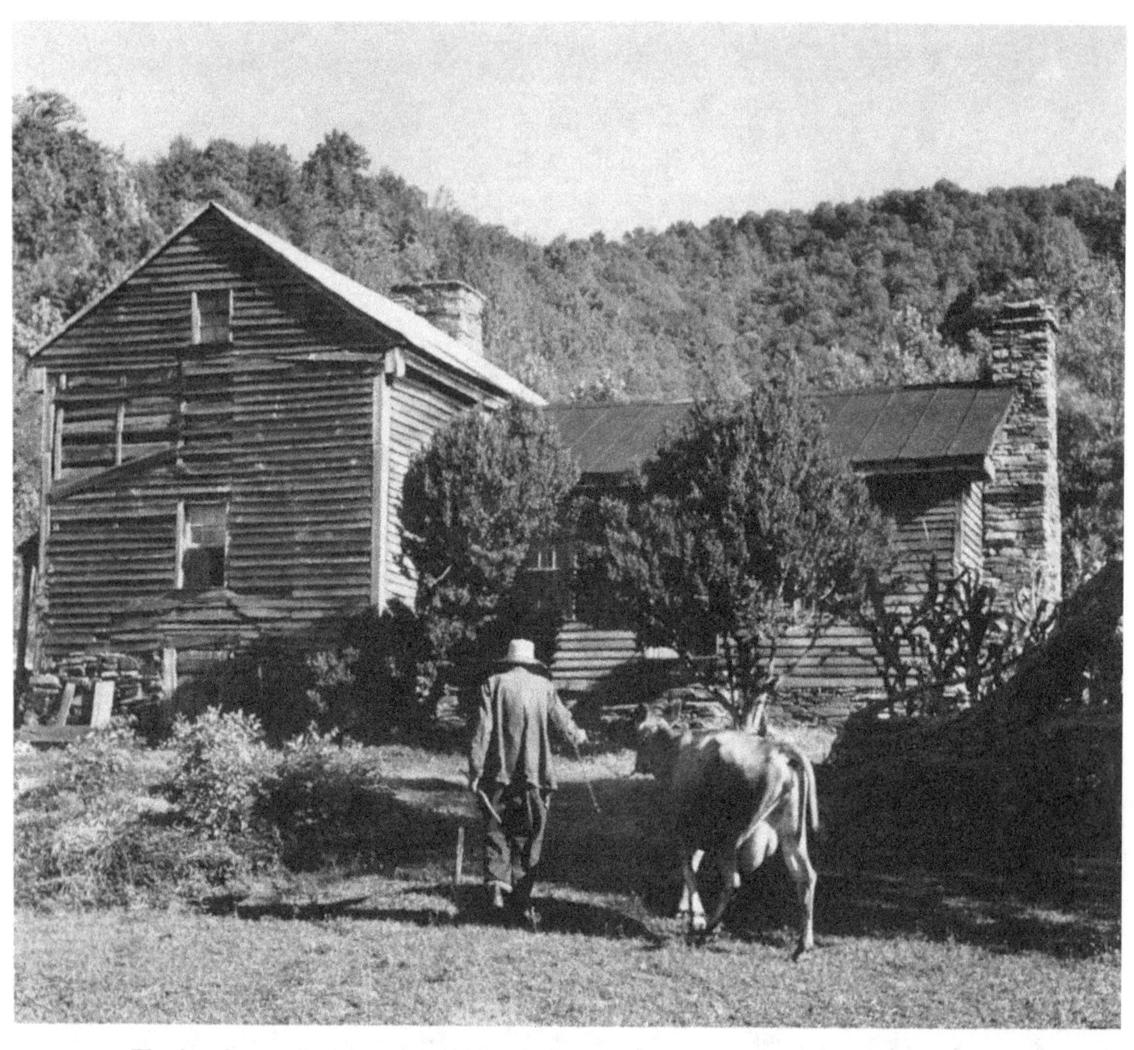

The late Buren Cockram, who lived on Raven's Den Creek in Patrick County [Virginia], heads his cow homeward at milkin' time. [1960.]

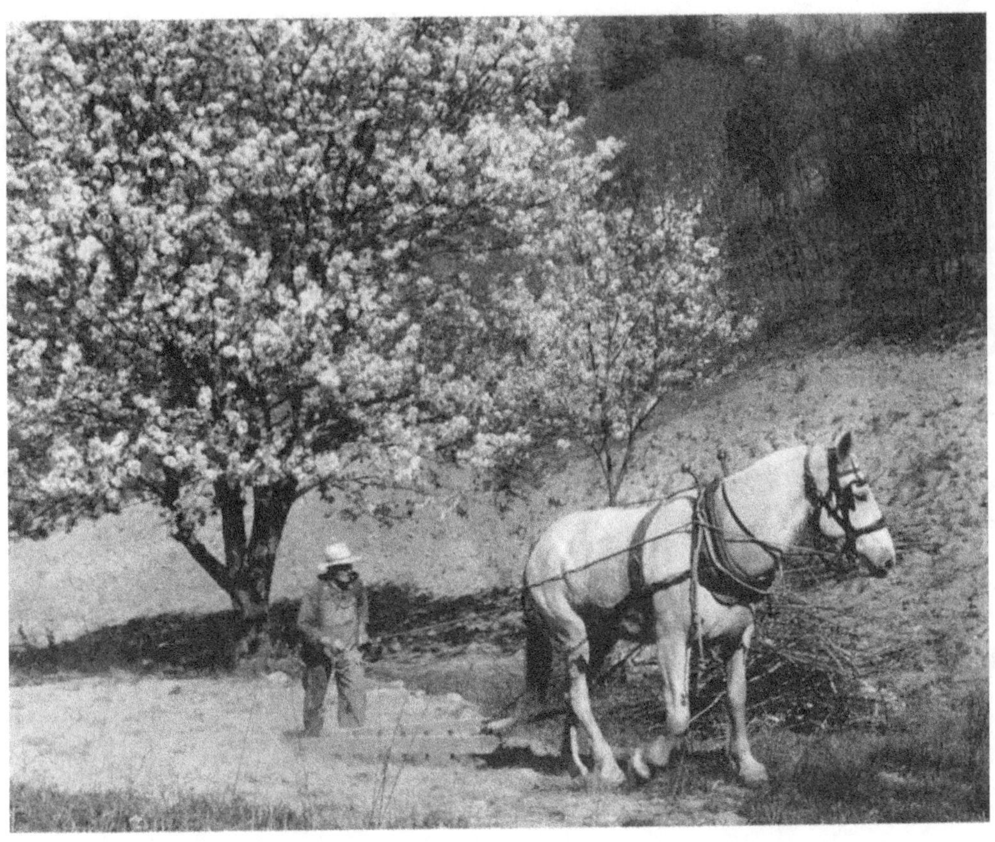

For people cooped up in canyons of steel and concrete, spring is a time for building dream castles in the air. Not so for Timothy Wirt; he has no time for dreaming, come spring; he has a world to build in growing things. [Ellett Creek, Virginia, 1944.]

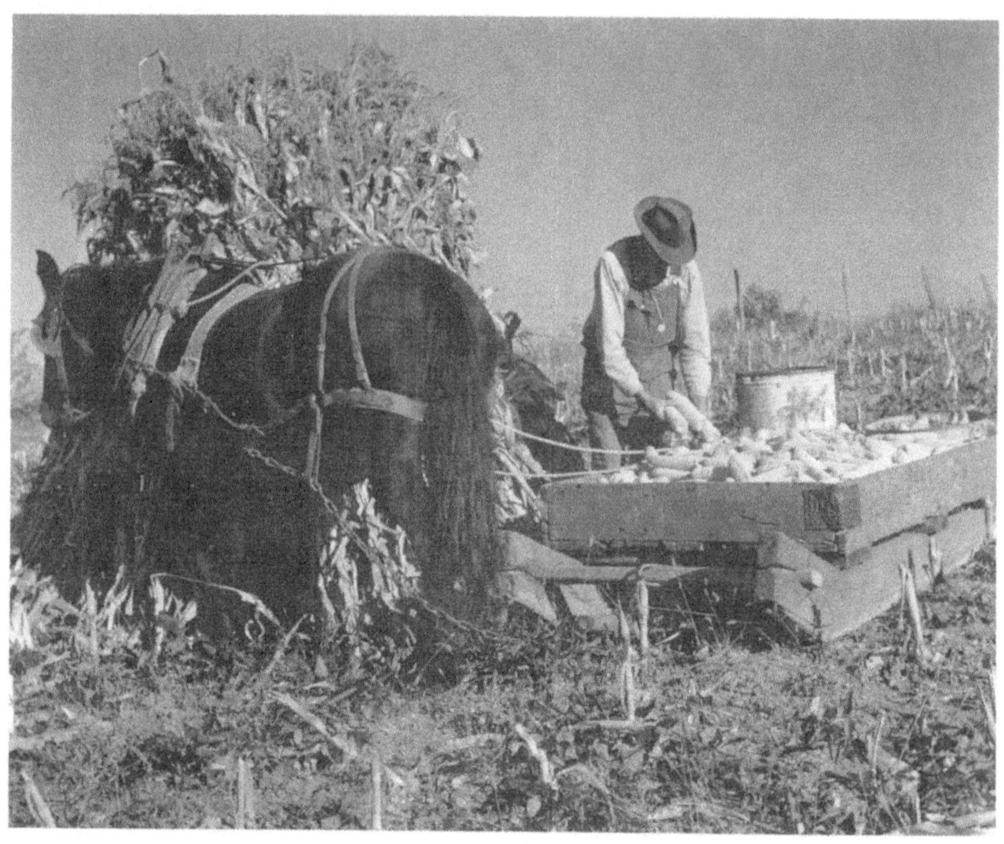

The first frost falls, maples on the fringe of the woods flame scarlet in the nip of an October morning. It's corn-gathering time in the hills and the crop is a bountiful one. [Near Riner, Virginia, 1950.]

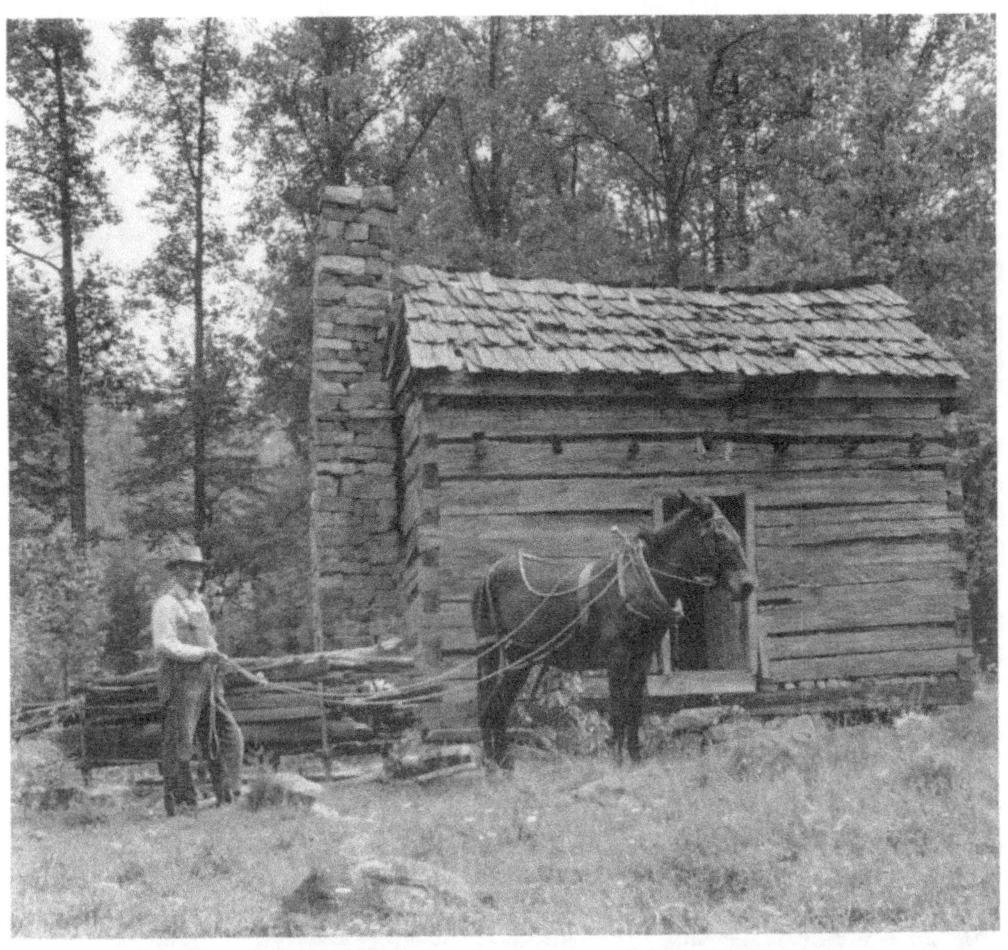

Jim Howard could always find another sled-full of firewood to keep the bite of winter away from his cabin. Like Thomas Jefferson Cupp, who lived across the mountain, Jim was a self-sufficient feller, not the sort to ask aught of any man. [Ewing, Virginia, 1939.]

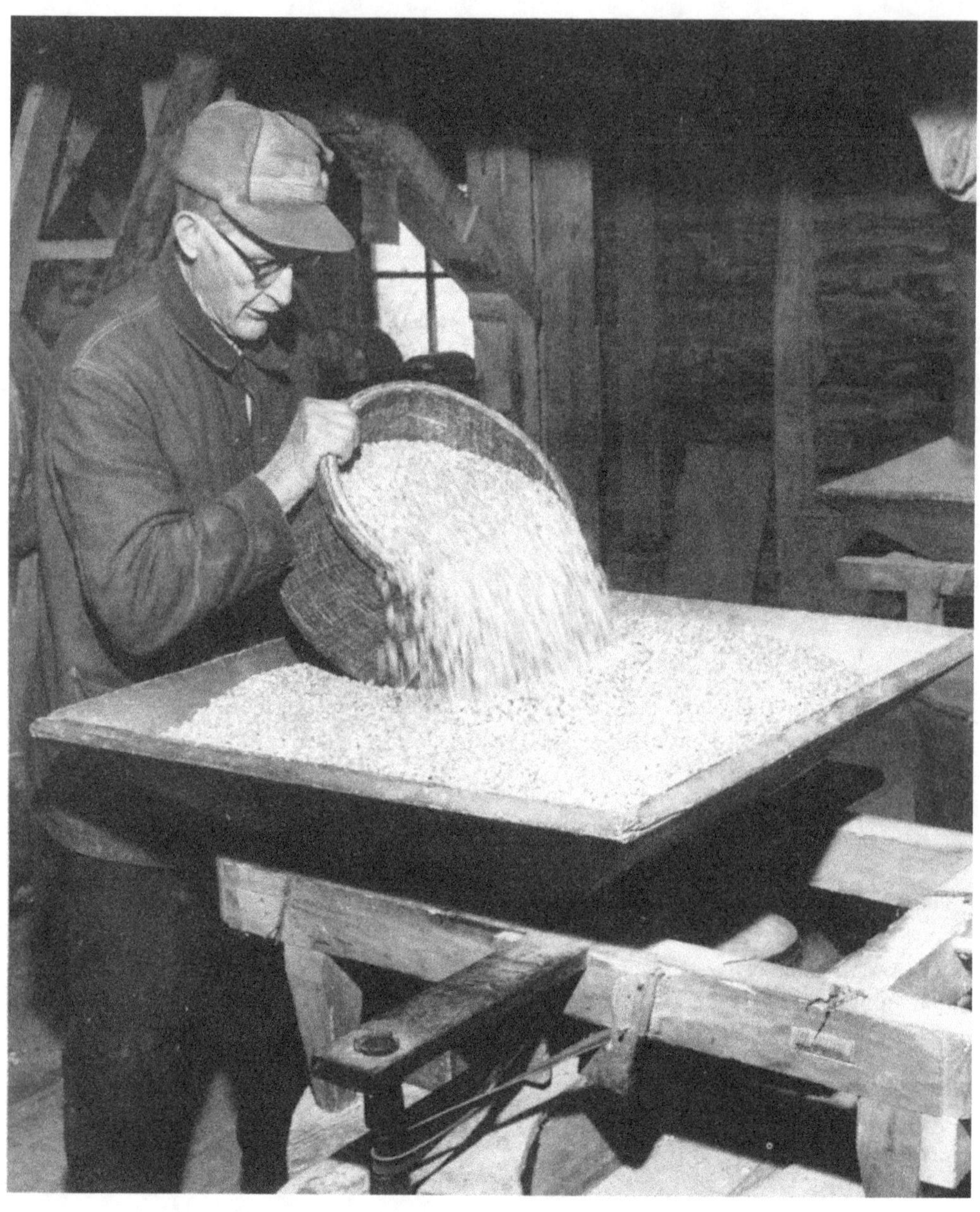

Mont Marshall pours another bushel of hickory-grain corn into the hopper of his gristmill. Mont has departed this life and his gristmill, too, is gone from the scene. We shall not behold another of his kind. [Groundhog Mountain, Virginia, 1955.]

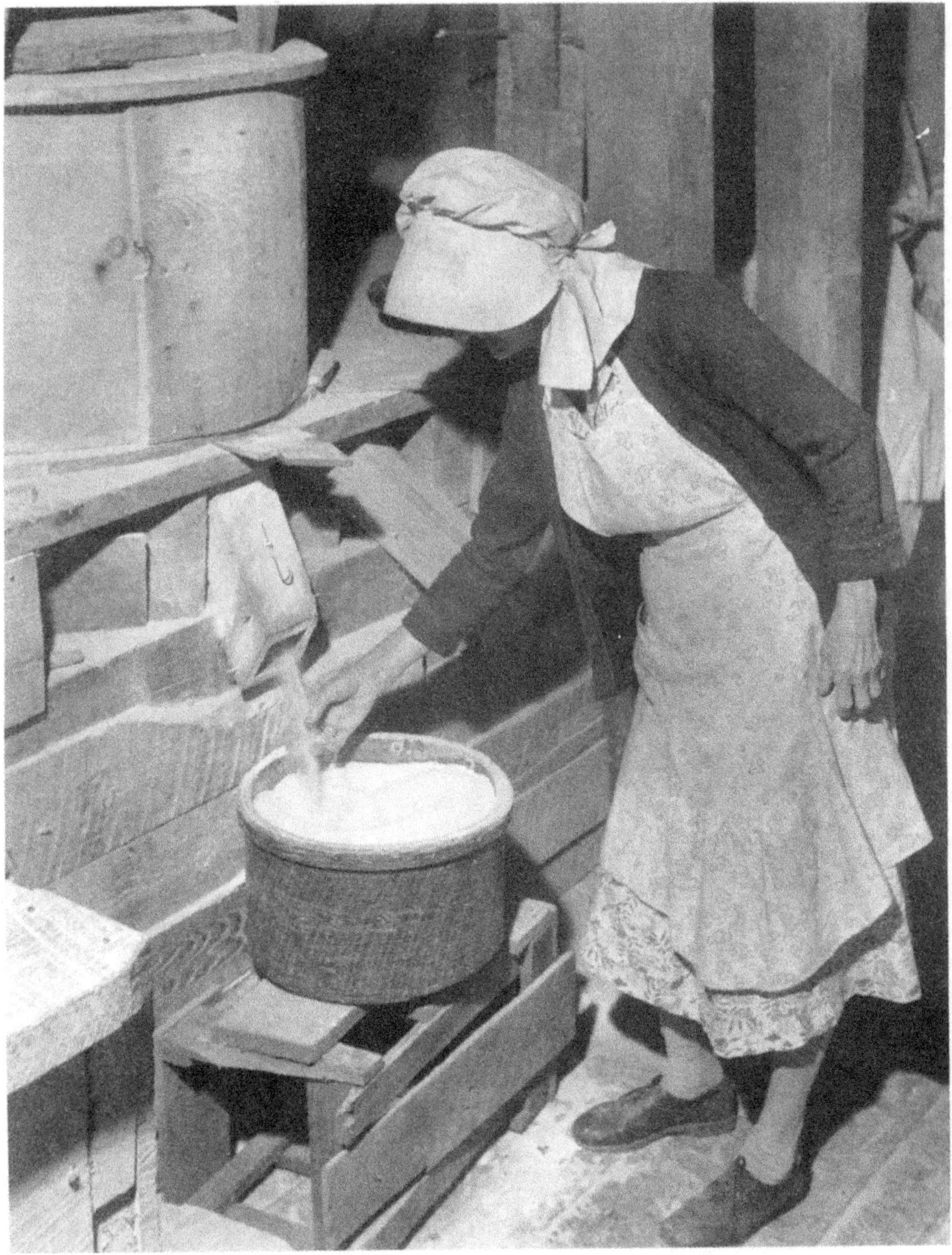

The late Belle Marshall tests the fineness of the meal pouring from the French-burr millstones of her husband's mill on Stone Mountain Creek south of the Blue Ridge Mountains.

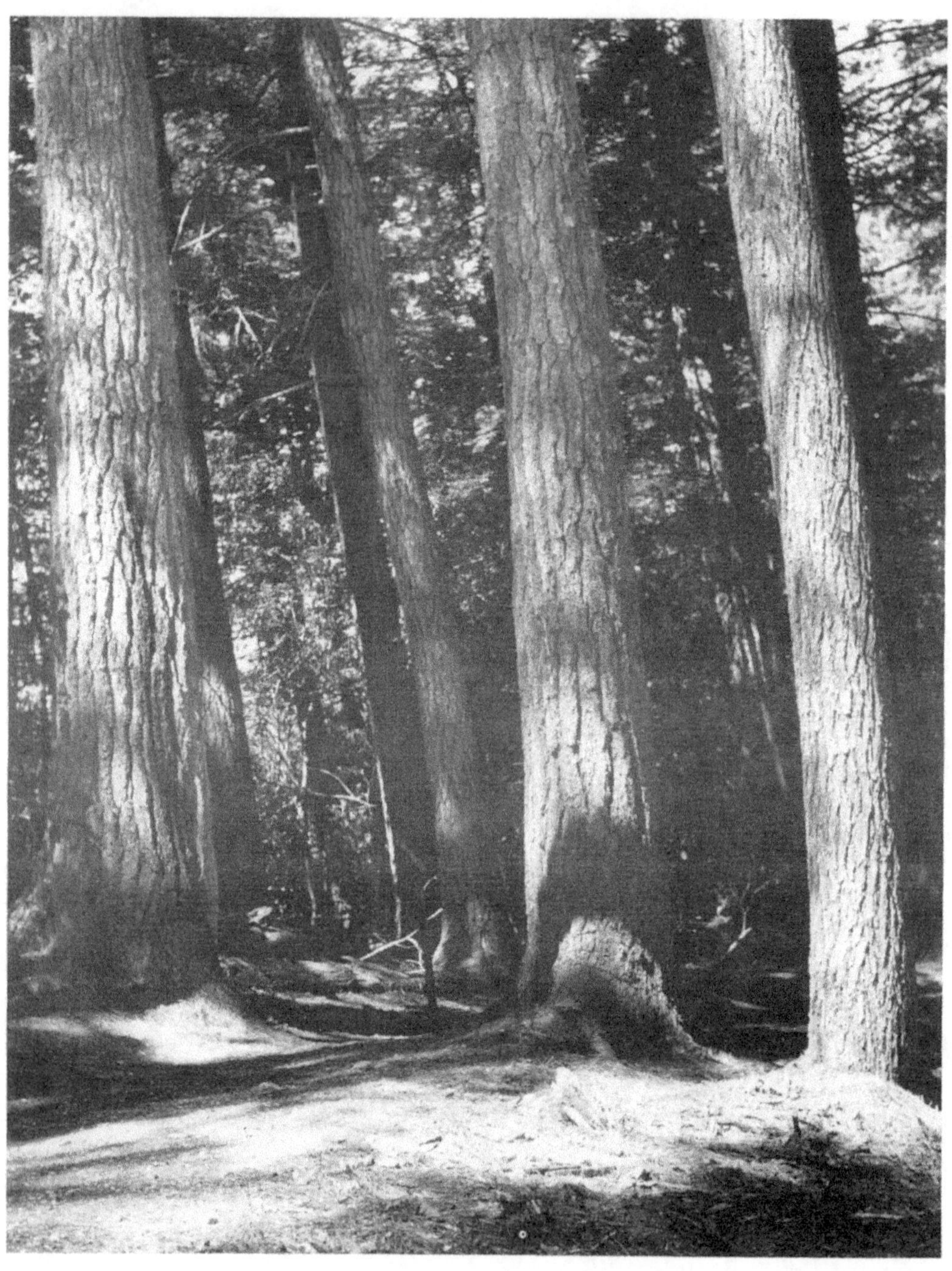

Passengers on the trip to Bald Knob are amazed to see huge forests of stately hemlocks and spruce, left to grow after the initial cutting. The trees crowd right down to track-side, their crowns oftimes overlapping. [Cass, West Virginia, 1968.]

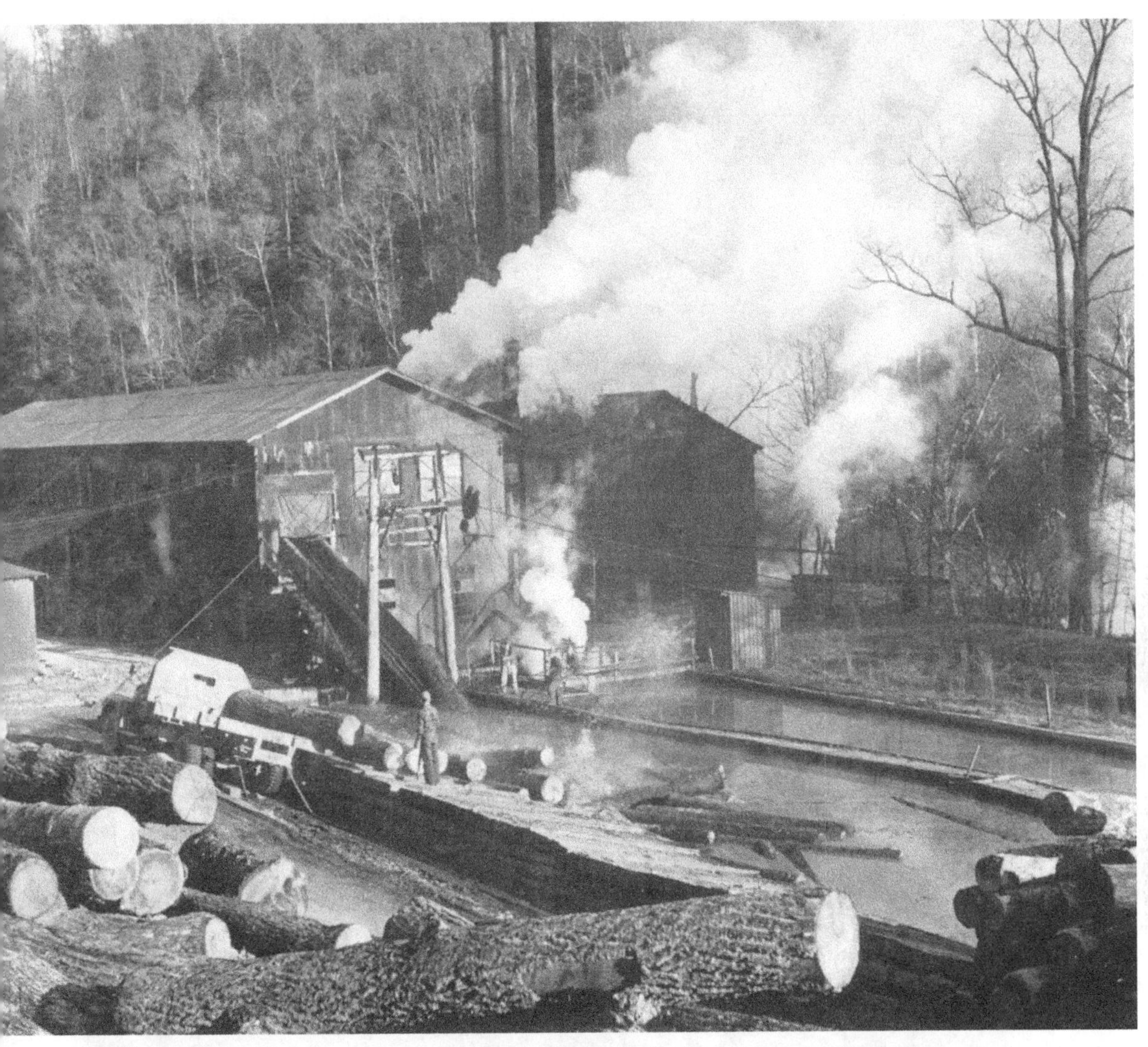

[Steam sawmill operation on the middle fork of the Kentucky River at Hyden, Kentucky, 1940.] Around the birth of the present century lumber companies discovered that the Cumberland Mountains were clothed with a wealth of timber; as many as five varieties of oak, three of poplar, along with white pine, hard and soft maple, hemlocks in the higher elevations, all were here awaiting harvest. The mountainsides of Eastern Kentucky had the largest growth of chestnut in the world, in the words of mountain folk "the best tree God every growed." Possessing straight flaw-free grain, and easy to rive into shingles and logs, lumber from the once spreading chestnut tree had high priority with lumber companies.

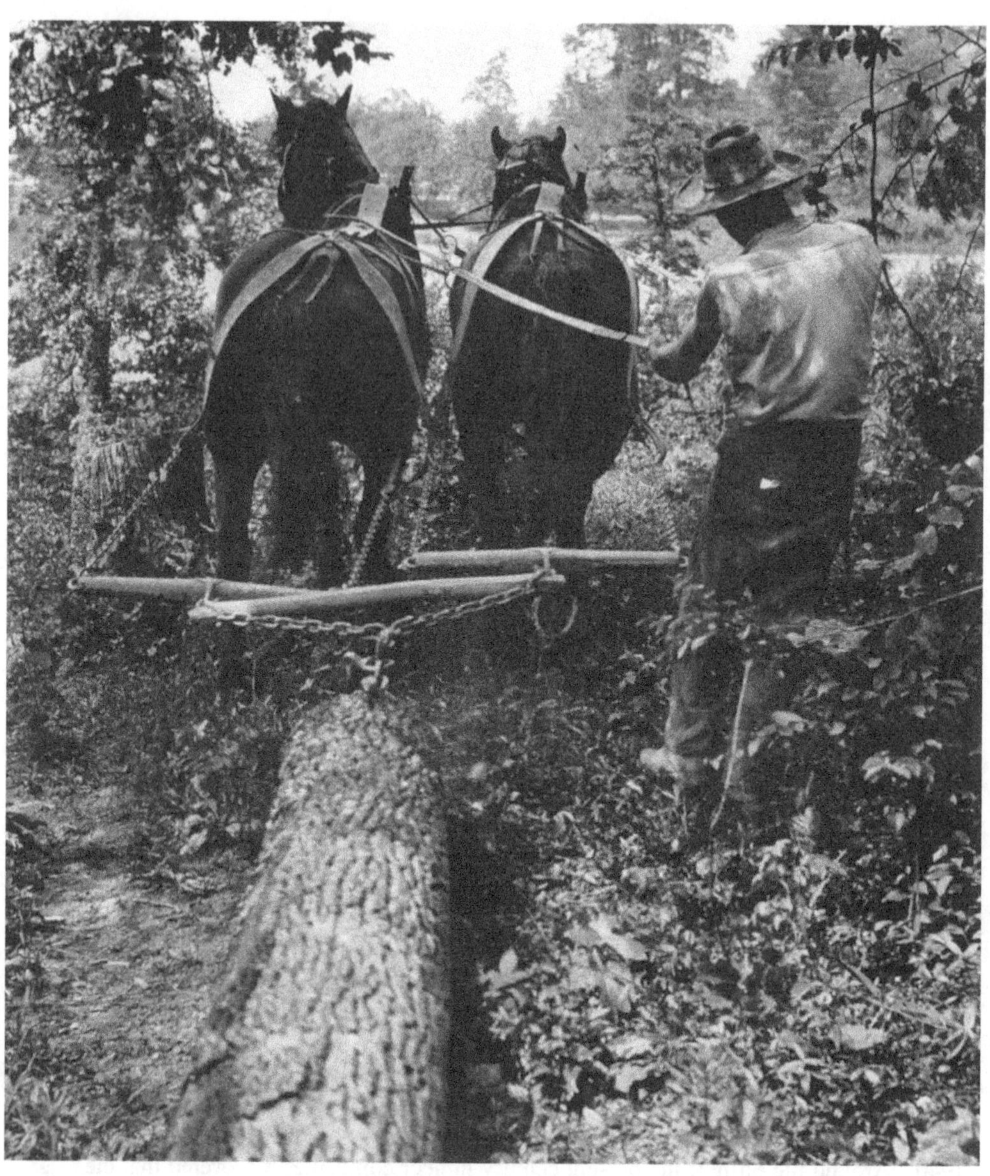

[Logging in the Cumberland Mountains of eastern Kentucky, 1939.] *Opposite,* Jack "Piney" Williams, like many other loggers imported from across the mountains by the lumber companies, was a wood hick, pure and simple. "Tough as a pine knot, rough and ready at all times for a fight or frolic, heady moonshine whiskey, cards, and women" were the descriptions of the wood hick during the glory days of logging in the mountains. The wood hick was characterized wherever he went by the clothes on his back. A woolen shirt was tucked into his trousers of tough duck, "snagged off" midway

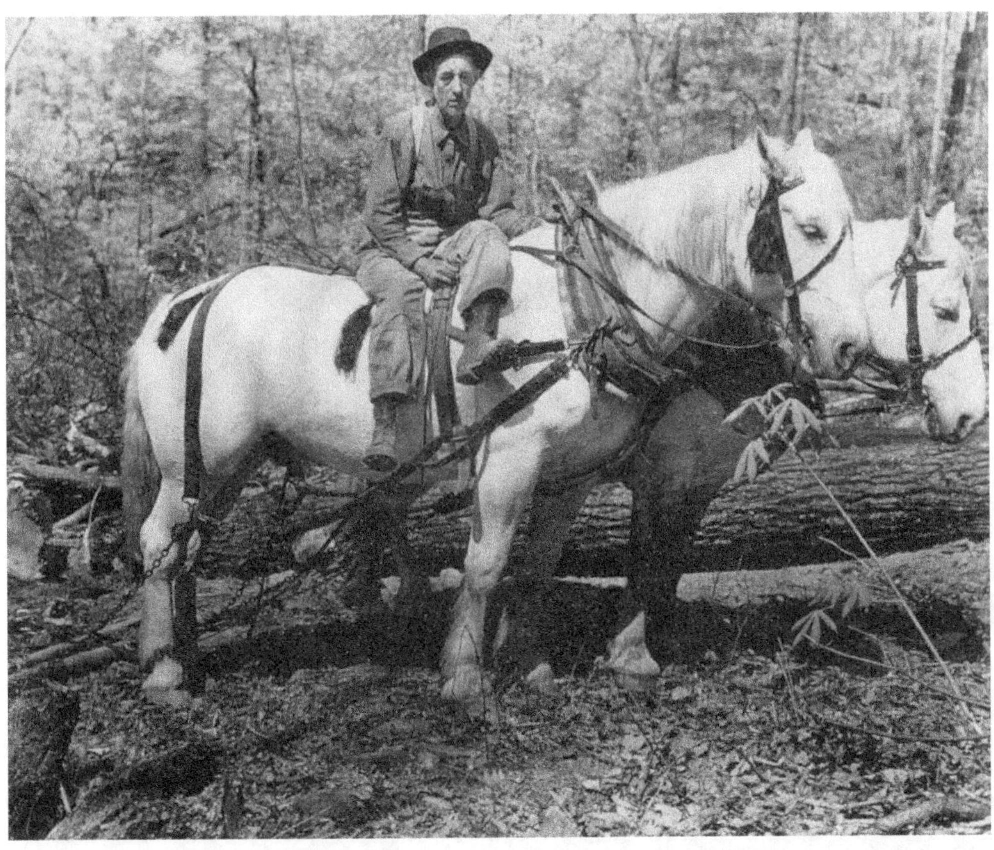

between his knees and ankles after one-time wearing. Buried about two inches into the bottoms of his snagged-off trousers, the wood hick wore the most cruel and lethal pair of boots created by man. Of Chippewa or AA Cutter make, his boots had twelve-inch uppers of full-grain cowhide. The soles were of three or four thicknesses of leather, nailed, sewed, hobnailed, and pegged into one laminated piece. Sharp-pointed steel caulks widely known as "corks" were added for sure footing over slippery logs. With such foot gear, cracking walnuts with a single stomp was no trick at all and in the frequent brawls in the camps many a logger had his hind parts lifted a foot or more off the ground with a swift kick from one of these armored boots. A high-crowned, wide-brimmed felt hat was another trademark of the wood hick, who "kept time" of the days worked by notching the brim of his hat with his pocket knife. When the notches circled the brim completely, he caught the first log train he could out of camp to spend his pay on a wild drinking, gambling, and hell-fer-certain spree on the town. When his money was gone, down to the last penny, the wood hick once again put on his corks and snagged trousers and returned to camp for another six months of hard work in the high timber. Of such mold, then, was the wood hick, the likes of whom we shall not behold again.

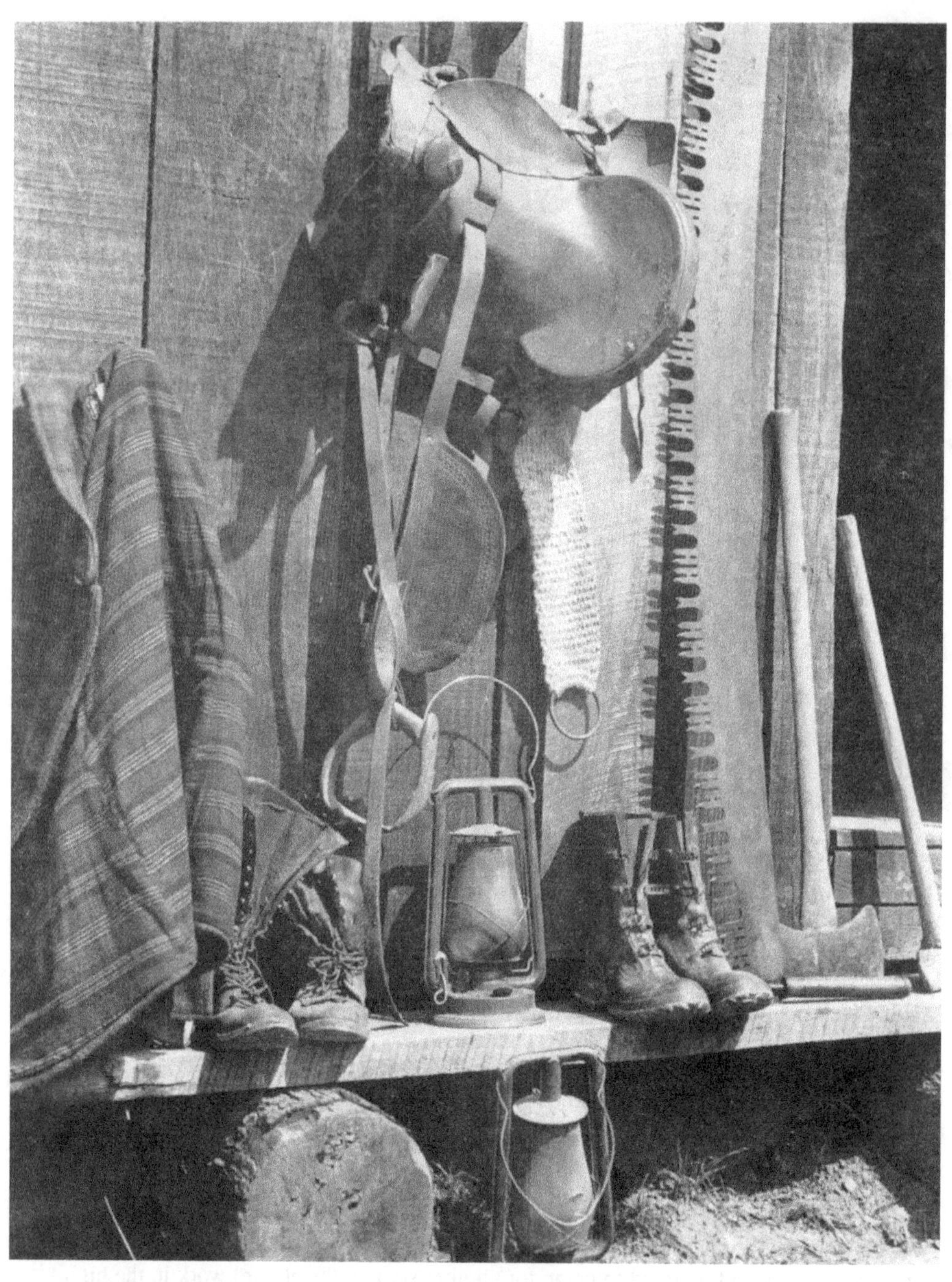

[A logger's equipment outside a bunk house in Clay County, Kentucky, 1940.]

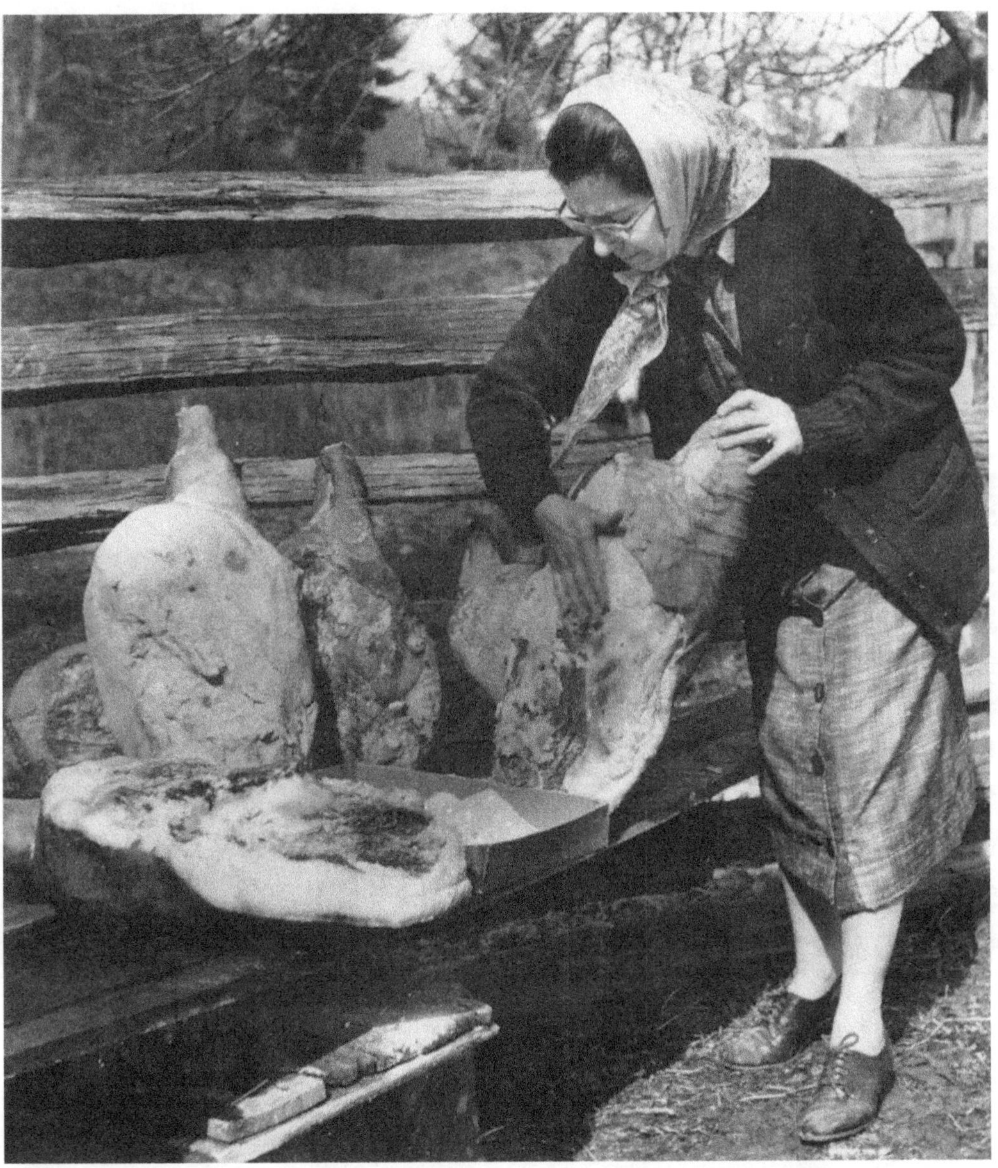

Evie Shelton cured hams the oldtime way and let them season in a well ventilated ham house. Finally, people in government who know all there is to know about such doin's made rules calling for both state and federal inspections. This killed Evie's business and that of farmers who raised the hogs. The business of raising hogs to supplement a mountain man's income has not been resurrected—may never be. [Copper Valley, Virginia, 1956.]

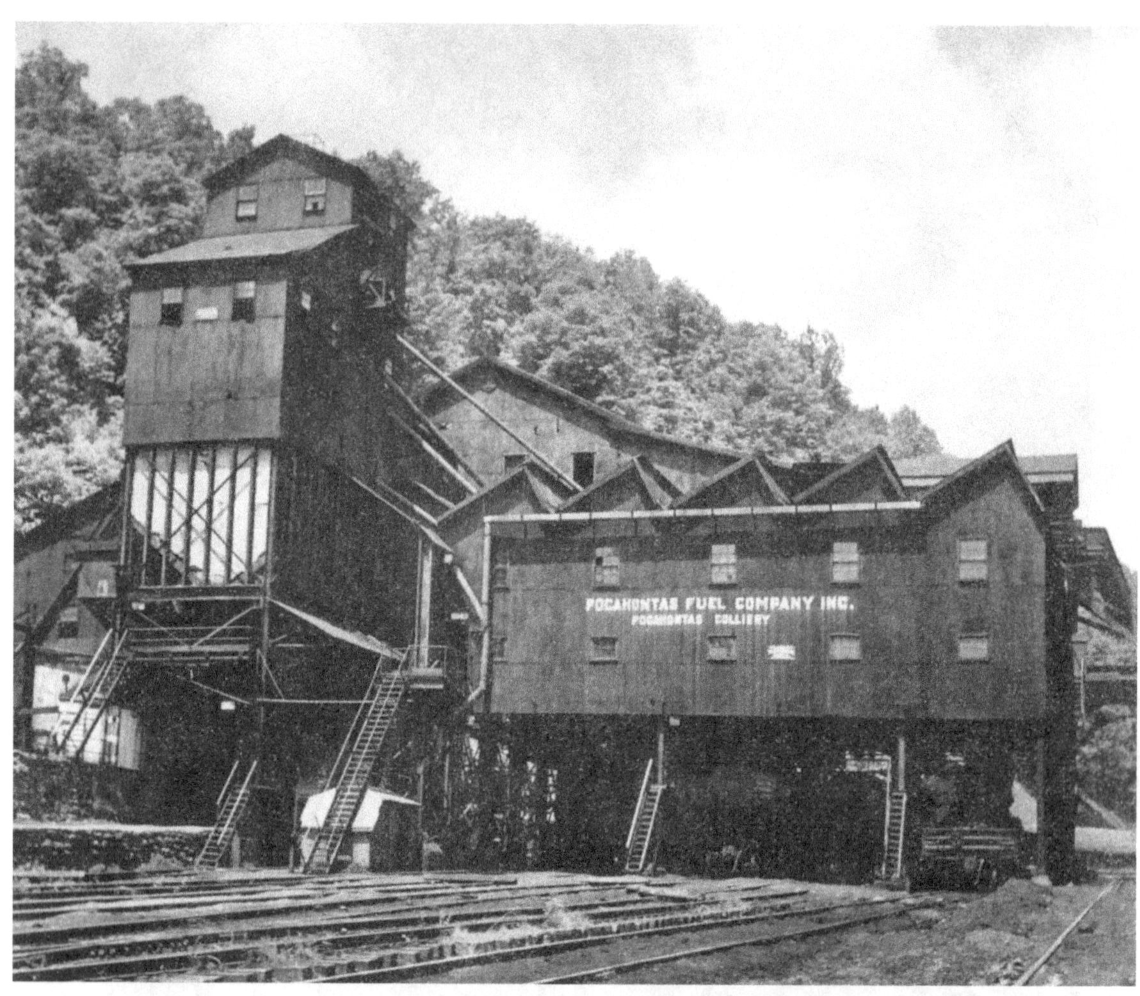

Preparation plant at Pocahontas, Virginia [1959]. Before this mine was worked out, more than forty million tons of coal passed through the preparation plant. In 1889, a methane explosion in the mine killed 113 miners and uncounted numbers of mules housed in a stable in the depths of the mine.

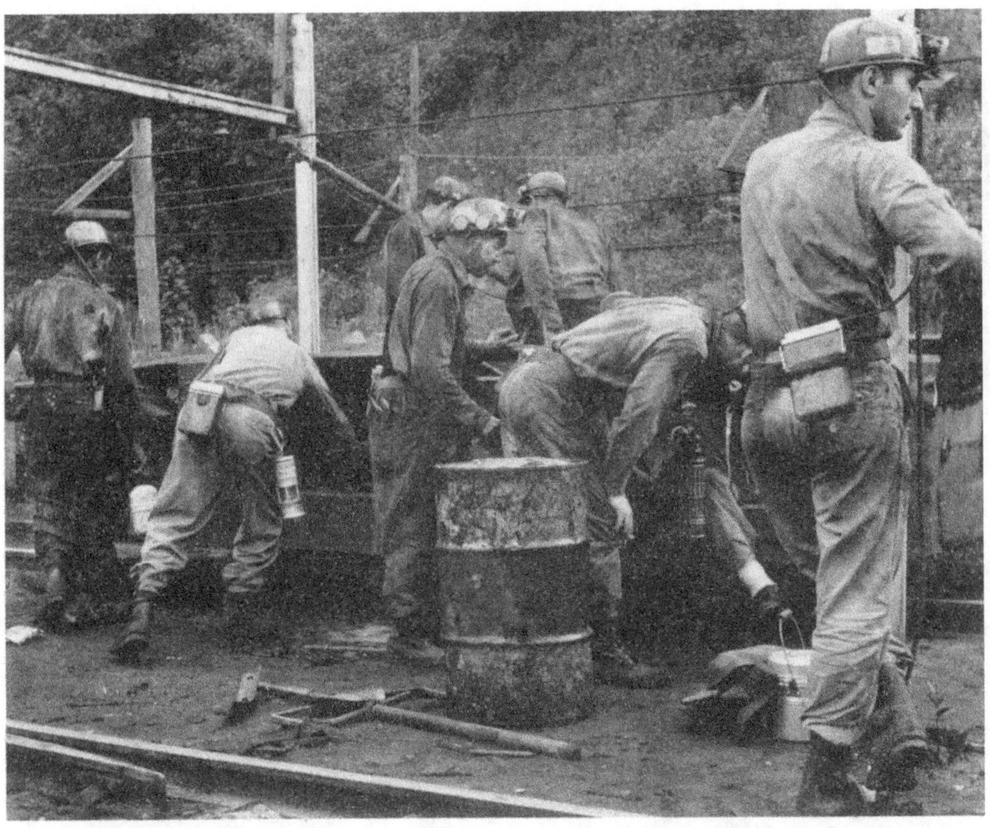

Coal miners entraining in shuttle cars bound for the main heading of Pocahontas Fuel Company's mine at Vivian, West Virginia [1966]. The lights dangling from the belts of two of the miners are safety lights used to detect buildups of deadly methane gas. Despite mine safety rules, gas and coal-dust explosions and the more frequent roof falls continue to exact toll of life or limb in the coal mines. A coal miner's life hangs on a very tenuous thread from the moment he enters the driftmouth of a mine until he comes out on the man trip.

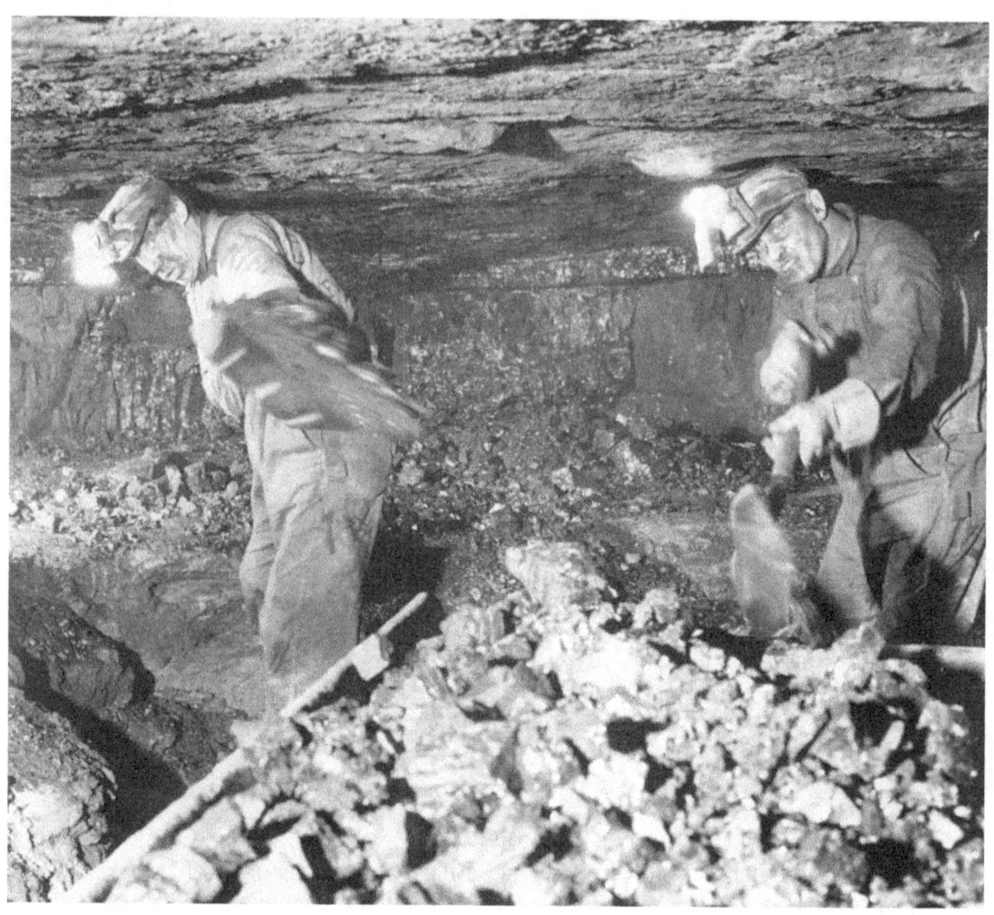

Despite the introduction of highly sophisticated machinery into the coal mines of Appalachia, here and there in small-seam mines the time-honored pick and shovel are used, mostly by miners too old to learn the operation of modern machinery. [Log Mountain area, 1941.]

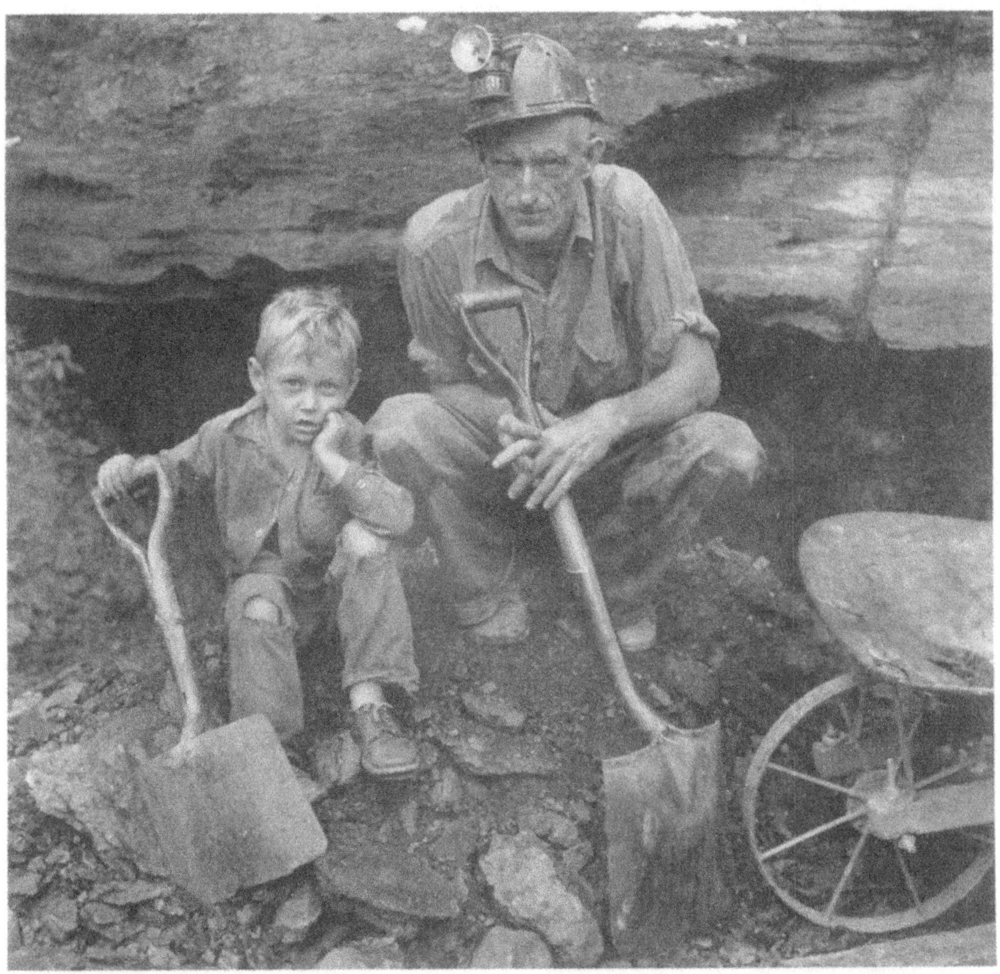

In 1949, rounding a sharp curve in the road leading to Pippa Passes, Kentucky, my attention was drawn to a wisp of vapor that seemed to come from a hole in the mountainside which turned out to be a small-seam coal mine. Looking into the entry, I saw a flickering light about a hundred feet from the driftmouth and a voice called, "Bet you want our picture!" The voice's owner could see a camera dangling from my neck. "Be there in a minute," the voice added, and presently a man wearing a carbide lamp atop his miner's cap appeared, followed by a tousle-headed boy, maybe eight years old. "Name's Teach Slone and this boy is my son," he said.

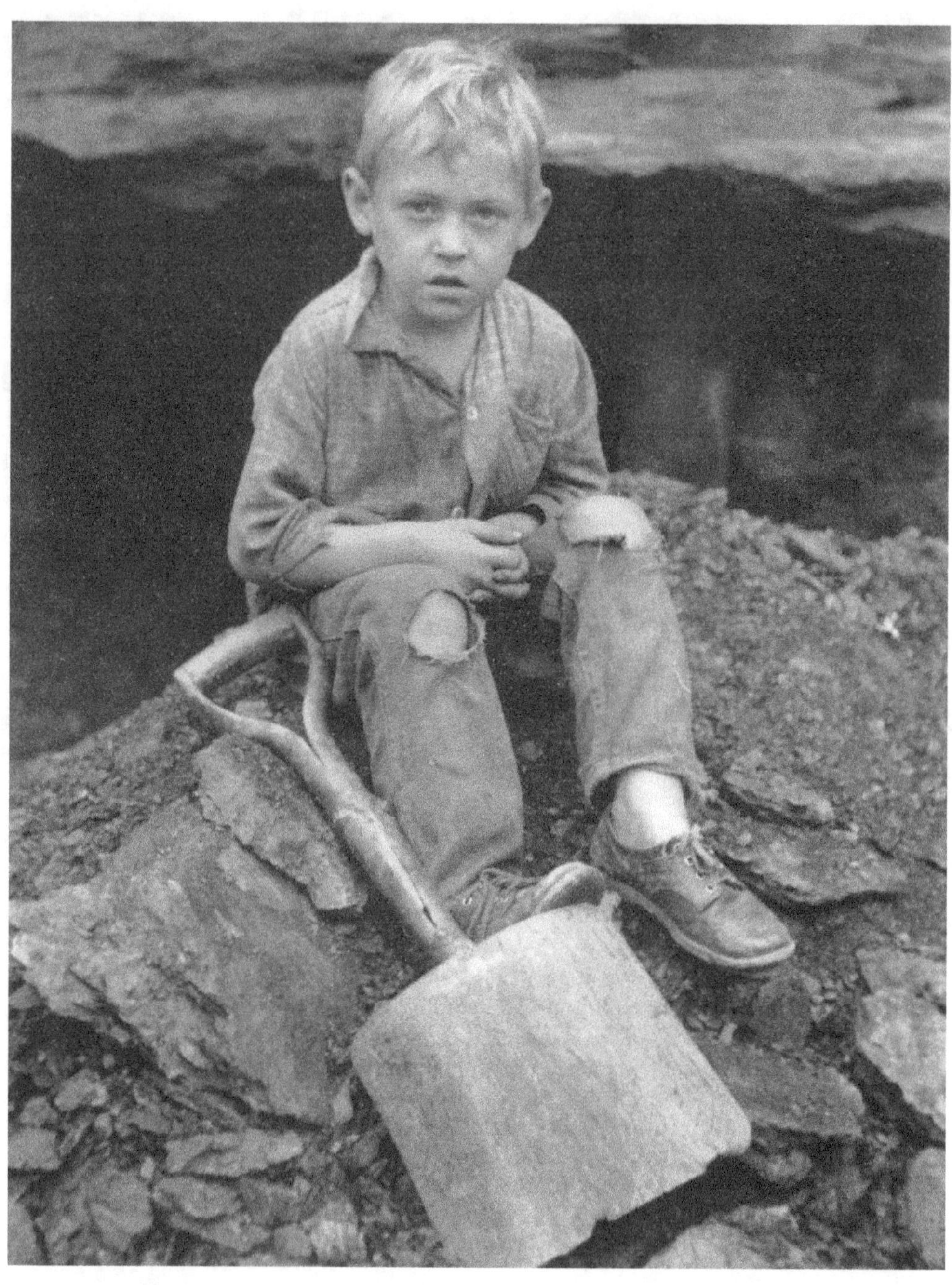

Lest it be construed differently, this tow-headed boy really was helping his father shovel coal in the mine just behind him. "With that sawed-off shovel of his'n he can load about as much coal as I can in this pencil-stripe mine," said his father.

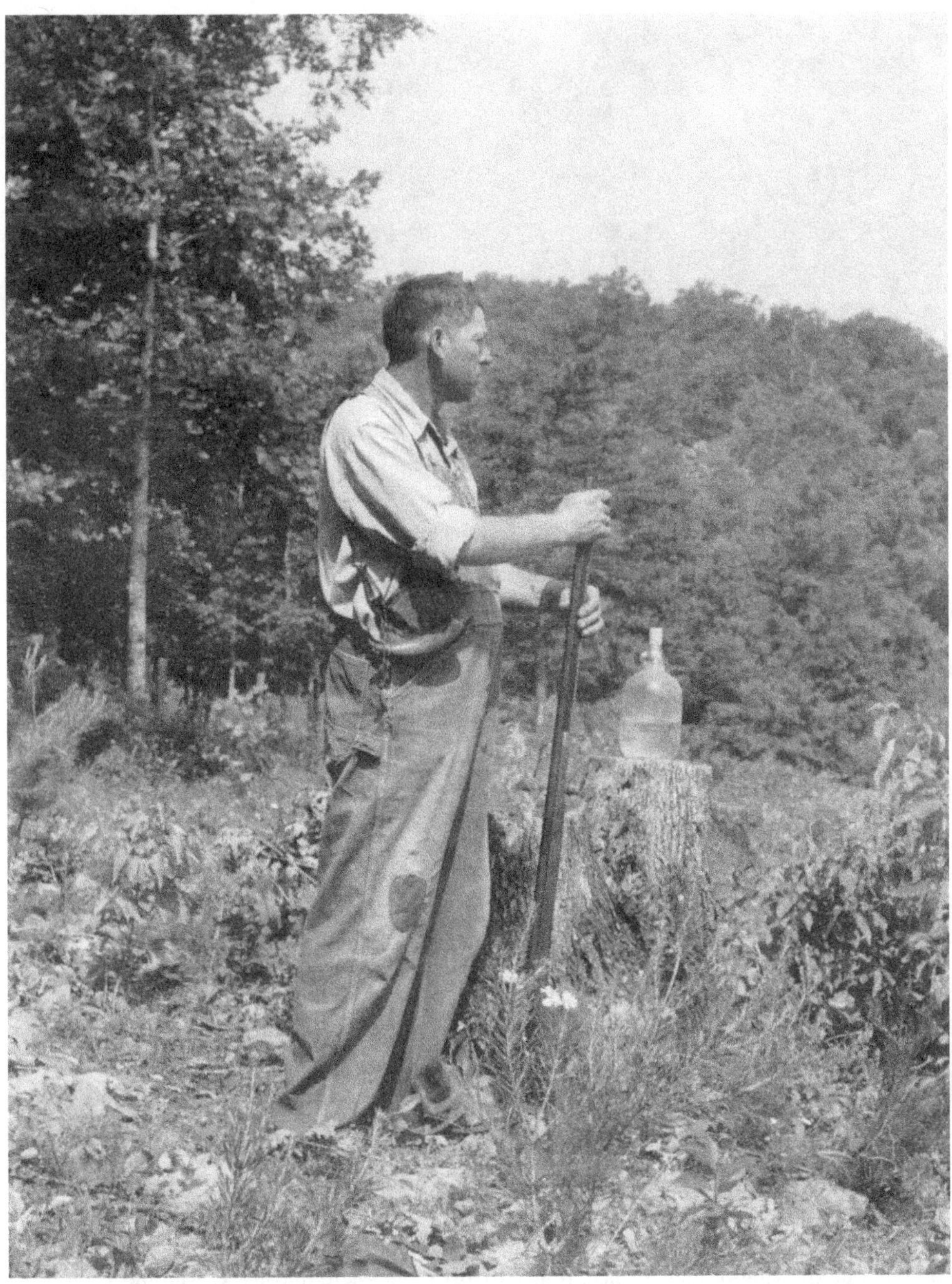

Oldtime moonshiners say there are two kinds of moonshiners, the "caught" and the "uncaught." To keep clear of the grabbing arms of the law, oldtimers post a guard on a hill overlooking the still site, who puts off a shot or two if a stranger is seen. [On Little Widgeon Creek in Patrick County, Virginia, 1959.]

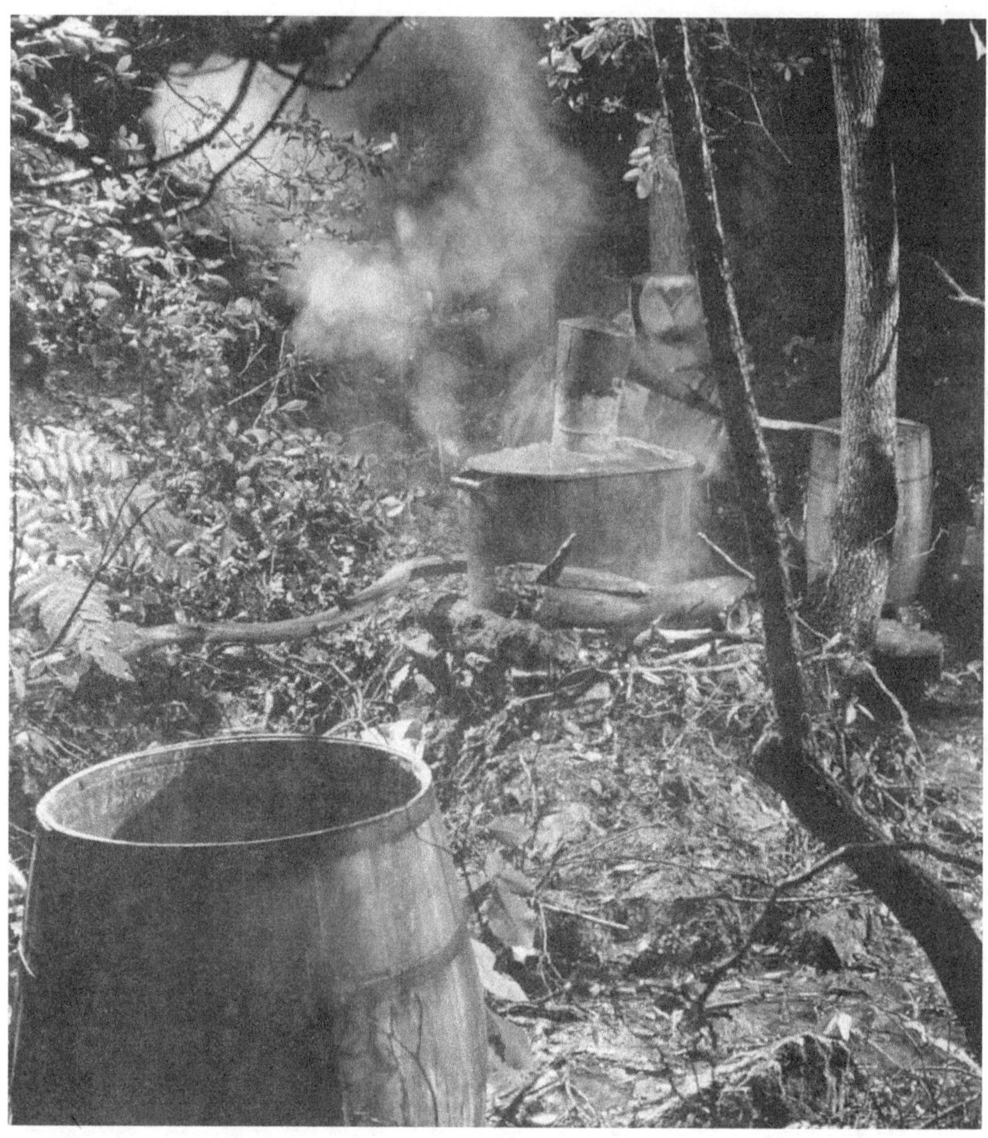

Like hoss collars and monkey wrenches, moonshine stills come in all sizes. This little feller, called a "mountain coffeepot," is all copper and produces better drinkin' likker than a big "submarine" still made of heavy sheet tin. Besides, the coffeepots are easier to conceal from the law. Actually, it's entirely possible to walk within thirty feet of this rig without knowing of its presence, if an expert fireman is in the shack. And most moonshiners are master fire builders. Between two suns, this still can turn out around twelve gallons of straight corn, given a rainless night. [Near Sinking Creek, Virginia, 1960.]

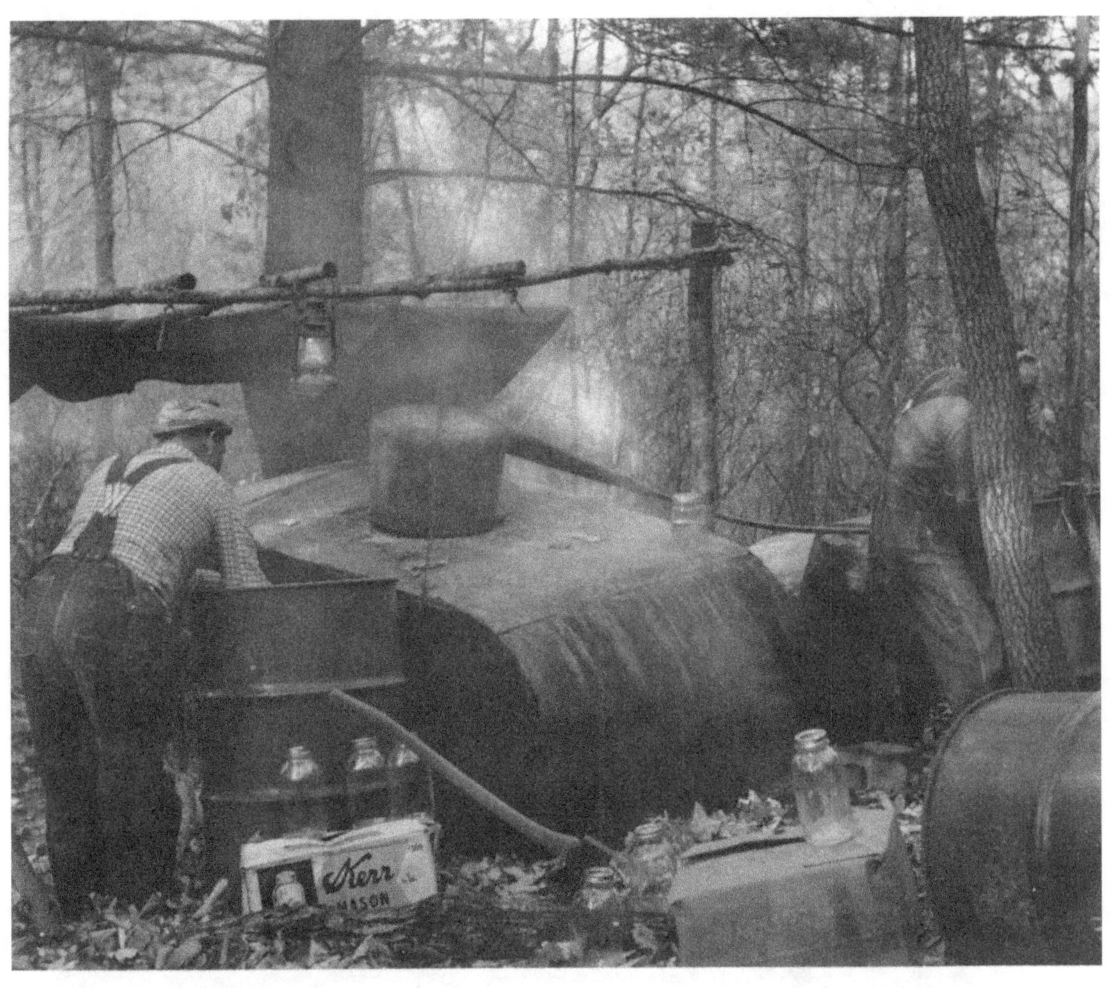

The moonshine still here is known as a "submarine" to mountain people generally; some folks label it a "black pot." Whatever the title, you can get for yourself around twenty cases of twelve half-gallons of singlefoot likker or apple flat brandy, whichever you might be runnin', for a night of hunkering down around your worm box—if your mash turns out like it oughta. [Near Craig's Creek, Virginia, 1959.]

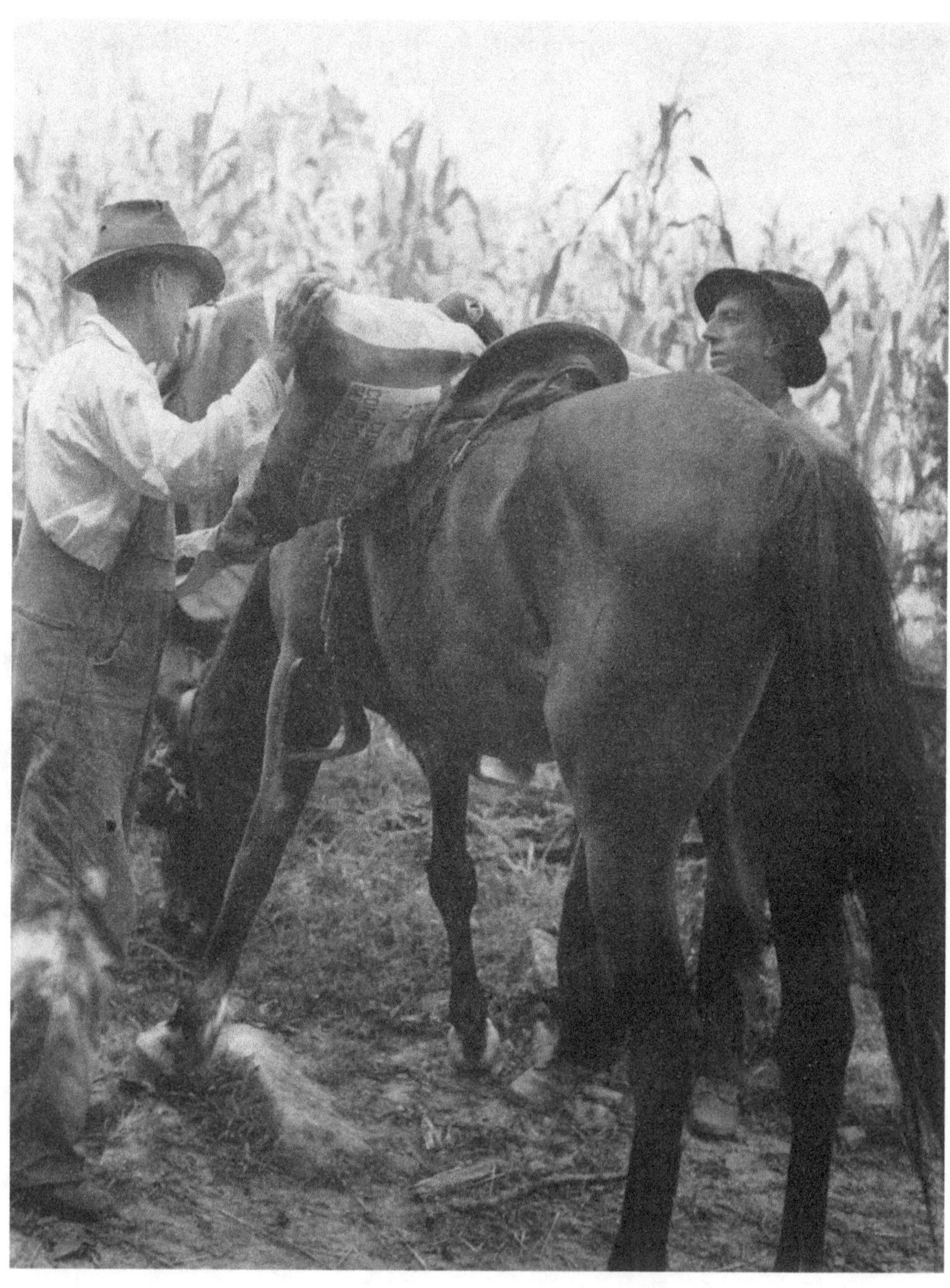

The late Jim Howard and Thomas Jefferson Cupp load apples on the back of a packhorse for a trip through Chadwell Gap and to the cabin of Tom Jeff, who will put off a run of apple flat brandy. Both of these friends are departed the halls of this life, but how well remembered are my visits with them. [Near Ewing, Virginia, 1942.]

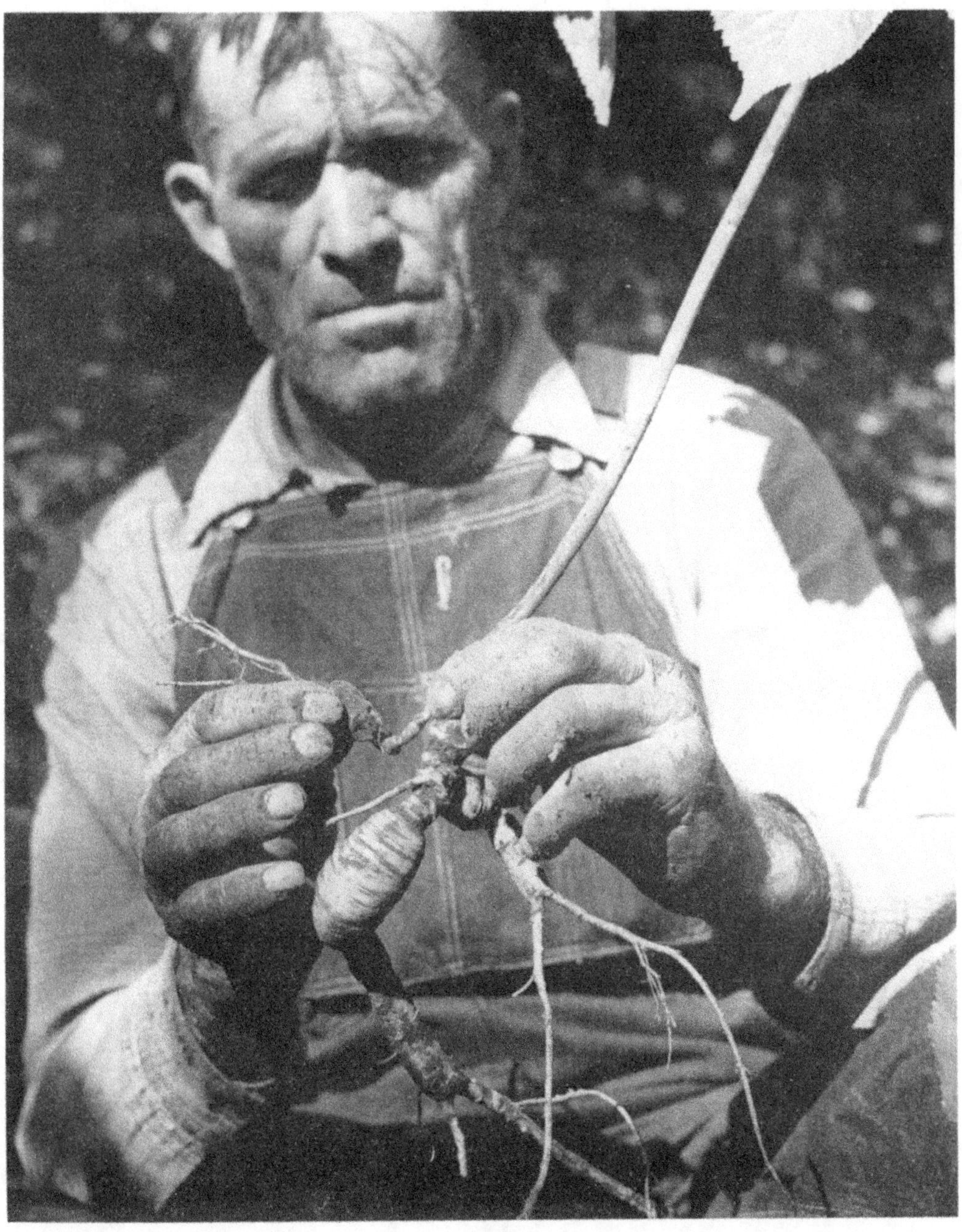

Green Wade was right proud of this wild ginseng root he dug on his place on Shooting Creek [near Tuggles Gap, Floyd-Patrick County, Virginia, 1954]. Ginseng was an article of commerce in biblical times, and the digging of the root was a way of life for many early settlers in Appalachia. Takes four pounds of this weird-shaped root, freshly dug, to make one pound of marketable root.

[Oak baskets made by Lera Rakes and her daughters at their home on Turkey Cock Creek, Franklin County, Virginia, 1956.]

Made by Hand

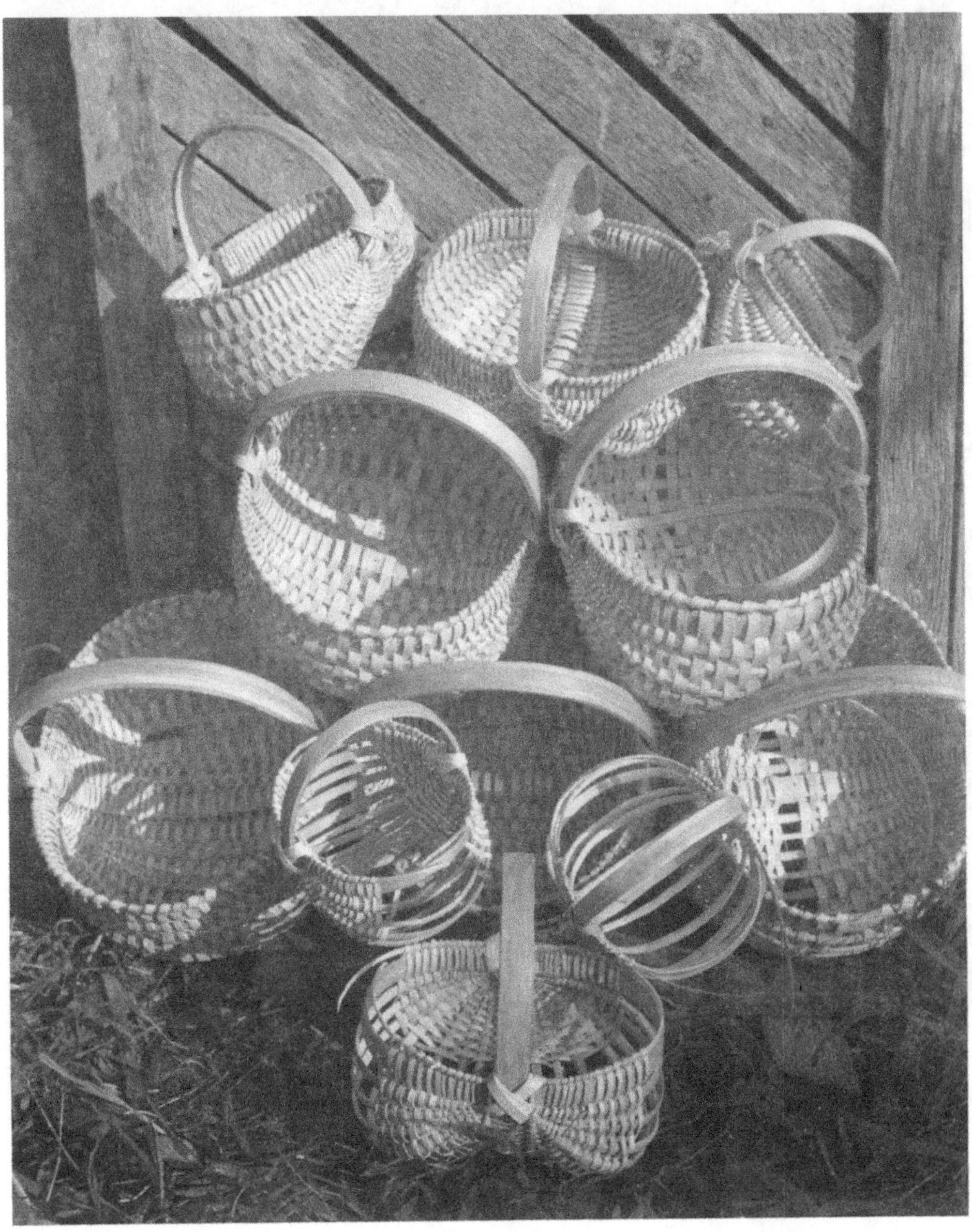

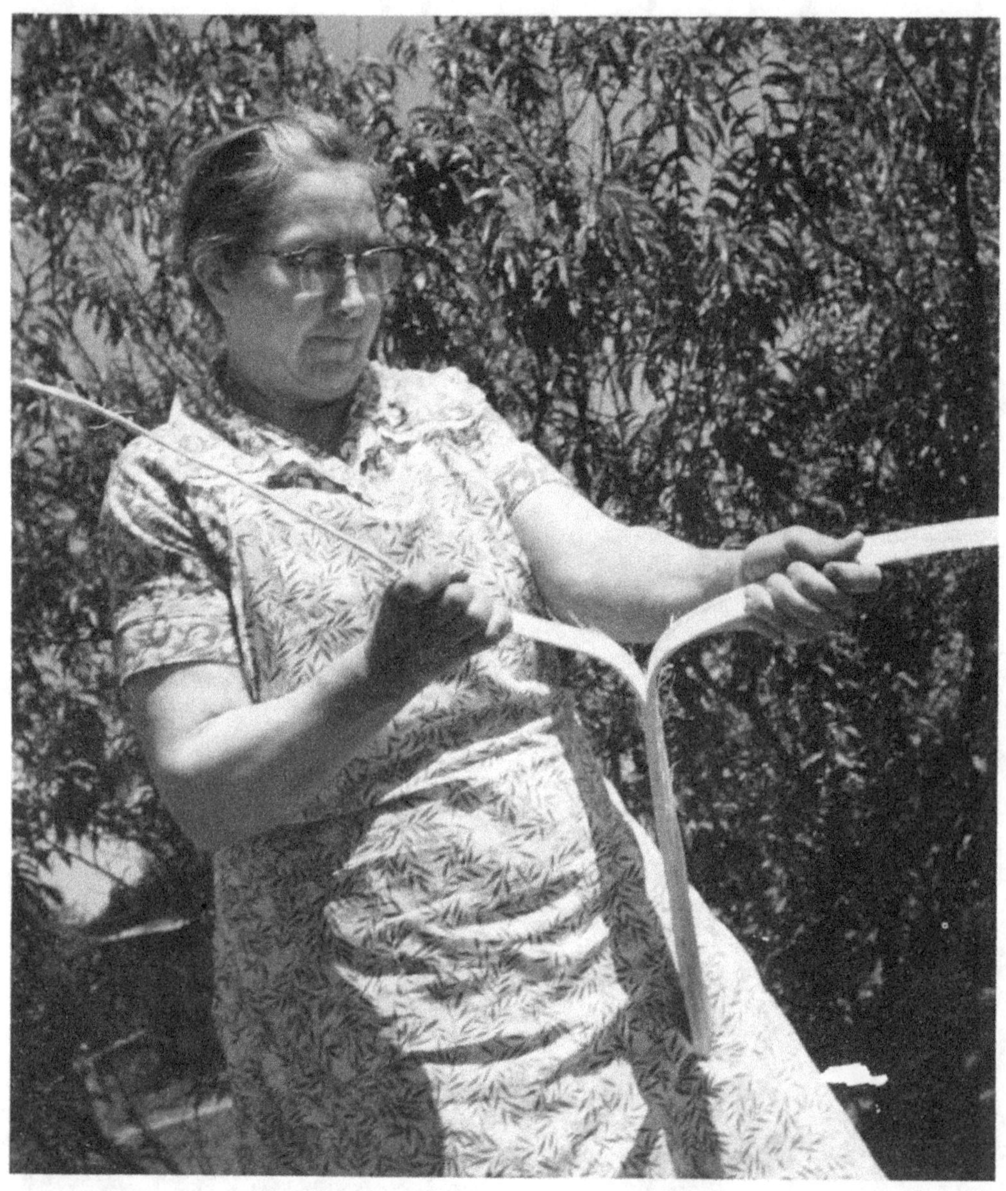

Takes a deft touch and strong hands and arms to rive off splits from a bolt of tough white oak. But Lera Rakes was riving splits while she was in pigtails, taught the skill by her mother.

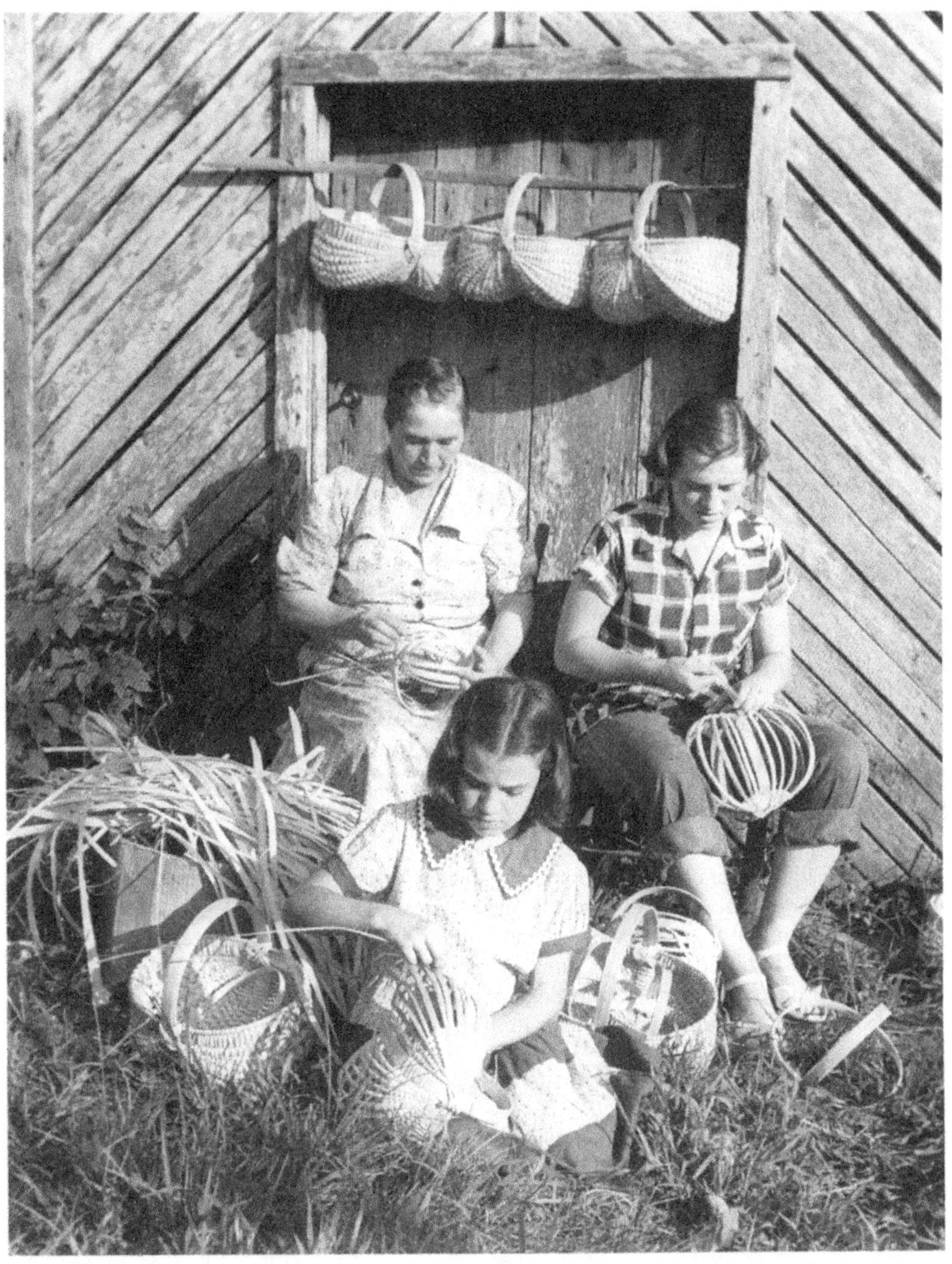

Lera Rakes and two of her children, Evonne and Sylvia, weave sturdy baskets from white oak splits. The baskets bring in money for school books, clothes, and many other necessities that stingy hillside land will not provide.

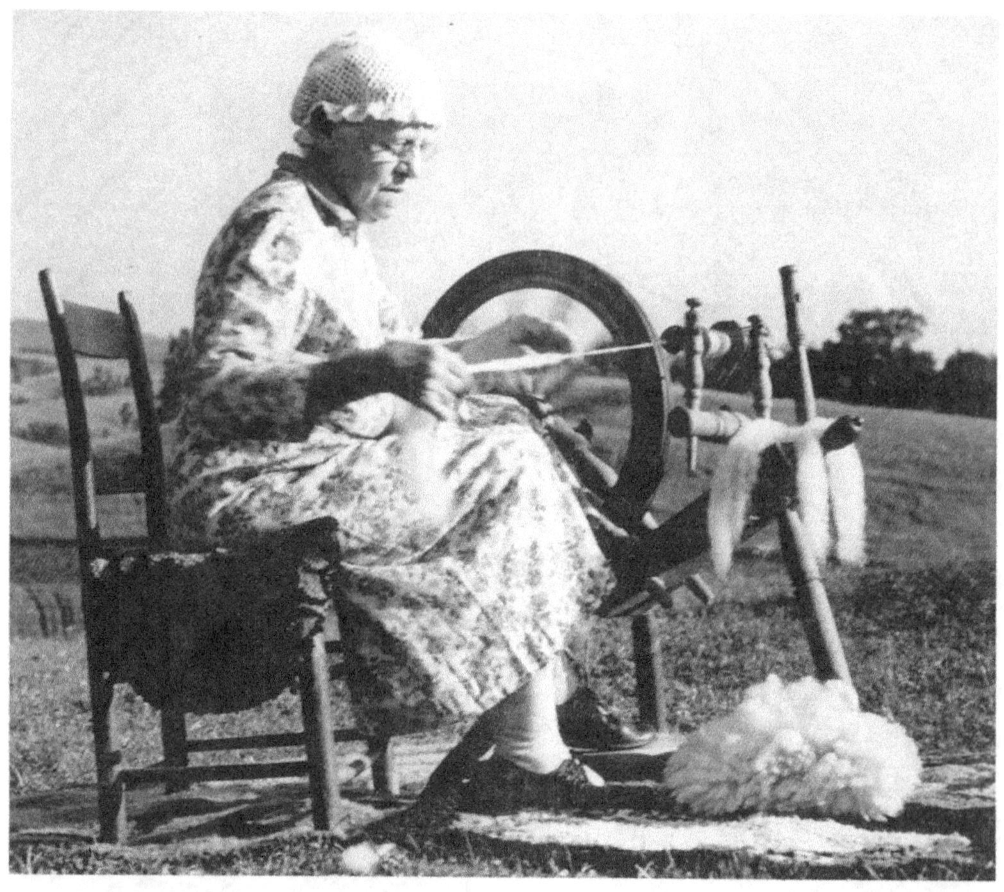

The late Callie Sowers and her mother and grandmother were self-sufficient people. Here she is spinning wool yarn into thread to fashion a coverlet for her bedroom. [Floyd County, Virginia, 1956.] *Opposite*, sew lines in rainbow form are chalked on a crazy quilt's top [at a quilting in Craig County, Virginia, 1957]. The crazy quilt had its origin in Colonial times, when cloth from England was so expensive that not an inch could be wasted. [Note the canning jars on the paling fence in the background, stored in this fashion for future use.]

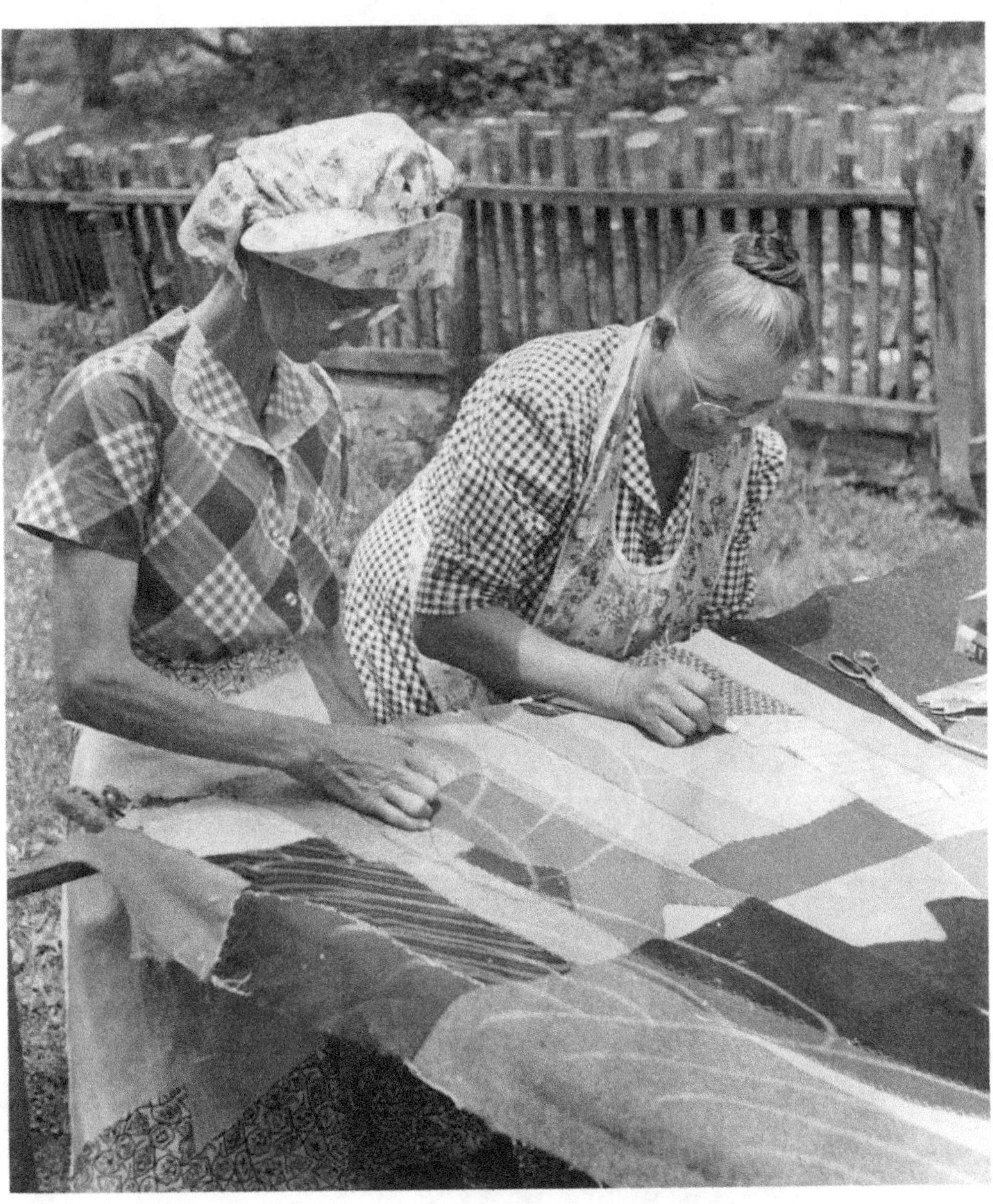

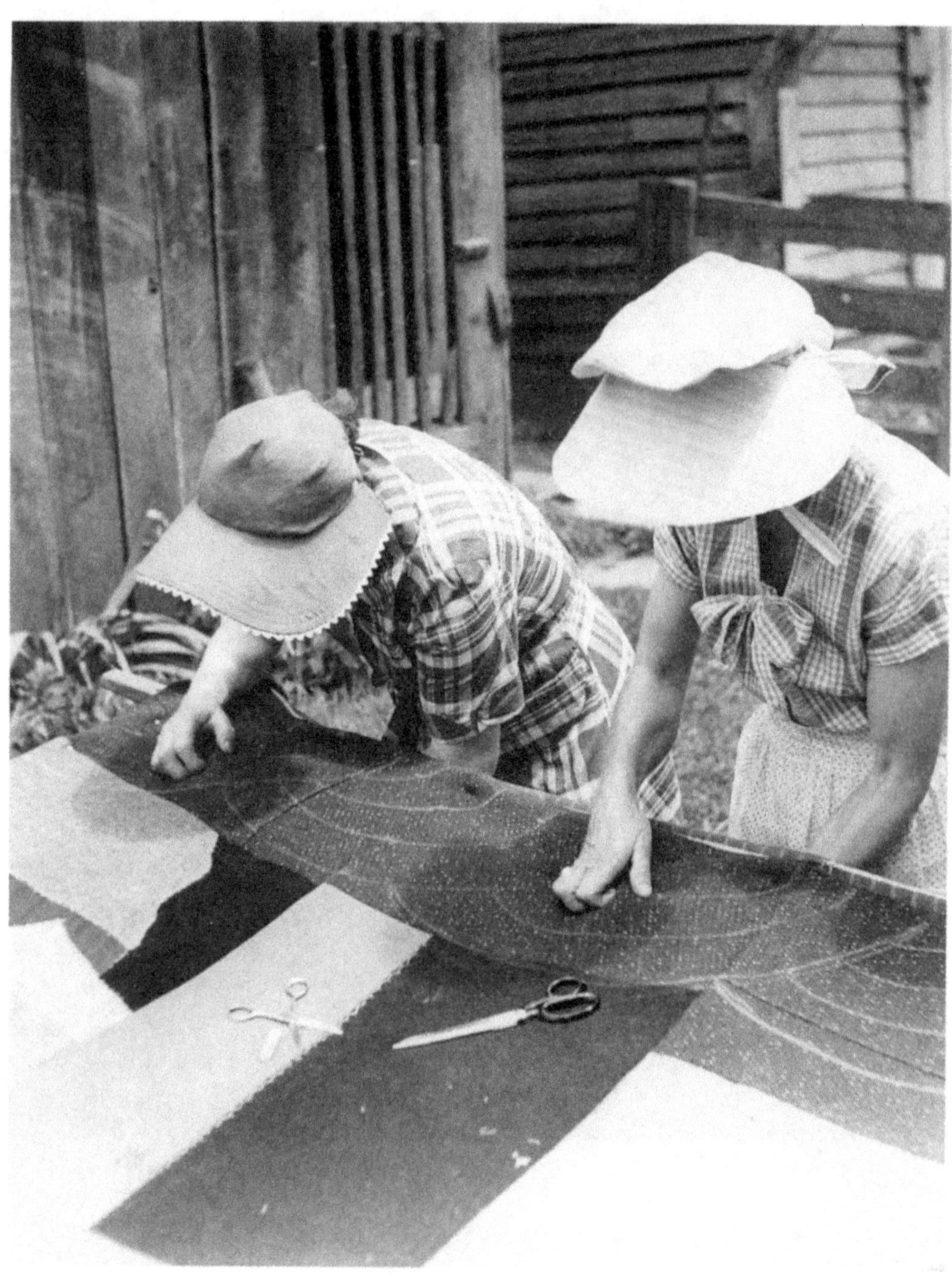

Quilters follow the sew lines marked in chalk on the quilt top.

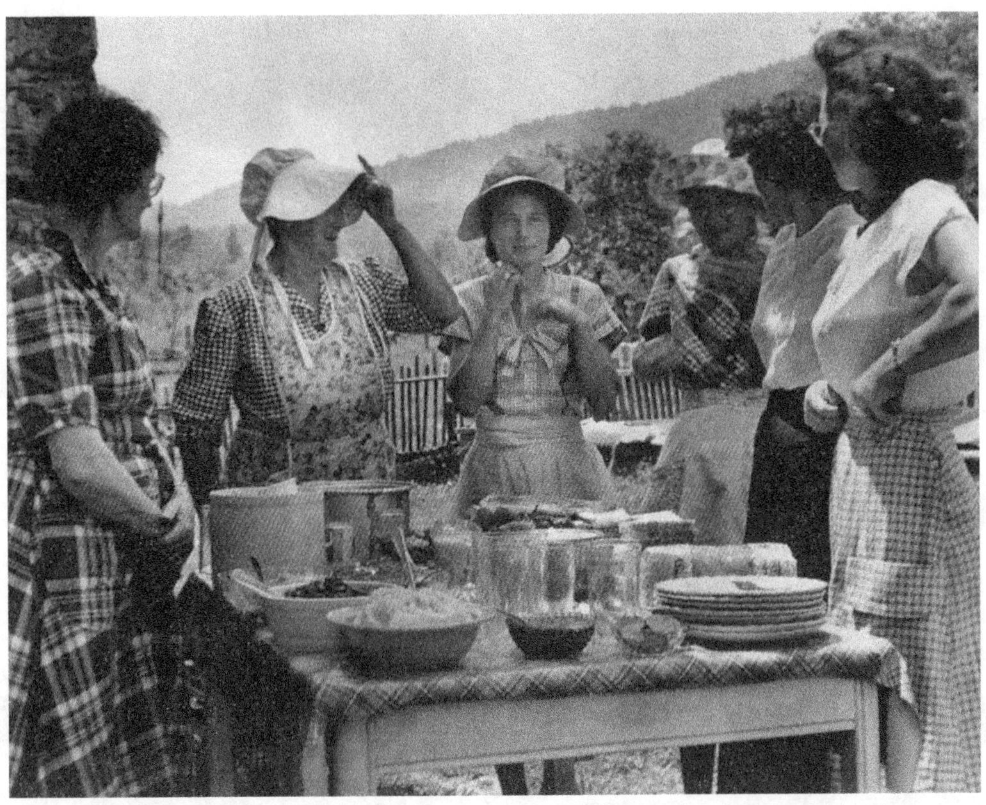

Dinner on the grounds is part of any quiltin' gathering of mountain women. Besides offering an opportunity for quilters to show off their favorite quilts, there is the chance to show off one's favorite fixins when the table is spread.

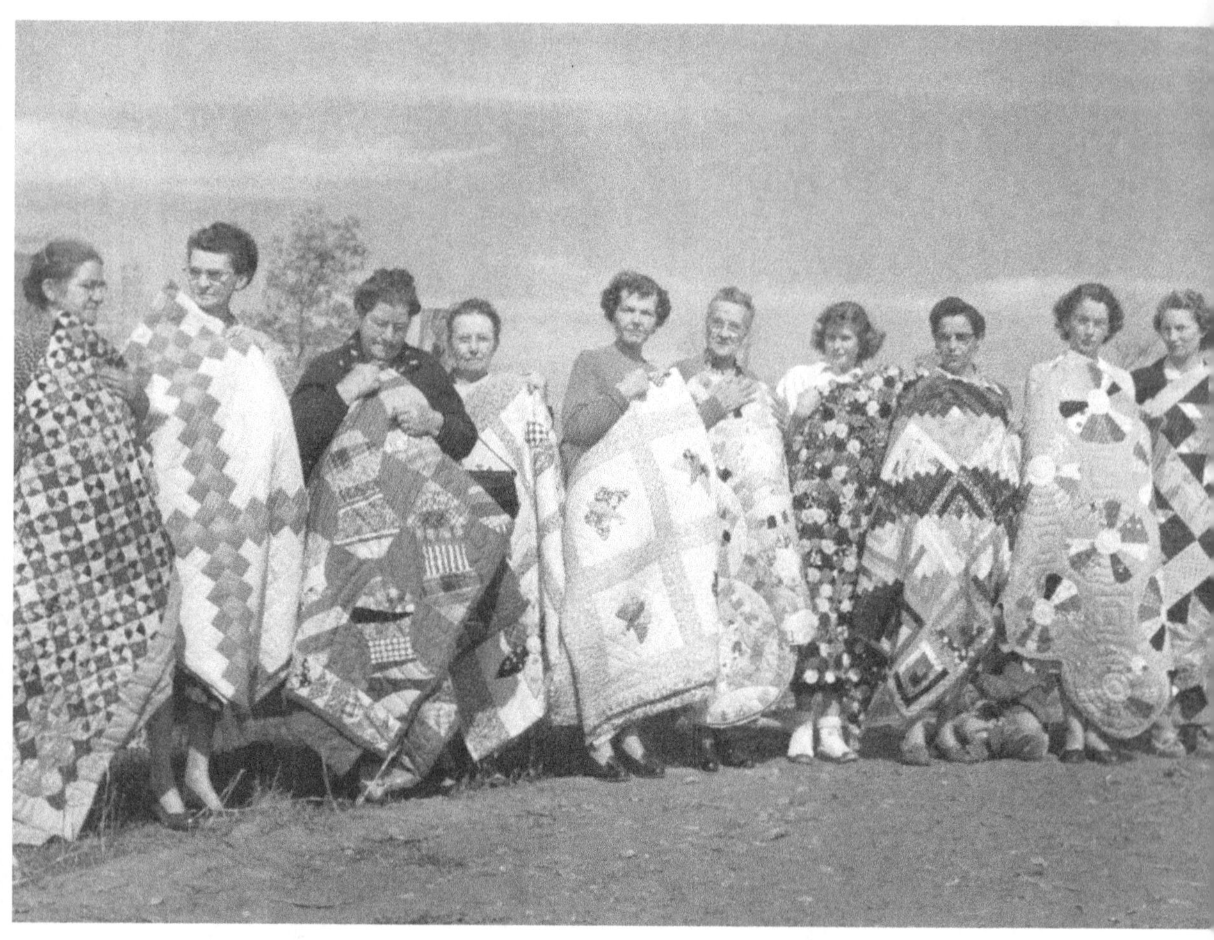

Quilters attending an all-day quiltin' session at the Charity Community Center [Patrick County, Virginia, 1957] display their show quilts for prizes offered by a magazine photographer.

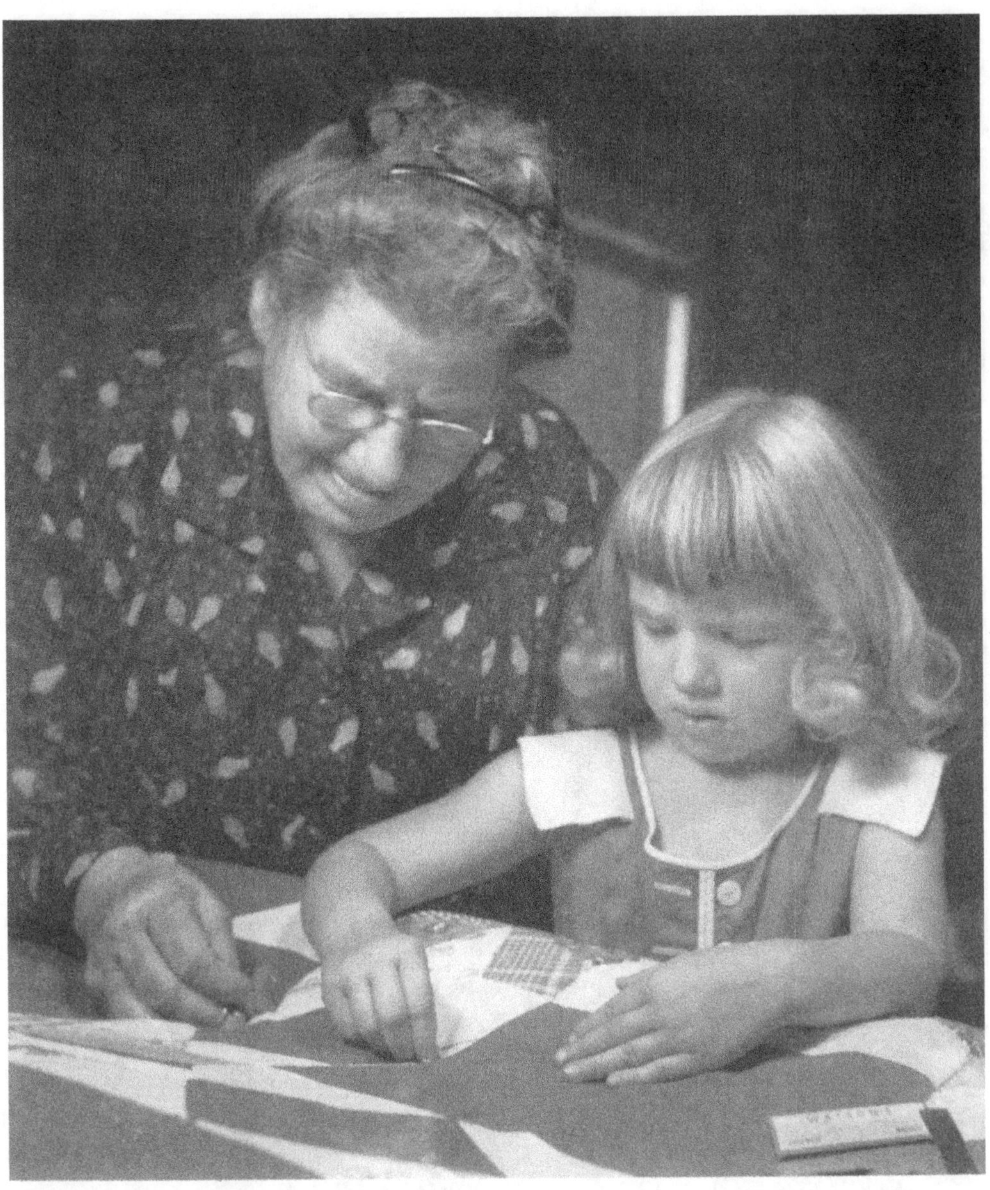

In the hill country, the very young are taught the skills handed down from Pilgrim times. Here Lillie Wood is showing her granddaughter a thing or two in the ageless art of quilting. [Patrick County, Virginia, 1957.]

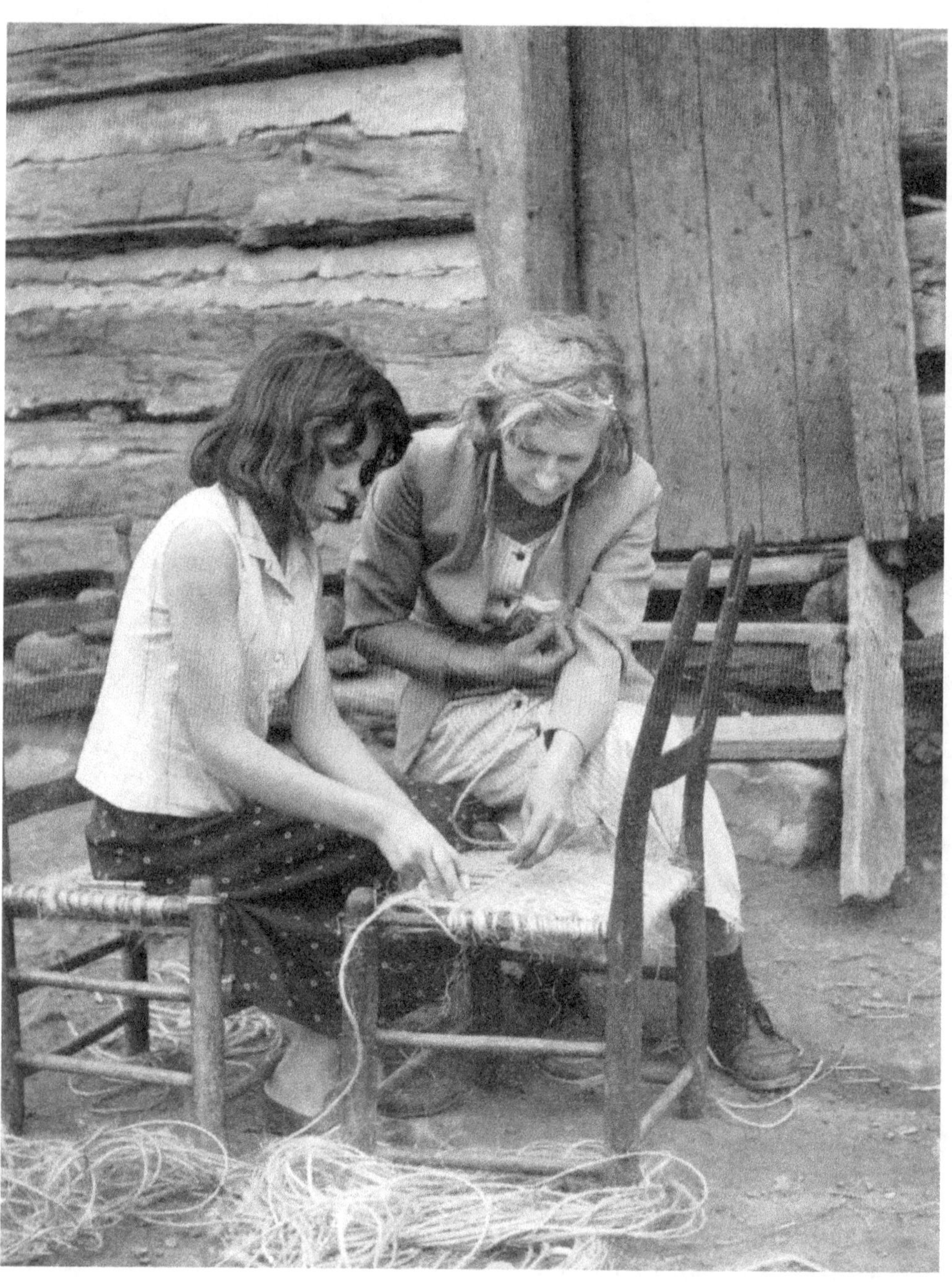

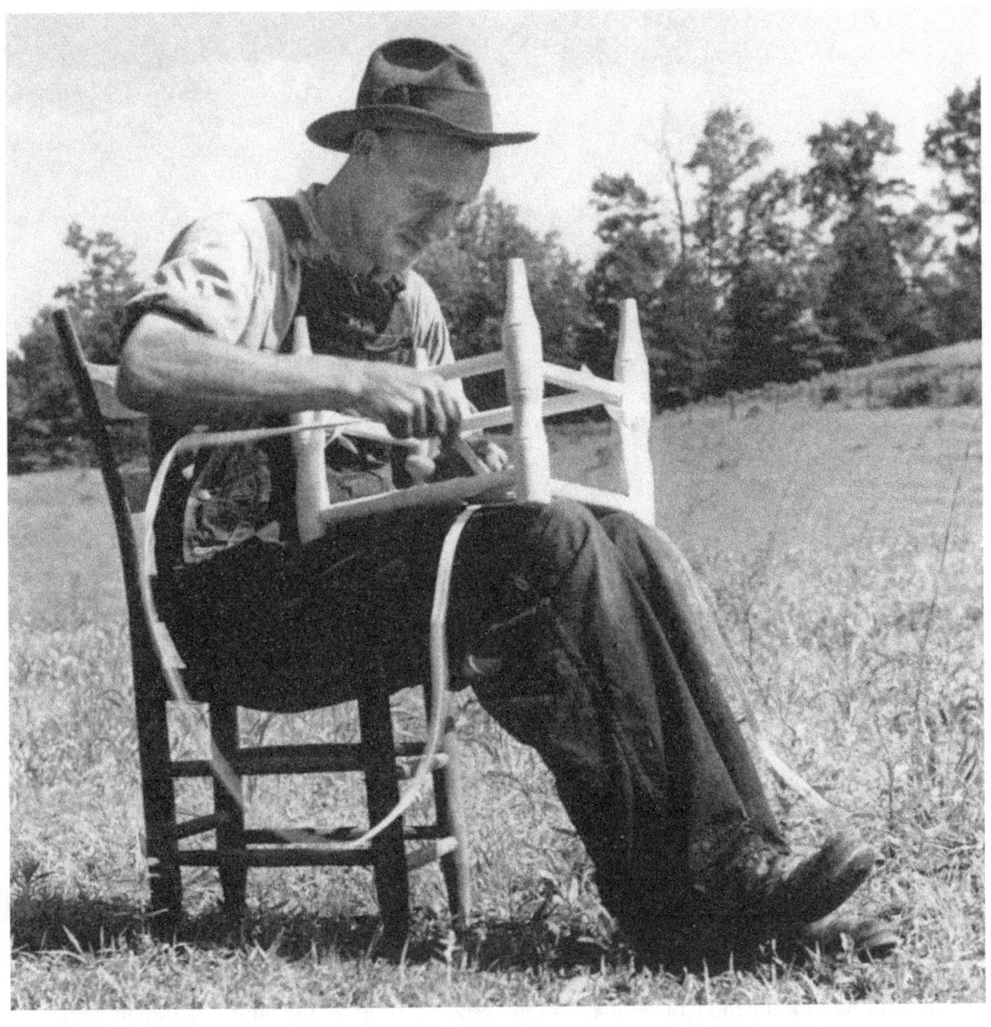

Opposite, Josie Caldwell shows her daughter Ethel how to bottom a chair with hay baling twine. [Craig County, Virginia, 1968.] *Above,* Fred McCarter used splits rived from tough white oak to bottom a footstool to match one of the chairs he made on his place in the Glades section of the Great Smokies. [1936.]

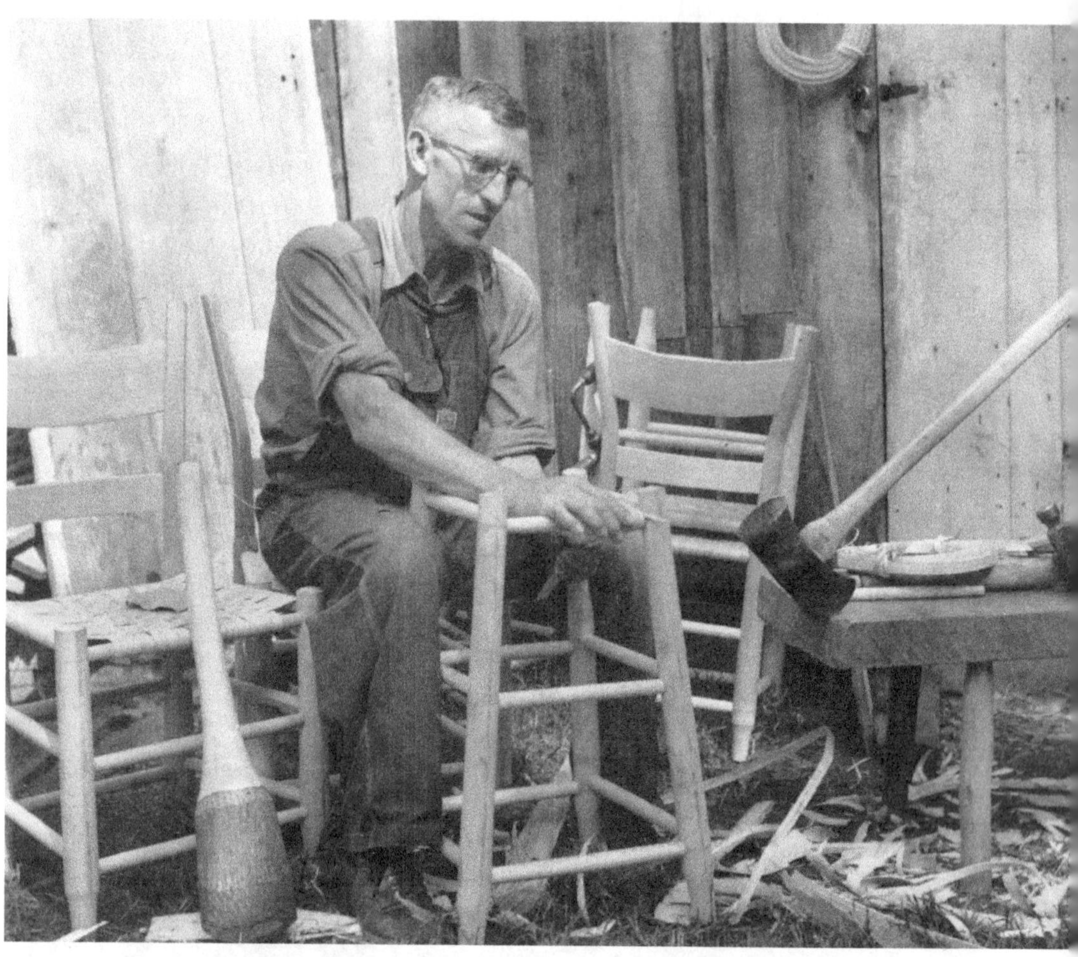

Rufus Duncan always knew how to make chairs, he said. Here he starts the weaving of a bottom for a tall kitchen chair he made in his wayside shop by the banks of Indian Creek [in Copper Valley, Virginia, 1960]. *Opposite,* Duncan bottoms a chair with white oak splits.

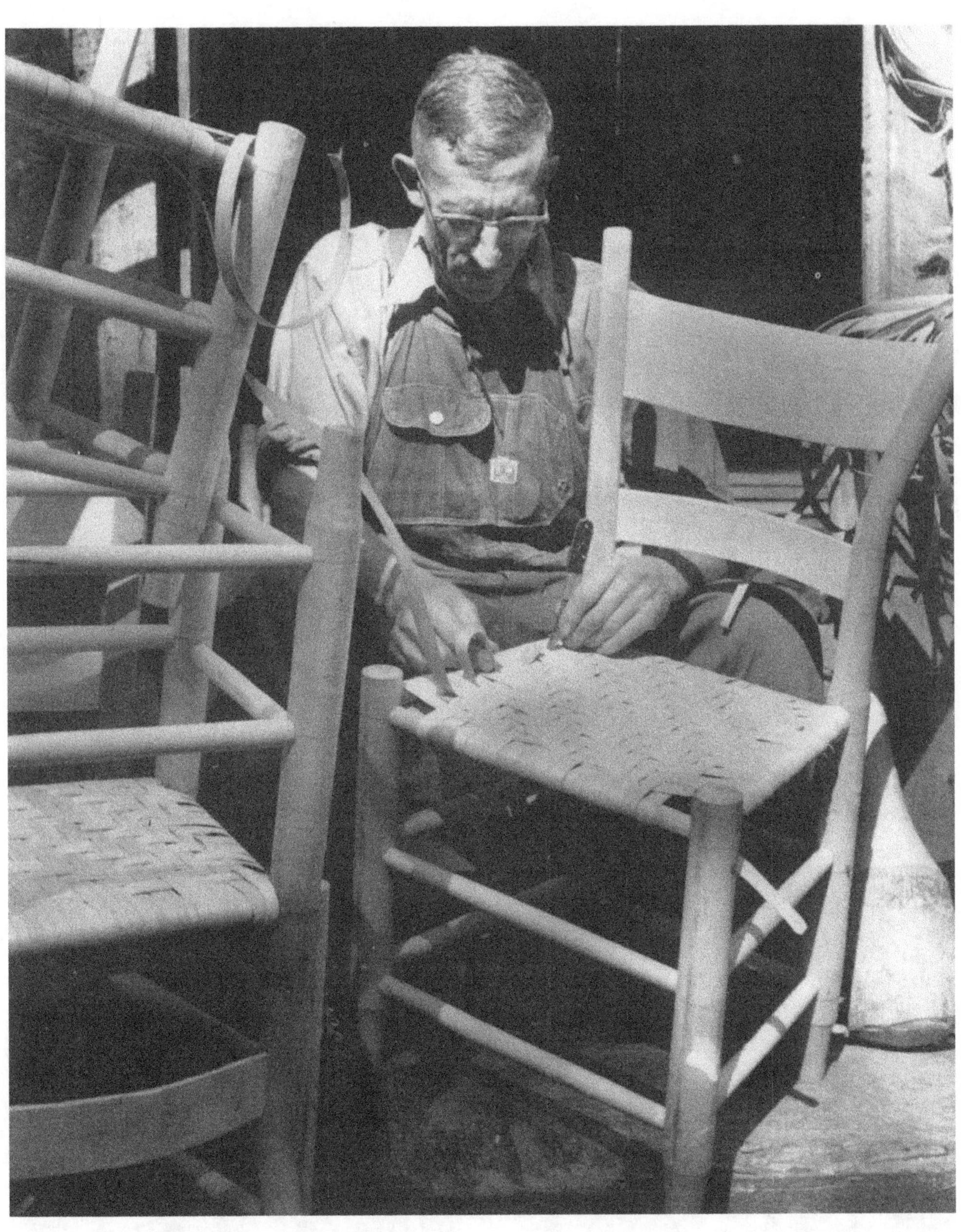

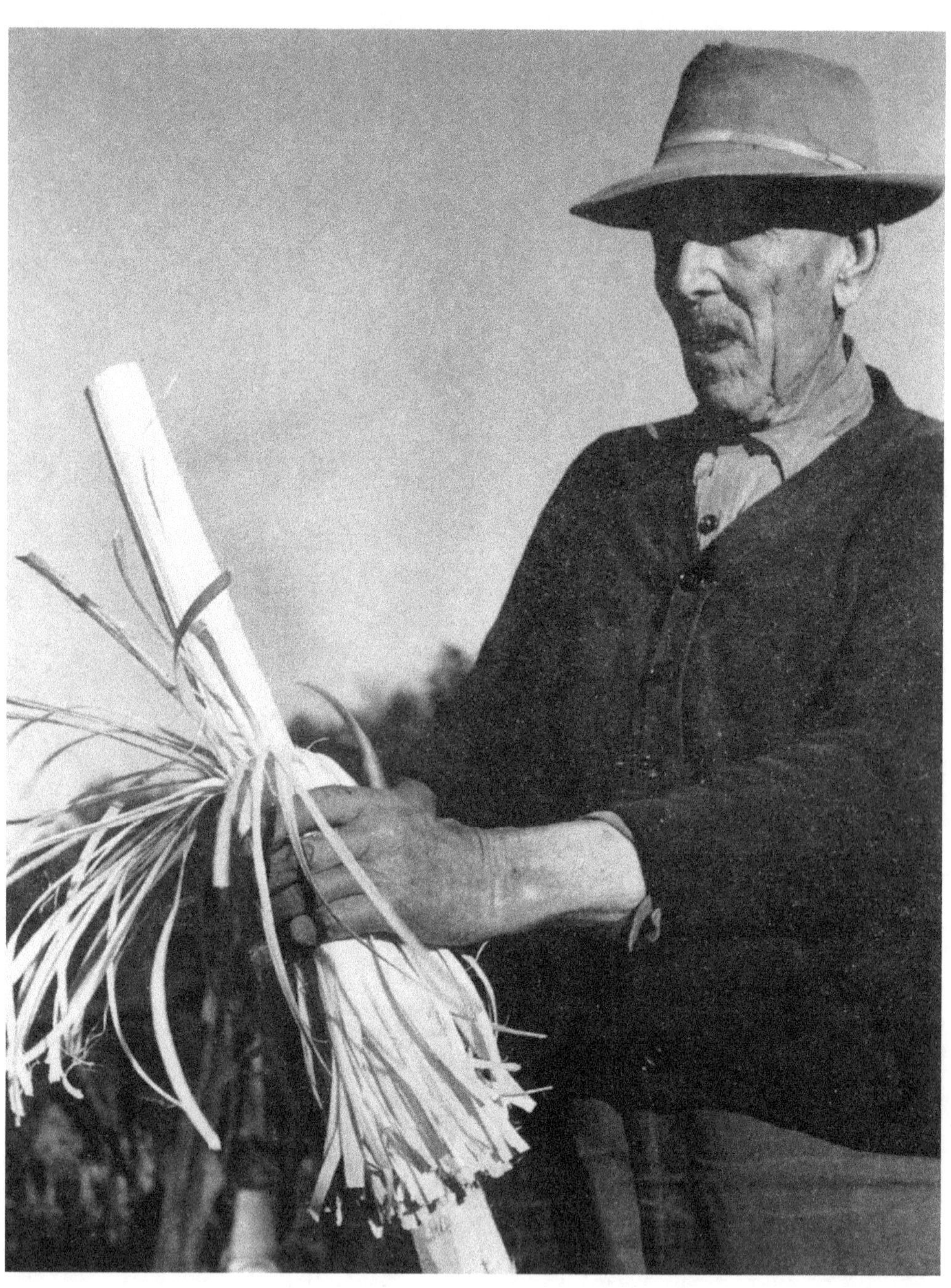

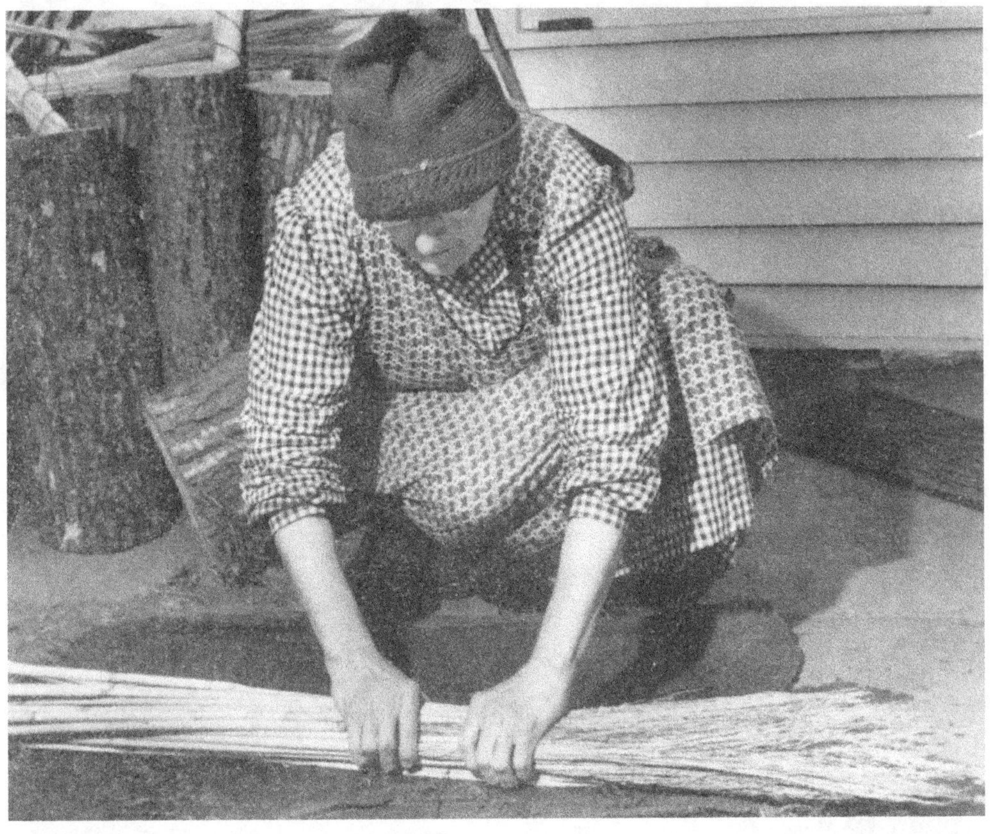

Opposite, Will Jones had unmatched skill in making the old things, like this oak hearth broom in one piece. You don't see things like this nowadays. [Craig's Creek, Virginia, 1968. *Above,* Mrs. Goode Hash of Runnet Bag Creek near Charity, Virginia, making a reed hearth broom, 1953.]

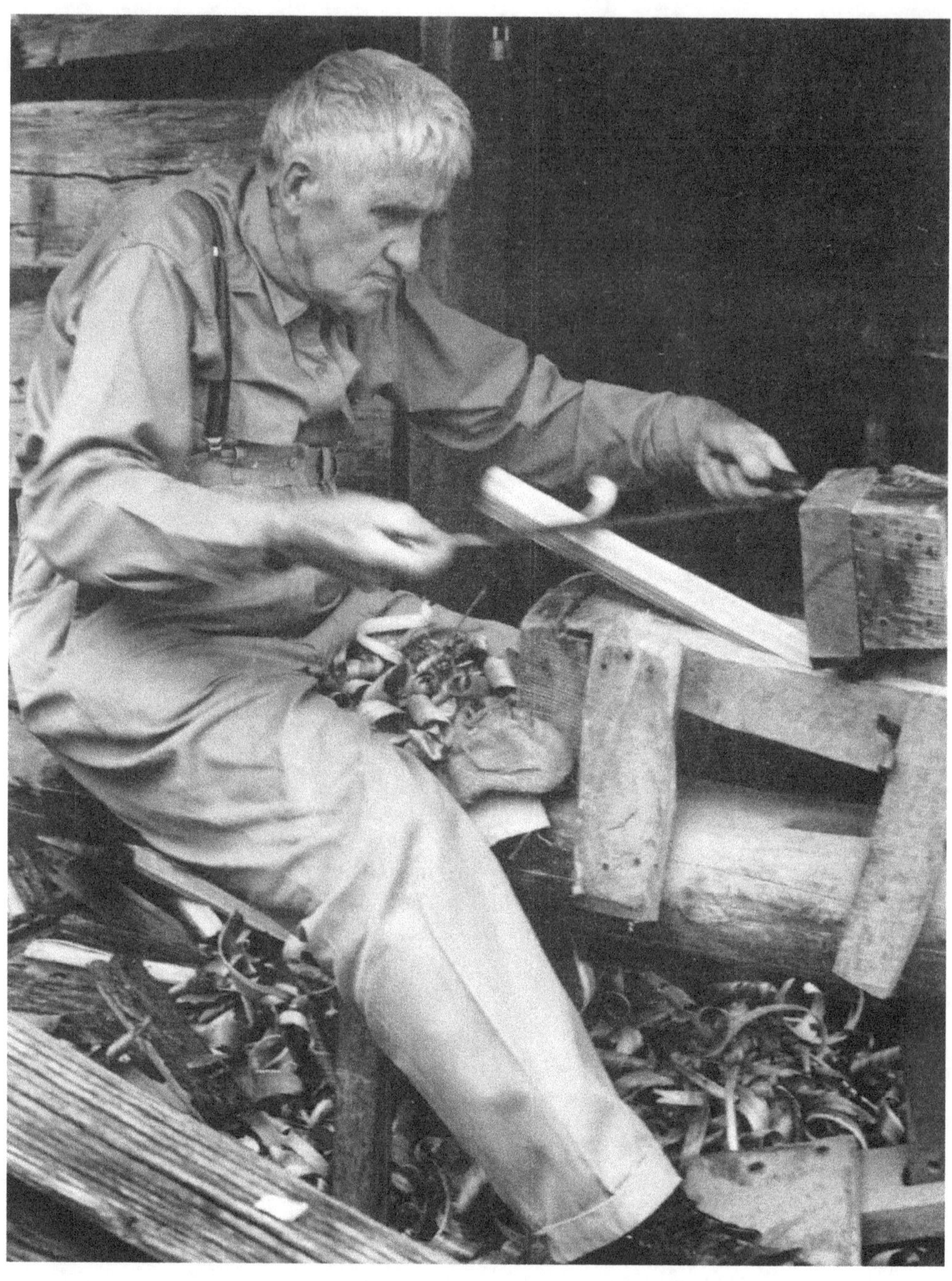

[Unknown craftsman smoothing wood with a drawing knife on a homemade shaving horse at the Highland Handicraft Fair, Asheville, North Carolina, 1965.]

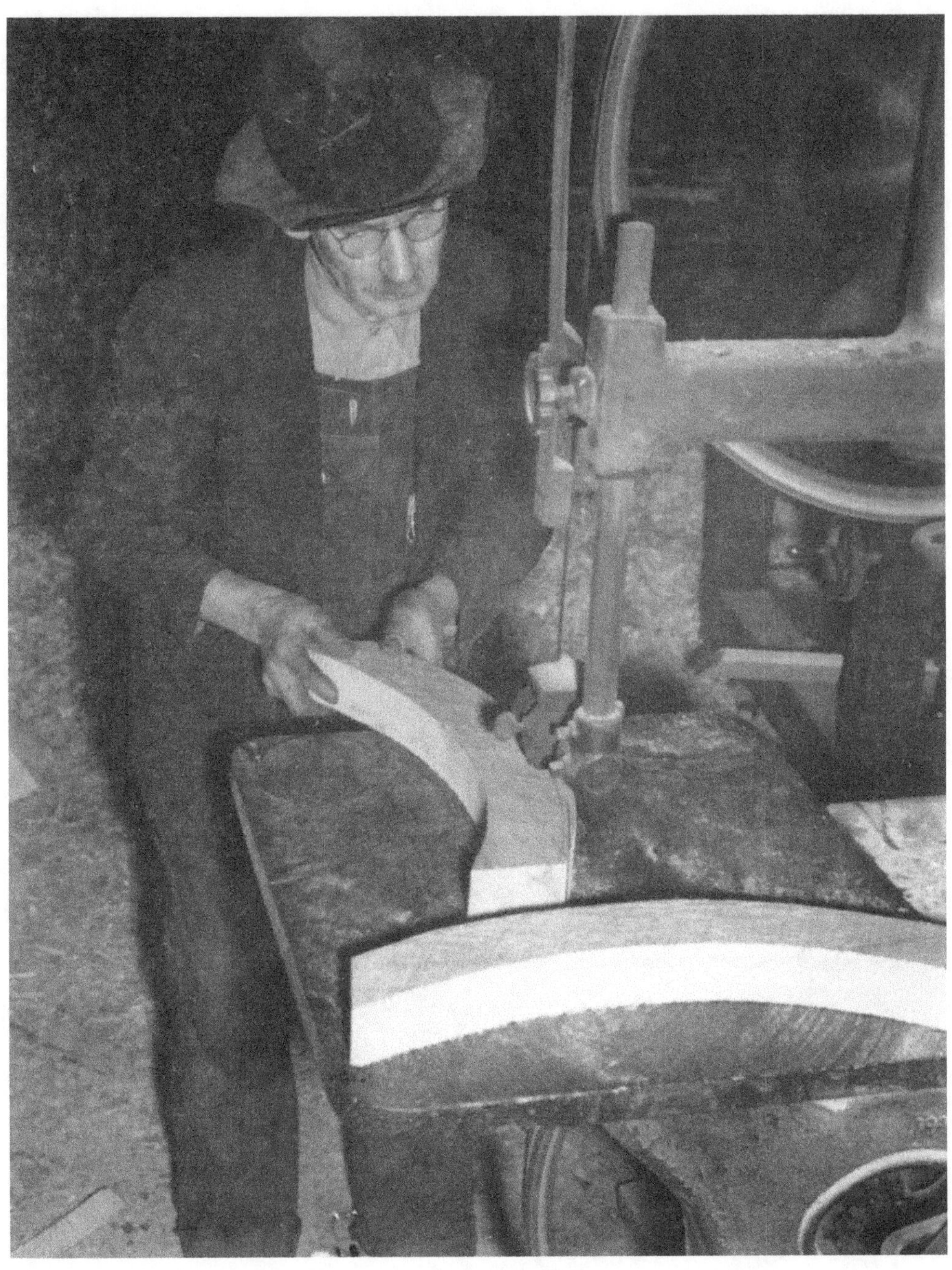

The late Winton "Preacher" Bolton, besides serving as pastor of a group of Hard-Shell Baptist churches, made wagons in his wayside shop at Cumberland Gap, Virginia. Here he is forming the rim of a wheel for one of the jolt wagons or trim buggies. [1941.]

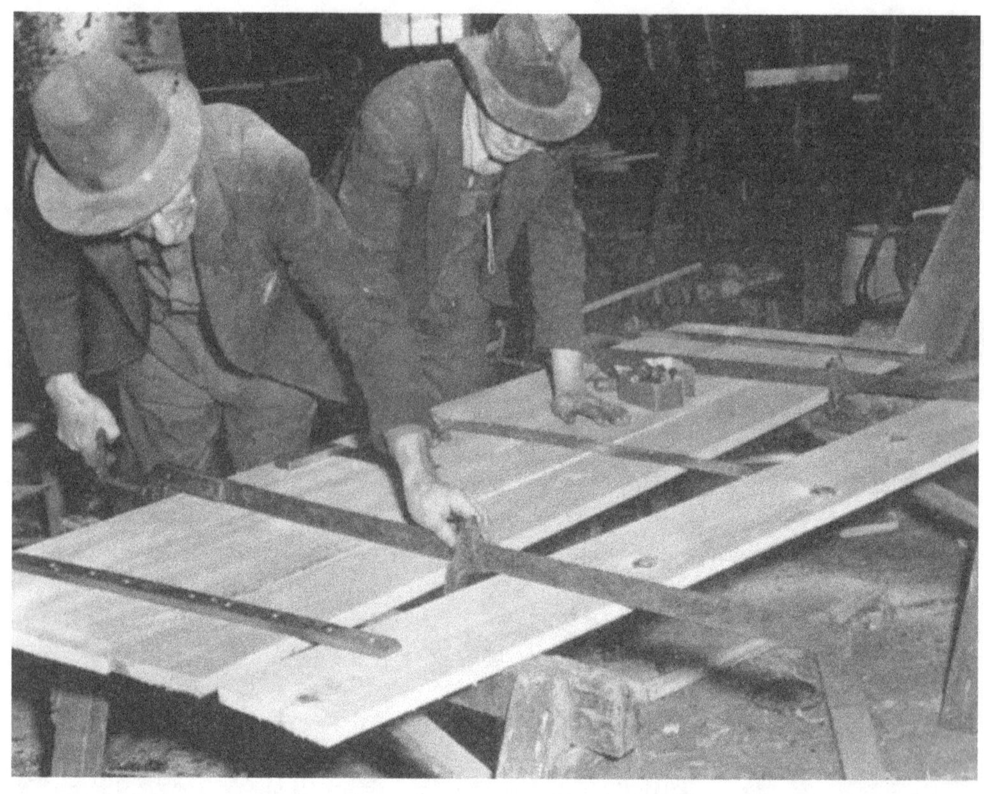

With the help of a neighbor, Wint Bolton lays out the bed for a wagon or buggy. *Opposite*, Winton Bolton was right proud of the trim buggies he made hisself.

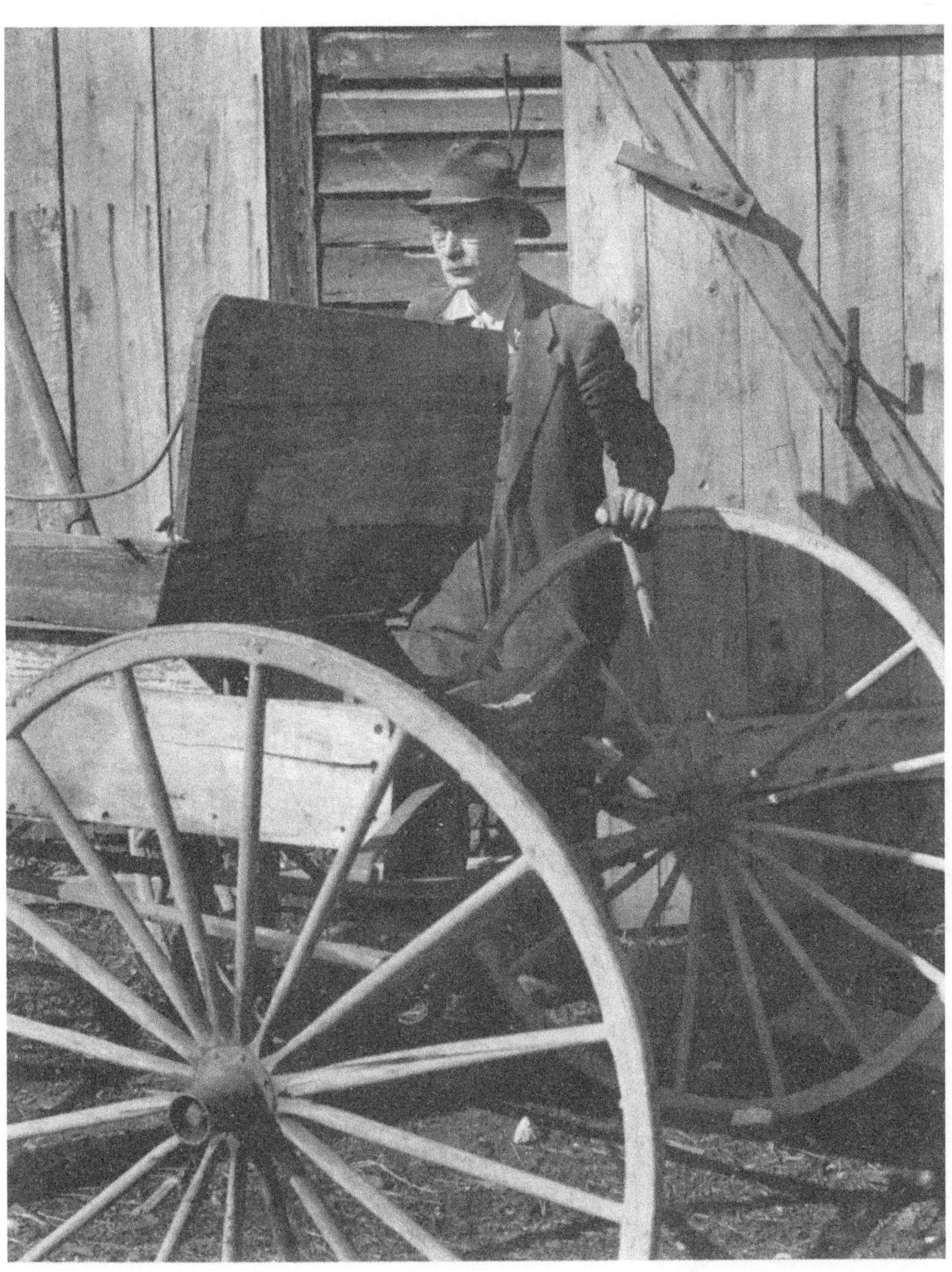

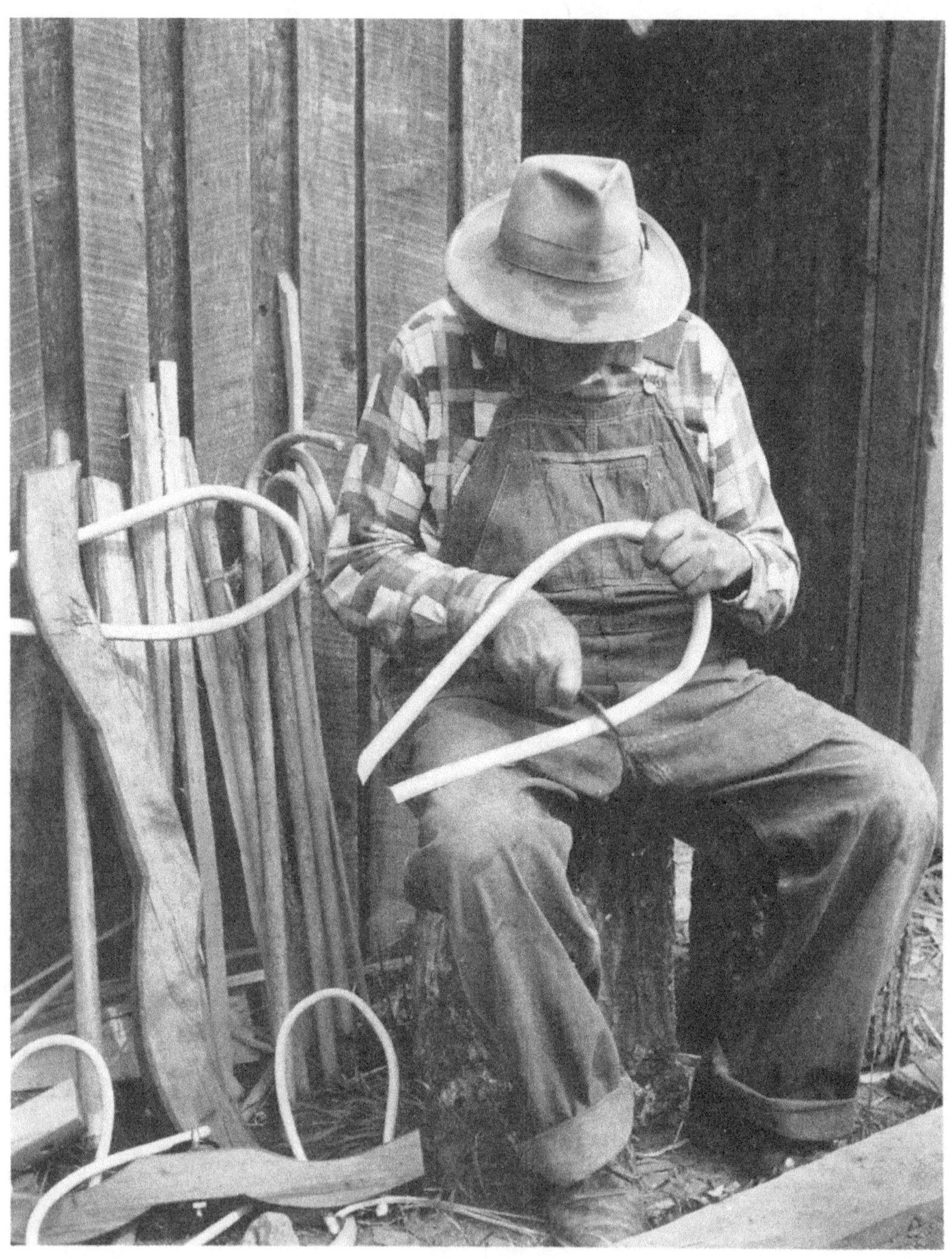

[Turner Boyd whittling ornamental ox yokes at his home in Floyd County, Virginia, 1963.]

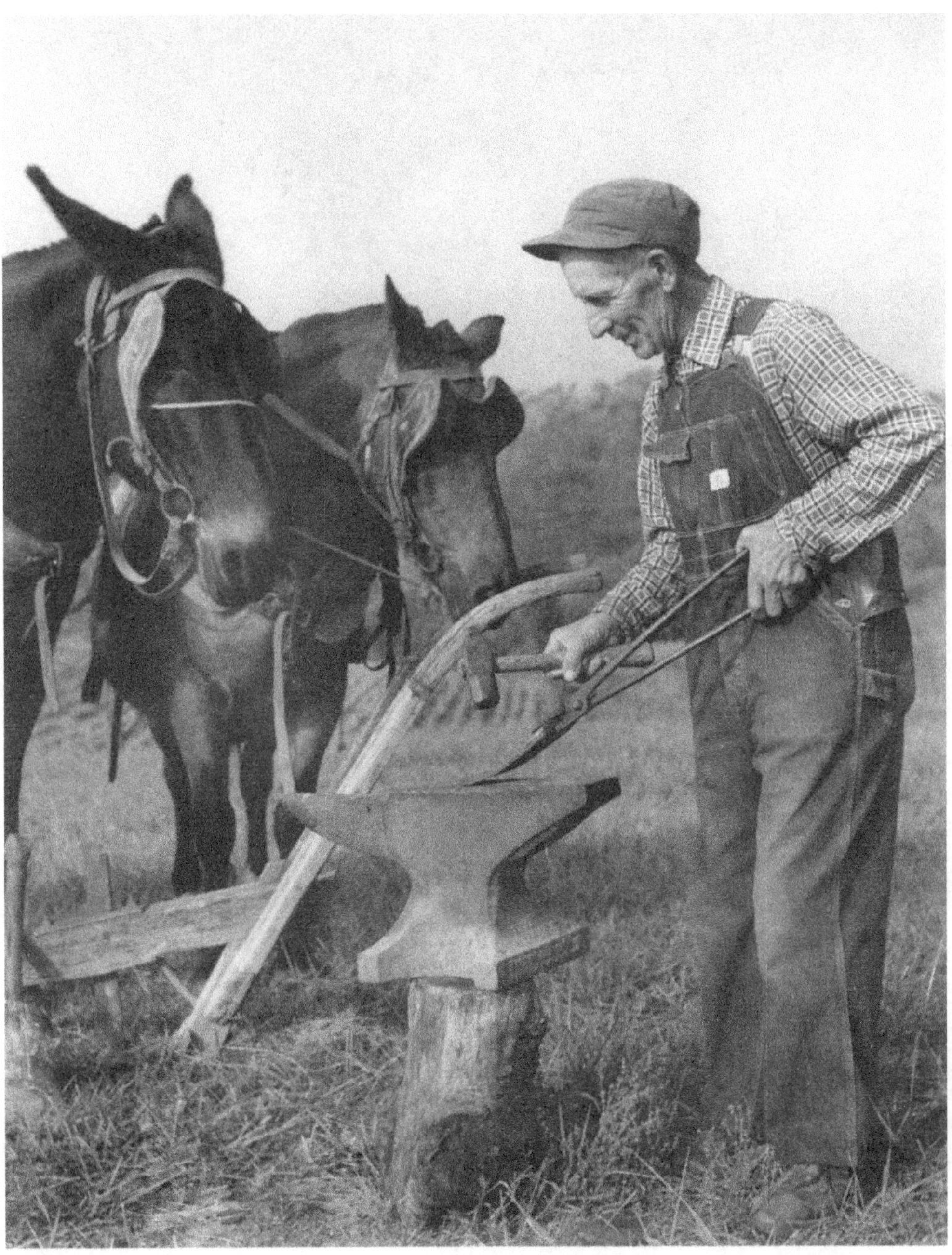

Robert Bowman was a bundle of tireless energy and know-how. What he needed around his hillbound farm he made hisself. Like he said, you've got to make out with what's on hand, do the best you can. He raised ten children, one of whom was my deceased wife, Alice, who had much the same way of doing things as her father. [Near Berea, Kentucky, 1959.]

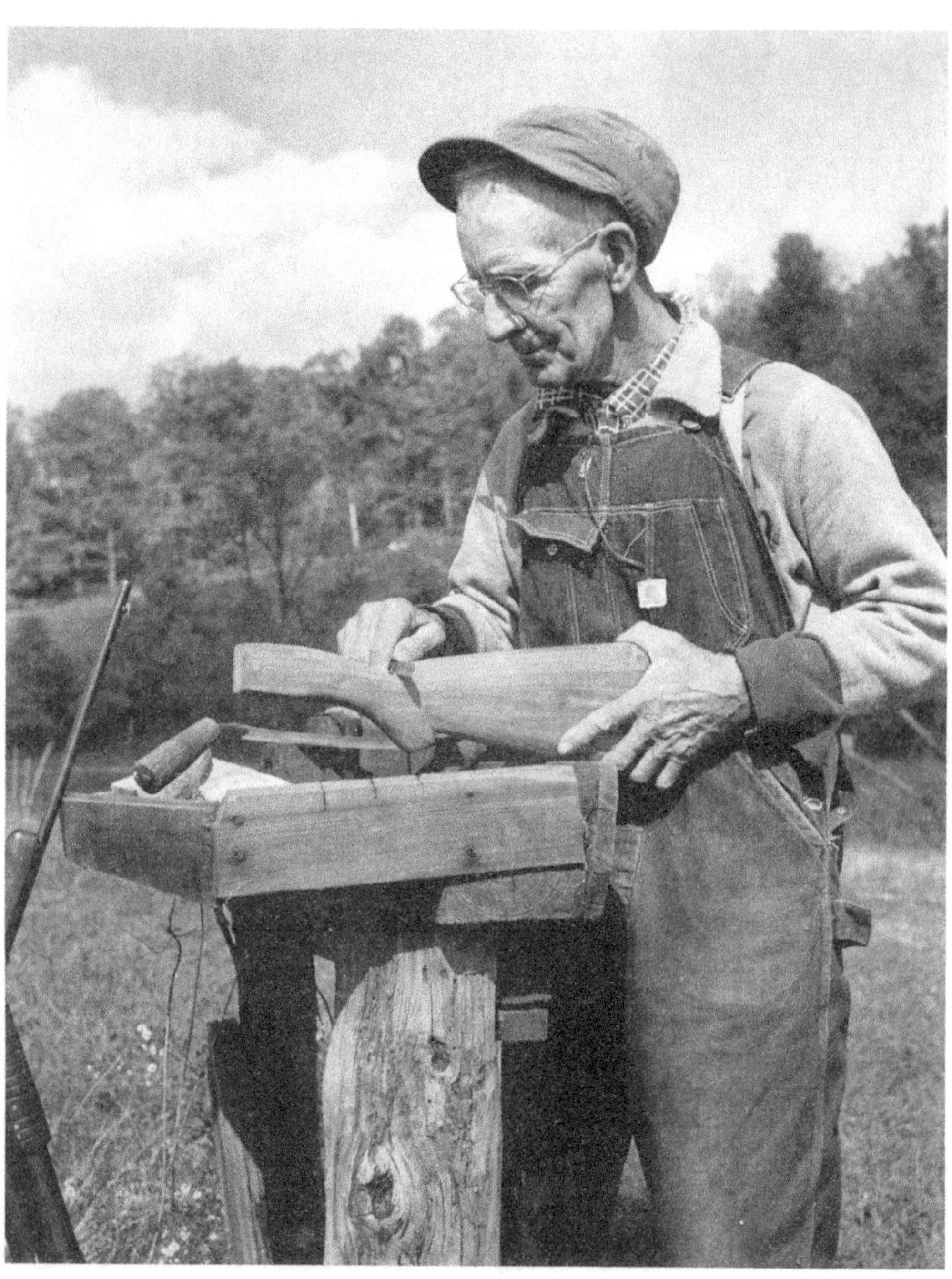

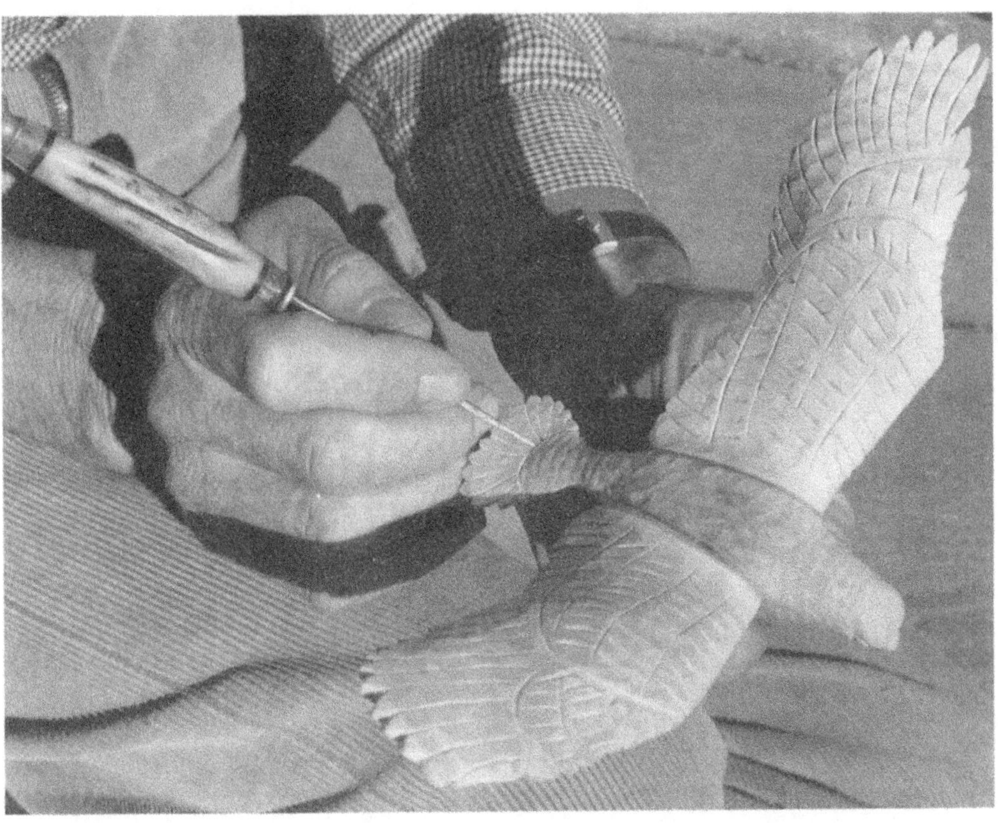

Like so many mountain-fetched-up men, Bob Bowman (*opposite*) was a virtuoso with a Barlow knife. Here he whittles a gunstock from a chunk of black walnut that growed on his farm. He may keep said gunstock for hisself, but then he might give it to some friend. [1959.] Among the many whittlers known to me, the late Harold Garnand (*above*) led the pack. Here he puts the finishing touches to a wild turkey whittled from Lombardy poplar. [Ellett Creek, Virginia, 1984.]

It's Court Day in Rocky Mount, county seat of Franklin County, Virginia. By sunup back country roads leading to Rocky Mount are clogged with gay buggies and horse- and mule-drawn jolt wagons. Some will be there to see if they're going to hang the jury or the man, others to meet old friends and engage in the time-honored ritual of swapping horses, mules, watches, and knives. Barnyard science and philosophy are exchanged at every hand: why it is that the ears of mules and man grow larger and more hairy with age; does the tail of a hog curve to the right or left; is the ham from the left side of a hog more tender than the right one? Hawkers will peddle for a quarter cures for what ails a feller—"blues, disappointment in love making, or a pain in one's bankpurse." [In his captions, Palmer has changed the locale of this photo often; it is probably Hyden, Kentucky, 1940.]

Mountain Rituals

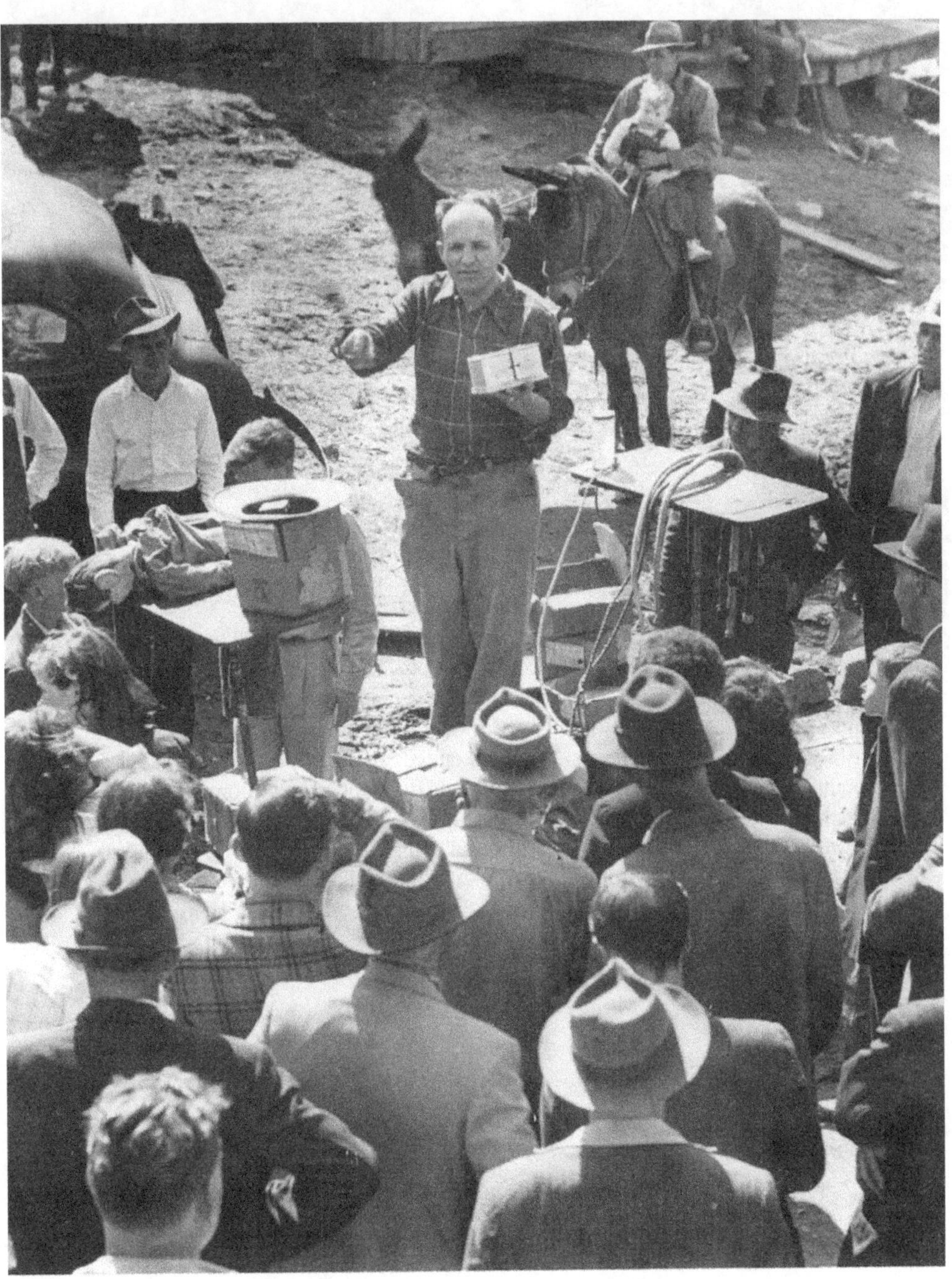

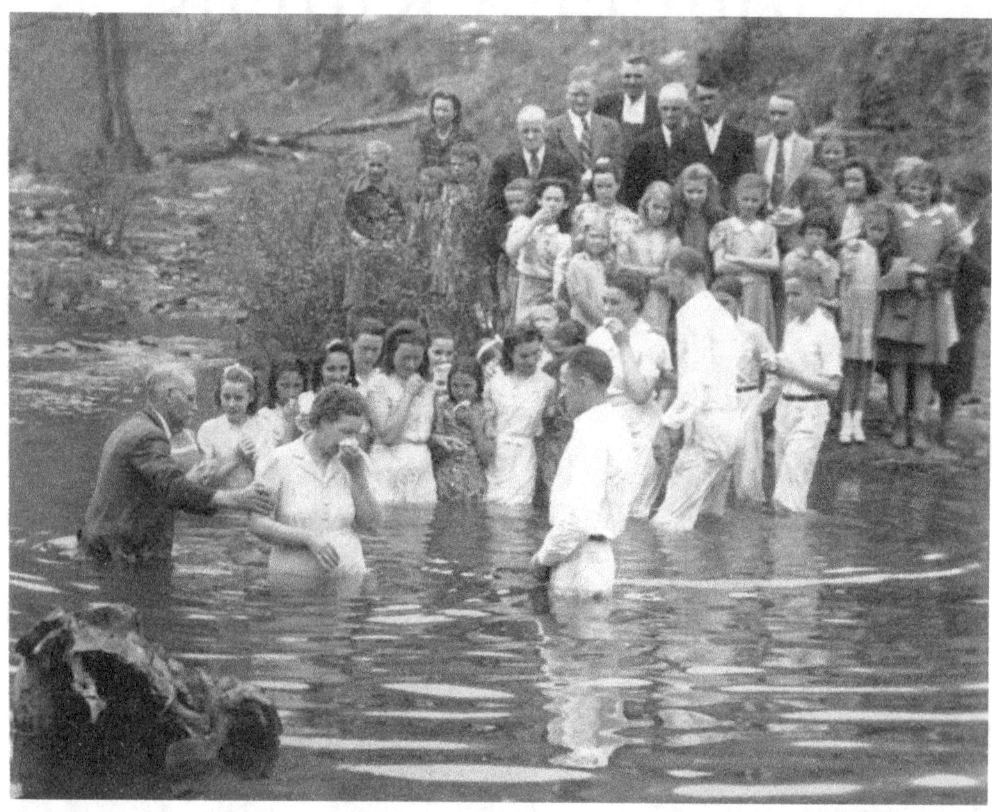

Baptizings are special events in the lives of mountain people, who have an inherent interest in what follows after their stay here is ended. A fit time to scare the sinful into full repentance for their wrong doin's, as funerals do, baptizings follow protracted revival meetings held by a preacher of homespun origin and scriptural beliefs. Wint "Preacher" Bolton was such a man, a member of a fast-vanishing breed of shouting and pulpit-banging preachers. He was here this hot mid-July day to baptize converts at a revival he held at the First Baptist Church across the ridge in Cumberland Gap. [Fern Creek, Kentucky, 1940.]

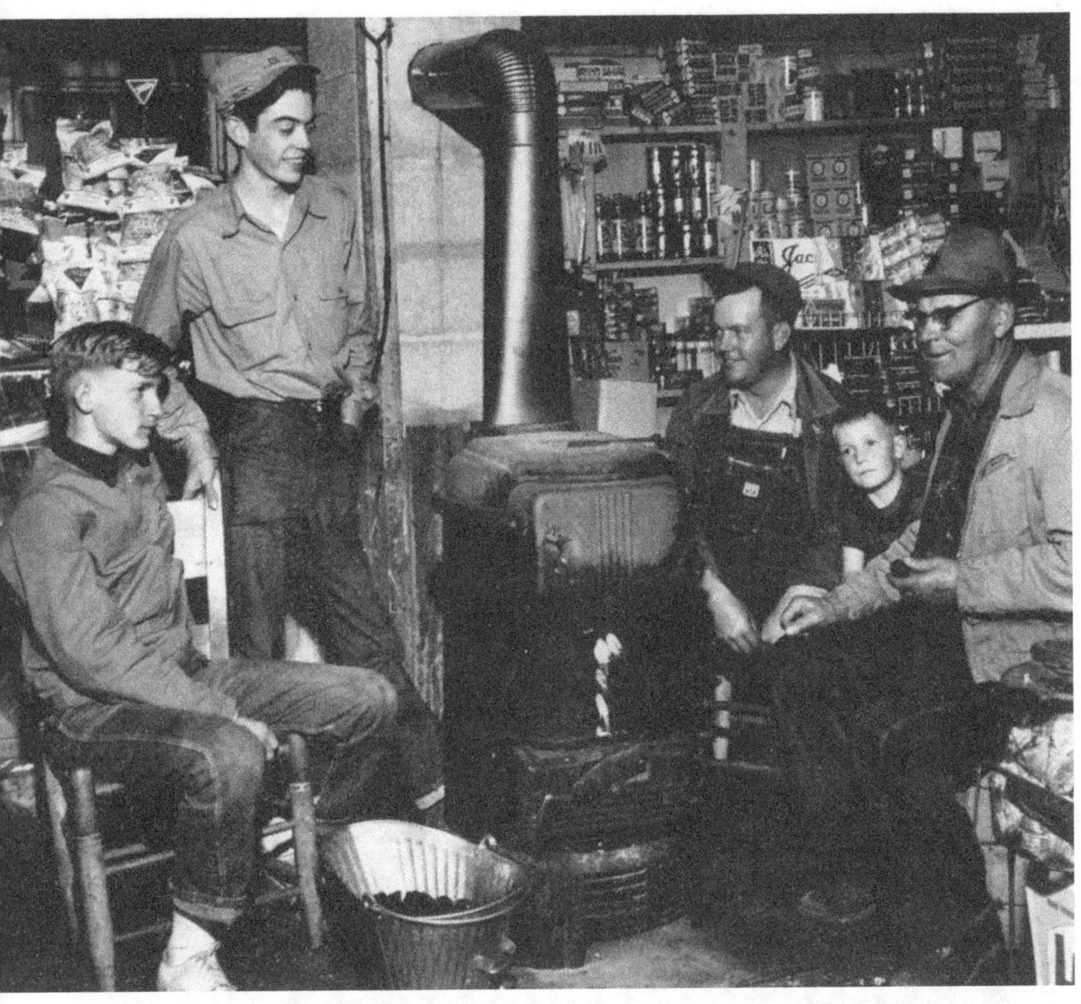

[At Evie Shelton's store in Floyd County, Virginia, 1955.] At the crossroads stores of the hill country, the mountain people gather around the year in good weather and foul, some to buy things their hilly acres won't grow, others to discuss the state of the union, swap guns and horses, or catch bigger fishes and chase faster foxes than ever swam in a stream or roamed in the forests. The all-wise storekeeper lends an ear the same as if he was hearing the tales for the first time.

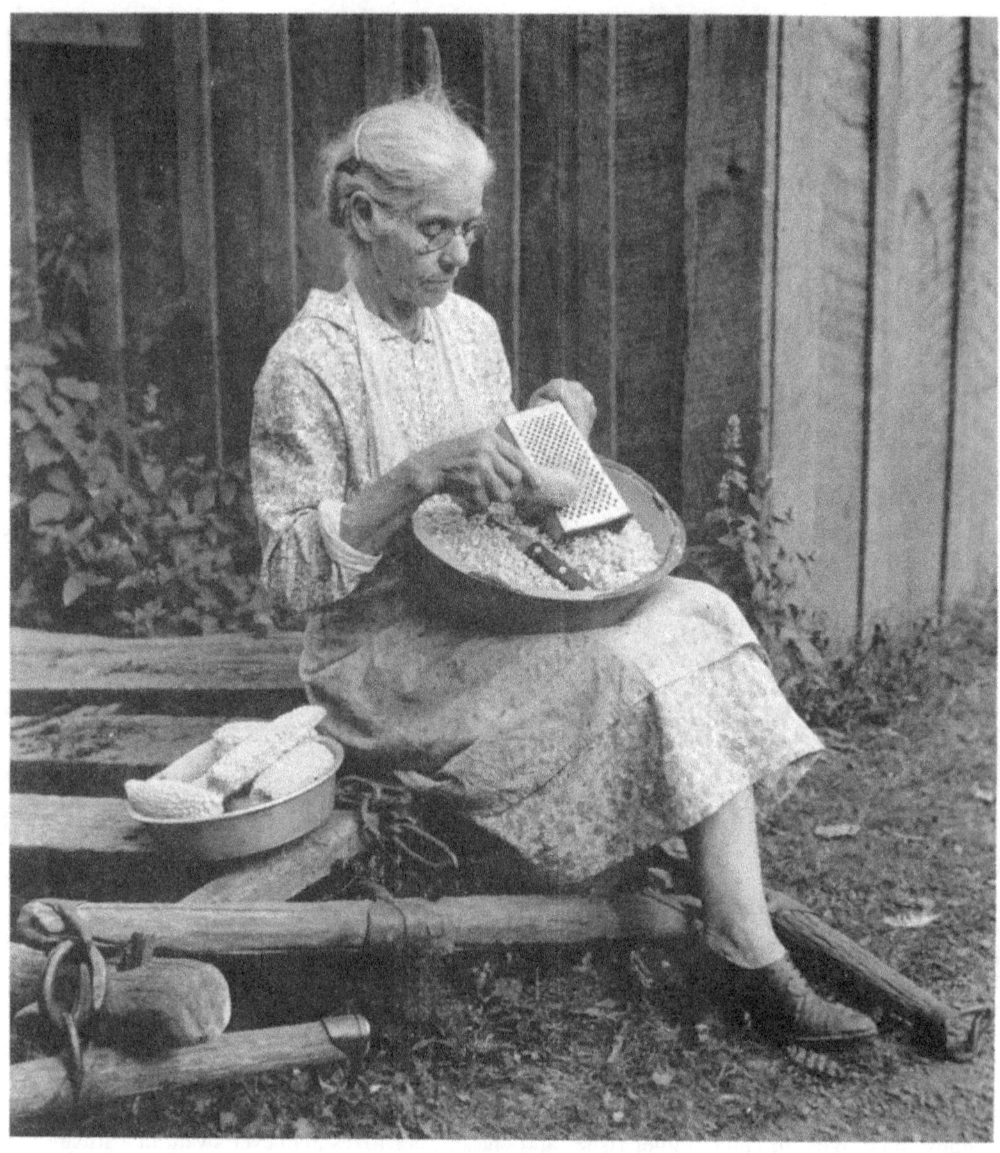

Lula Conrad, following a recipe handed down from her mother and grandmother, makes a batch of grit bread. Six ears of corn just beyond the milk stage are gritted to yield 2½ cups of scraped kernels, bran included. Over the kernels sift 1 cup presifted flour, plus 2 tsp. of sugar, 1¼ tsp. of salt and then 1½ tsp. of baking powder. Stir in one well-beaten egg together with ¼ cup of melted lard. Pour this mixture into a shallow pan and bake at 425 for about 30 minutes. Call in your young'uns and serve with thick slabs of country churned butter. [Sugar Grove, Virginia, 1954.]

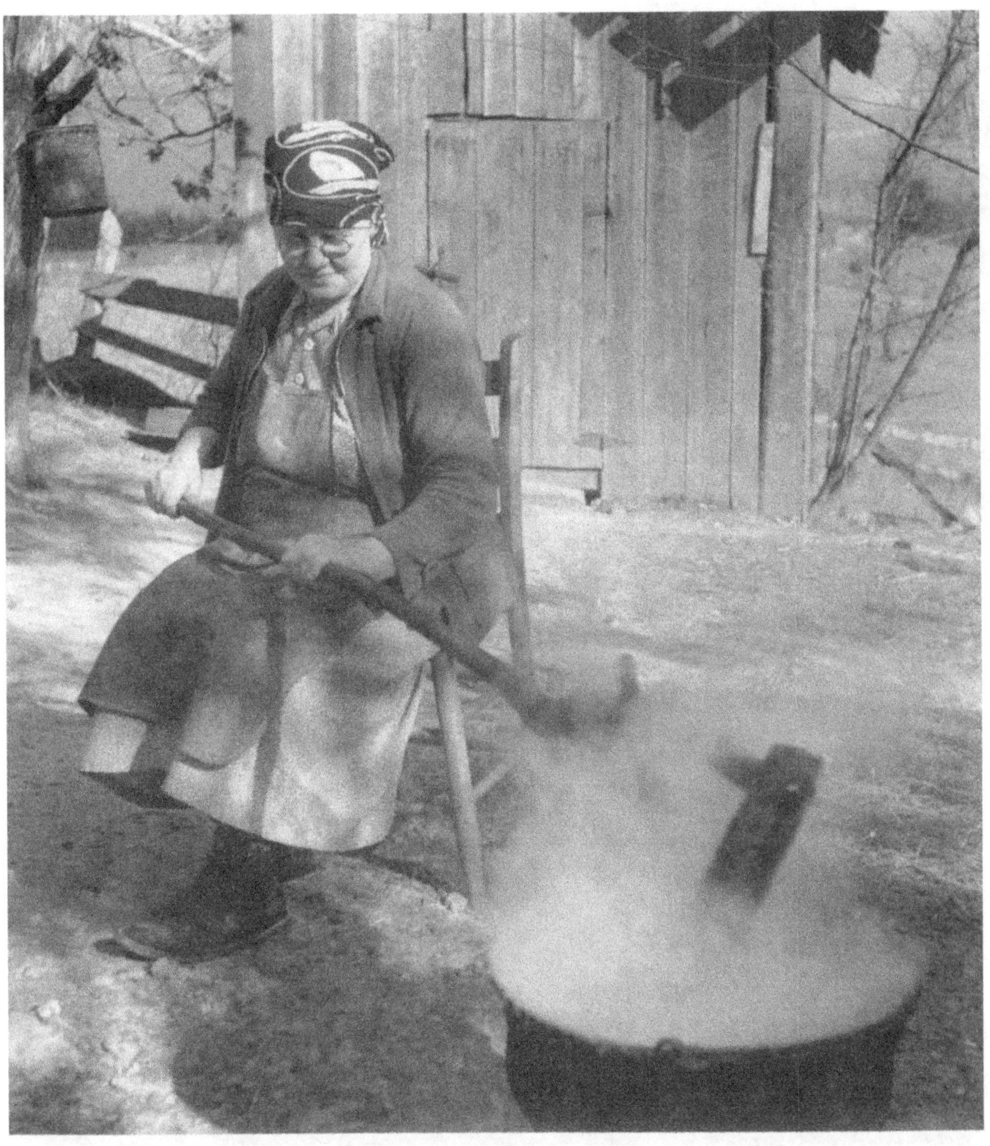

Aunt Nora Treece boils down a kettleful of apple butter against a time when snowdrifts will be banked up against the walls of her home. [1940.]

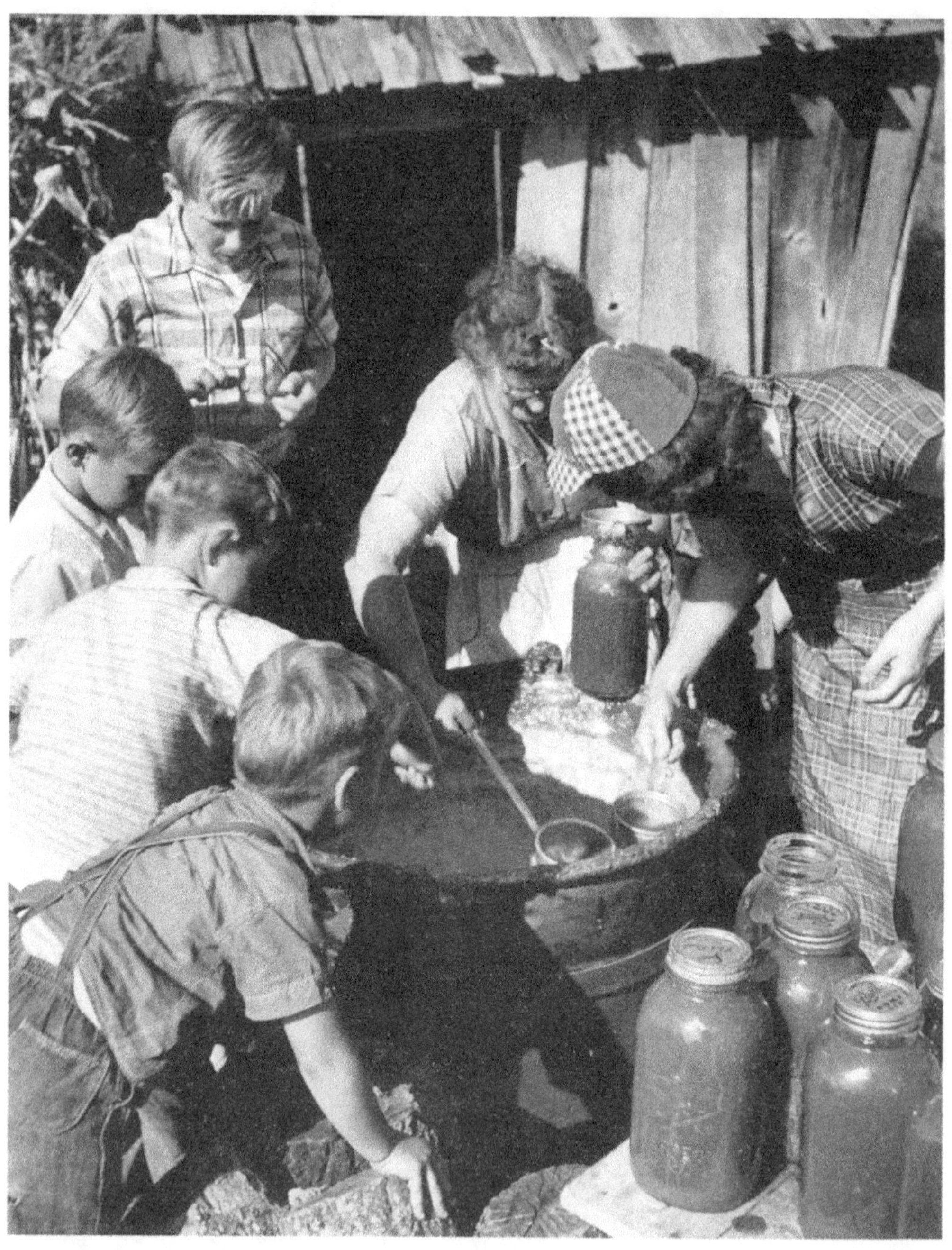

When the womenfolks around Woolwine, Virginia, stage an apple butter stir-off they use two twenty-gallon copper kettles to bile down this time-honored delicacy. [1954.]

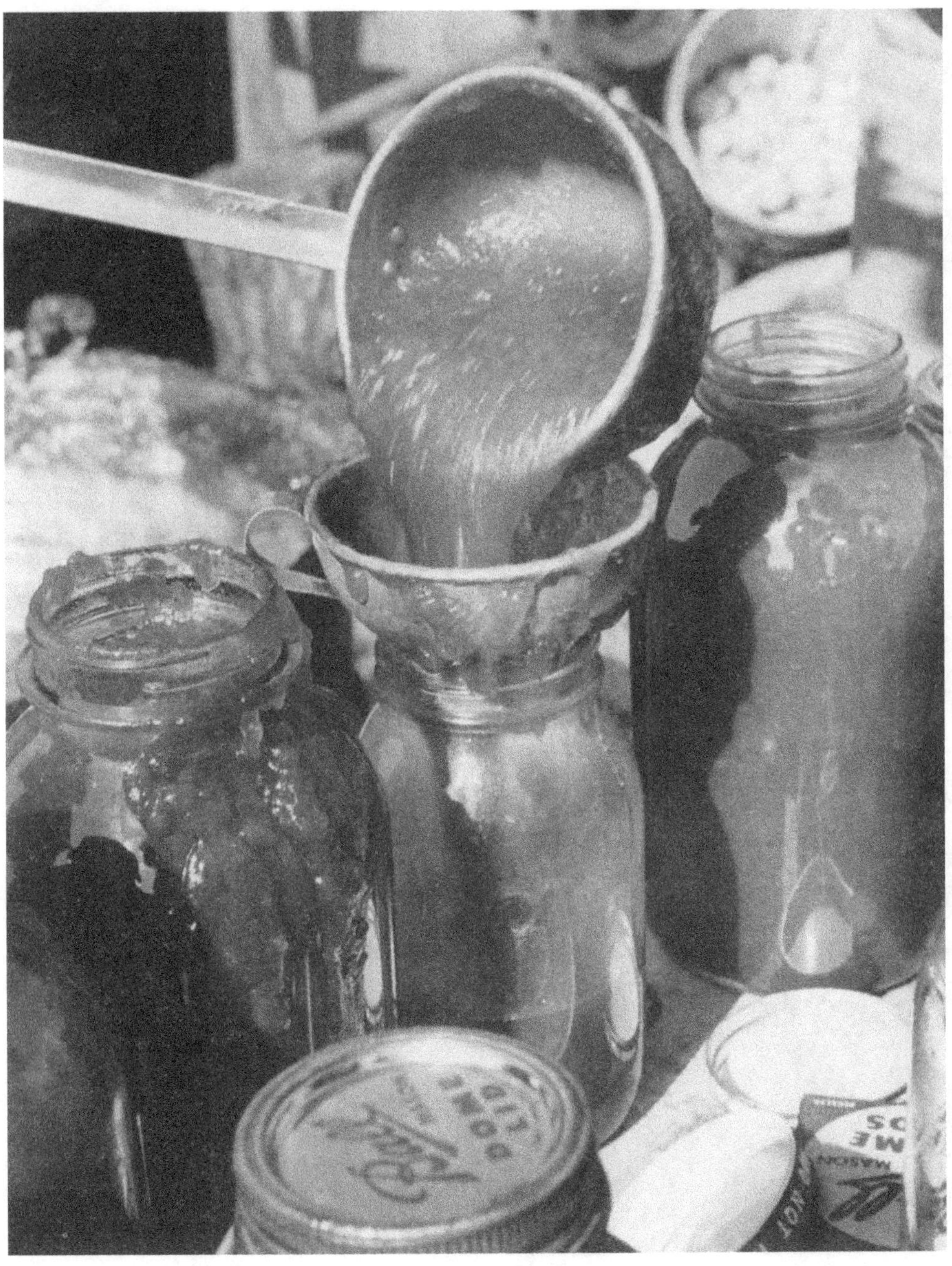

Piping hot apple butter is ladled into fruit jars against winter's need.

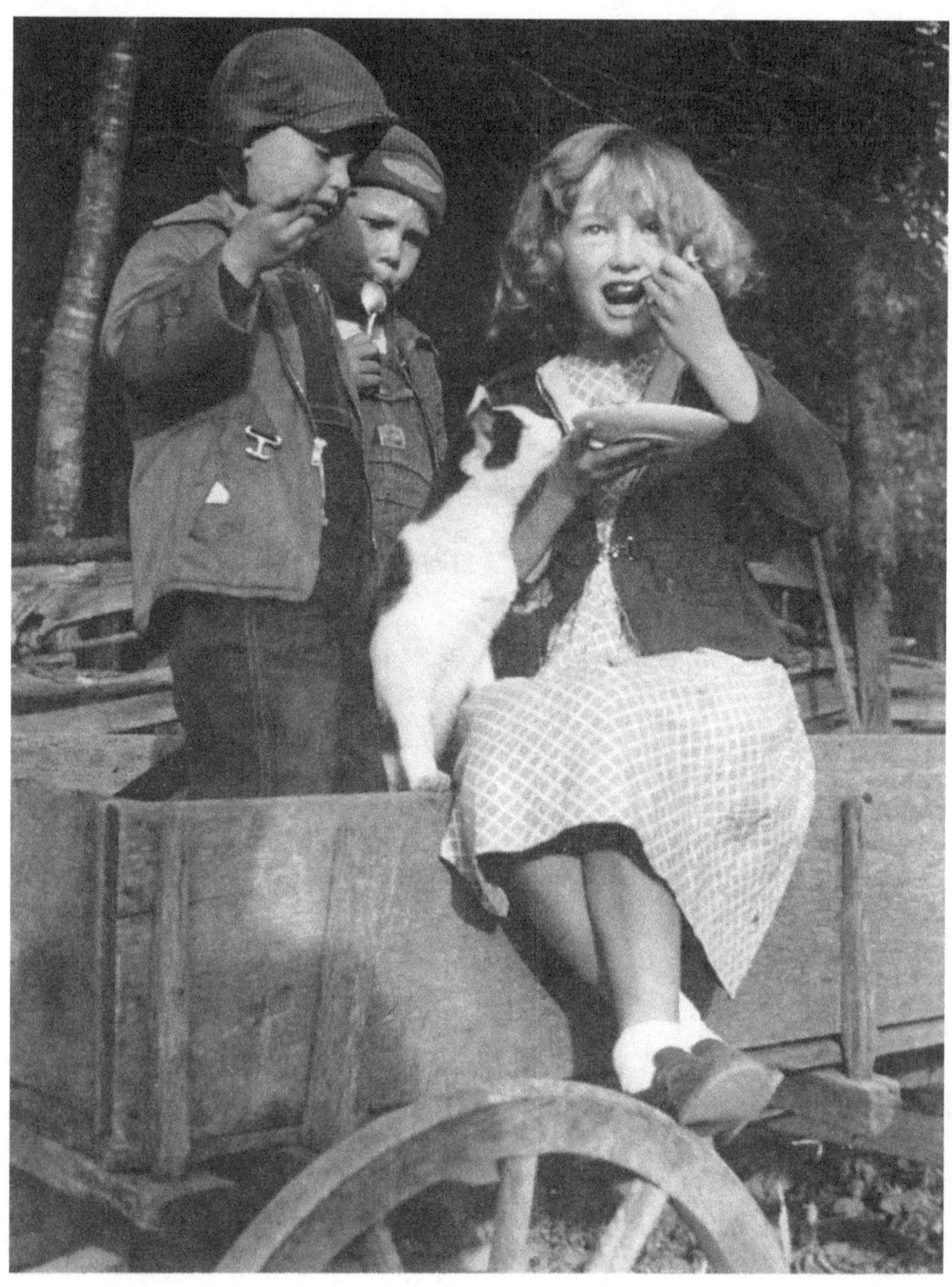

There's always a covey of very young on hand to test the fresh apple butter. "Mom, this is the best apple butter you ever made."

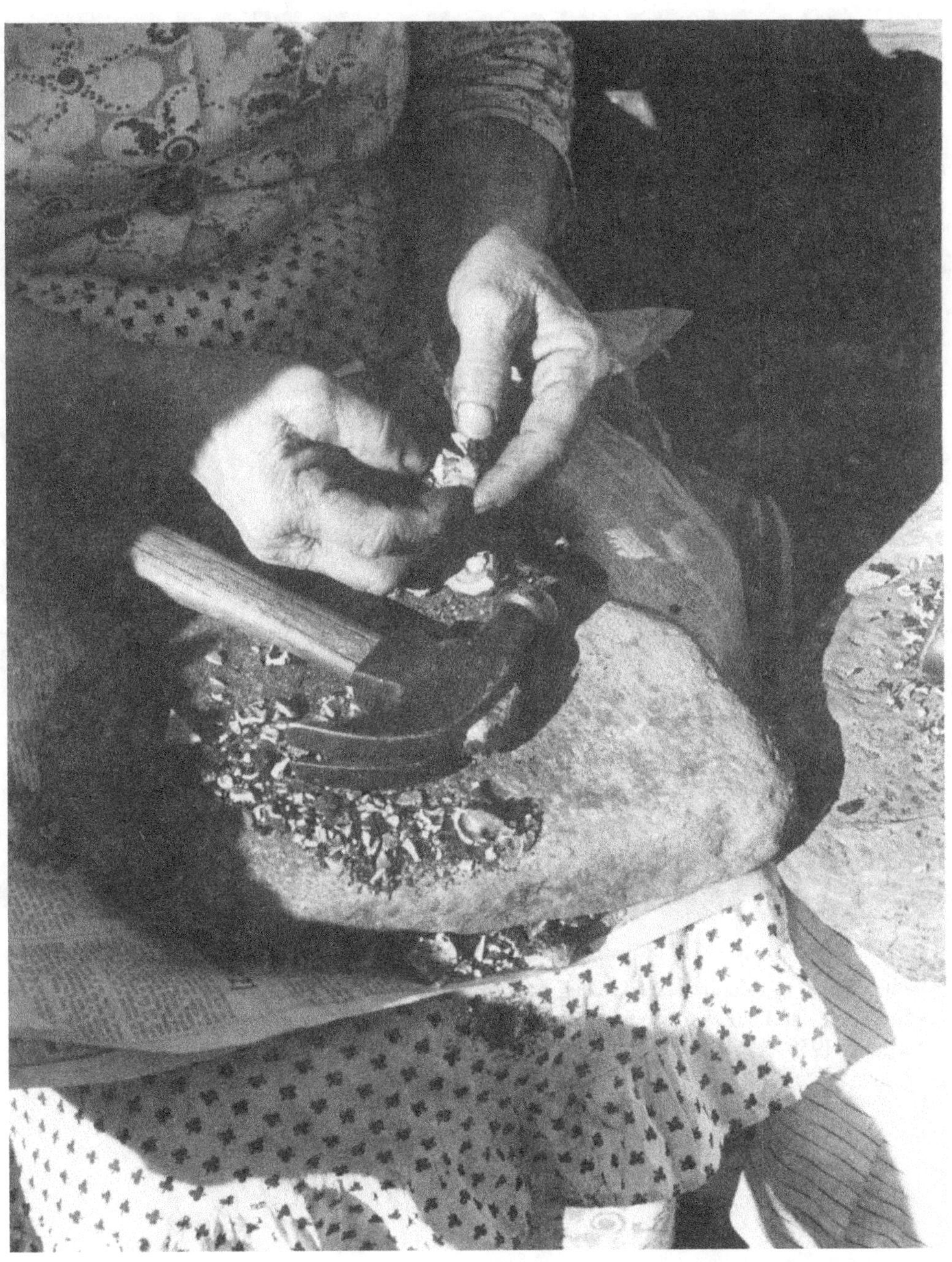

Walnut cracking. [1950.]

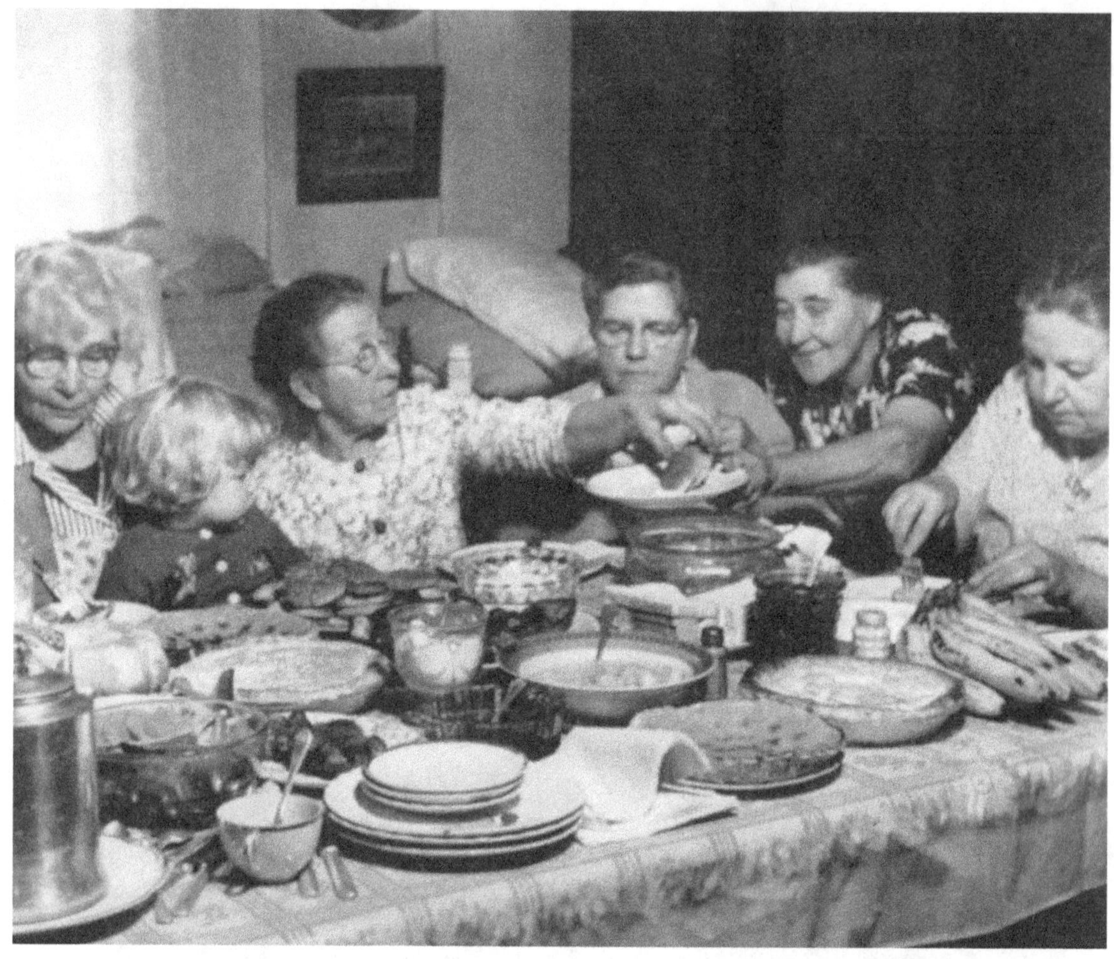

Walnut crackers take time out for a potluck lunch of country fried chicken and baked ham, deviled eggs and pickled beets, possum grape jelly and blackberry jam, and enough pies and cakes to stock a bakery. [At the DeHarts' home, Patrick County, Virginia, 1950.]

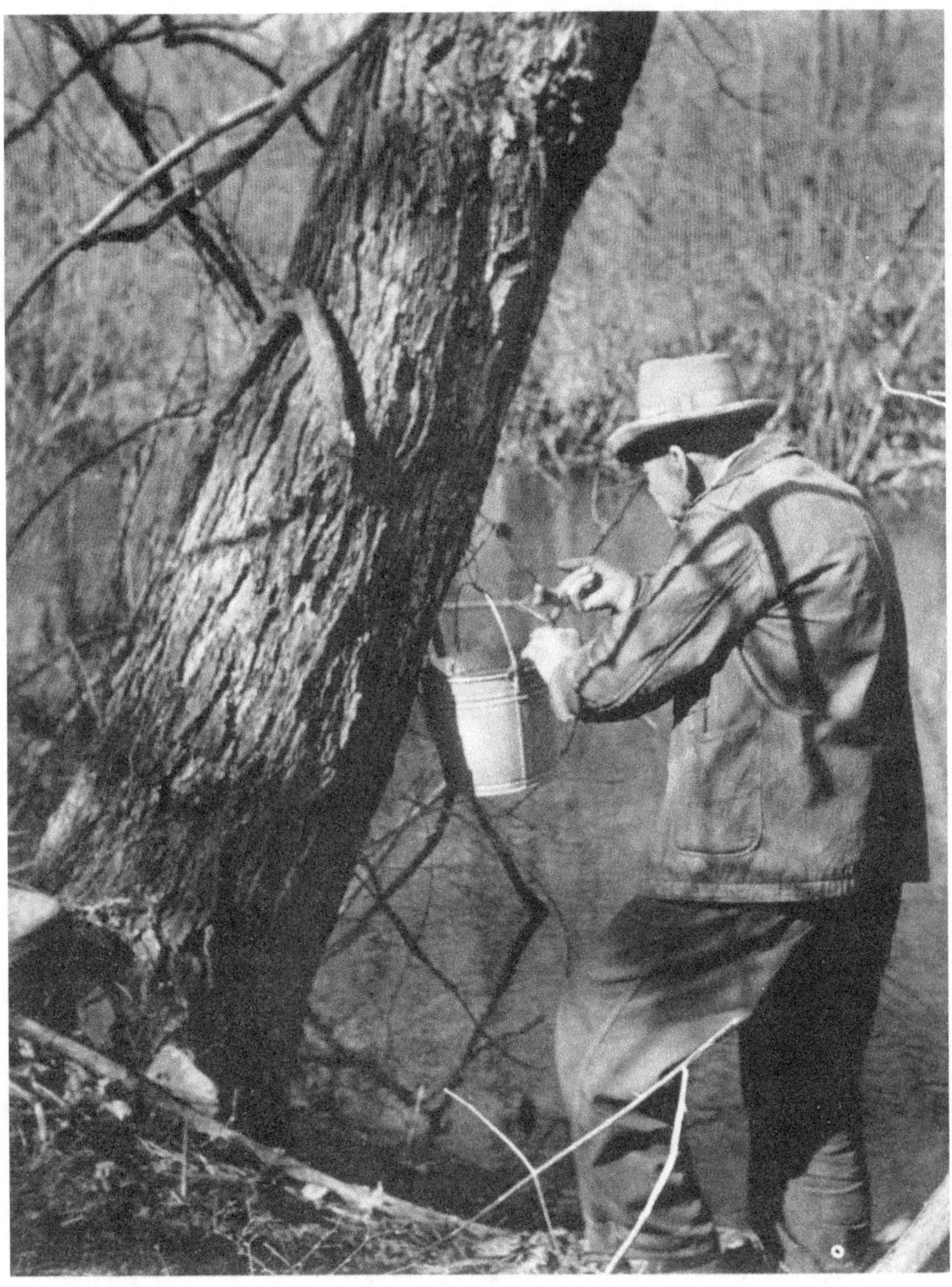

Clinton McPherson fastens a ten-quart bucket to a sugar maple tree on his place on Craig's Creek [Virginia, 1959]. Given a cold night followed by a warm day, a bucket will fill in about twelve hours.

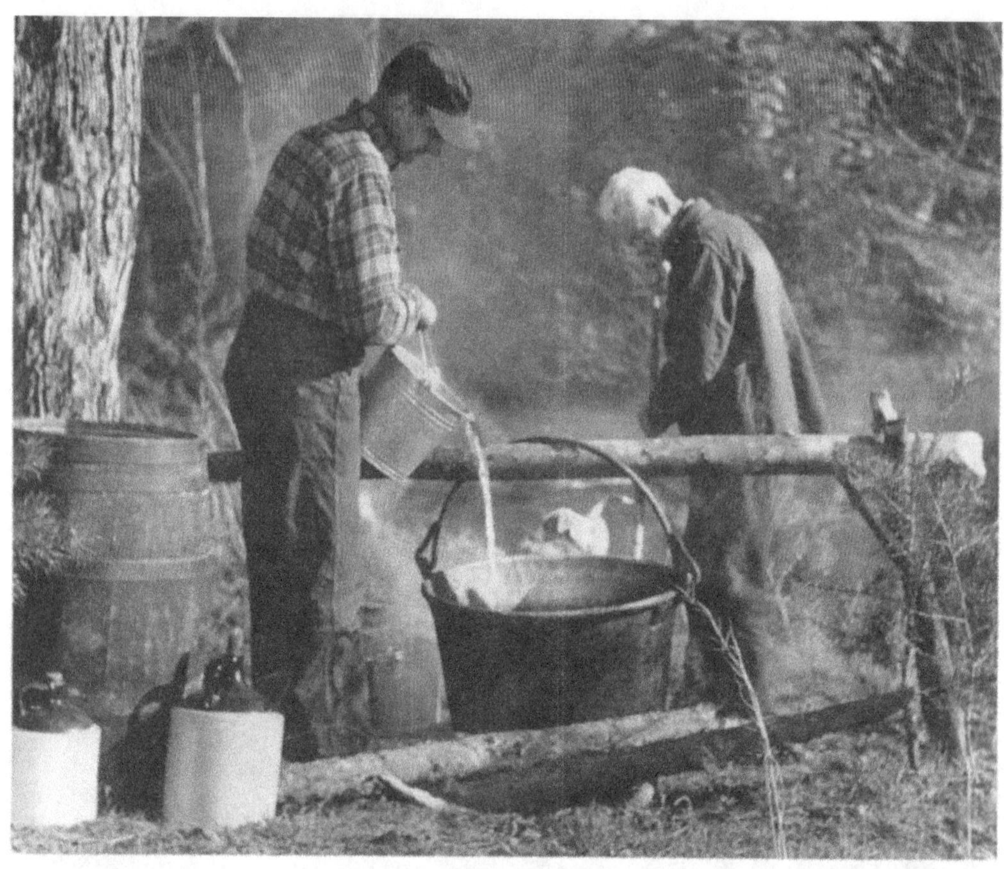

Clinton McPherson and his son-in-law, Raymond Ray, tap their maple trees along the creek and gather the clear, almost tasteless sap to boil down in huge copper kettles. Takes forty gallons of the maple "water" to turn out a gallon of syrup, this after day-long stirring of the kettle over a slow fire. Rather a hard way for a feller to get a dollar or two to keep the wolf from his cabin door.

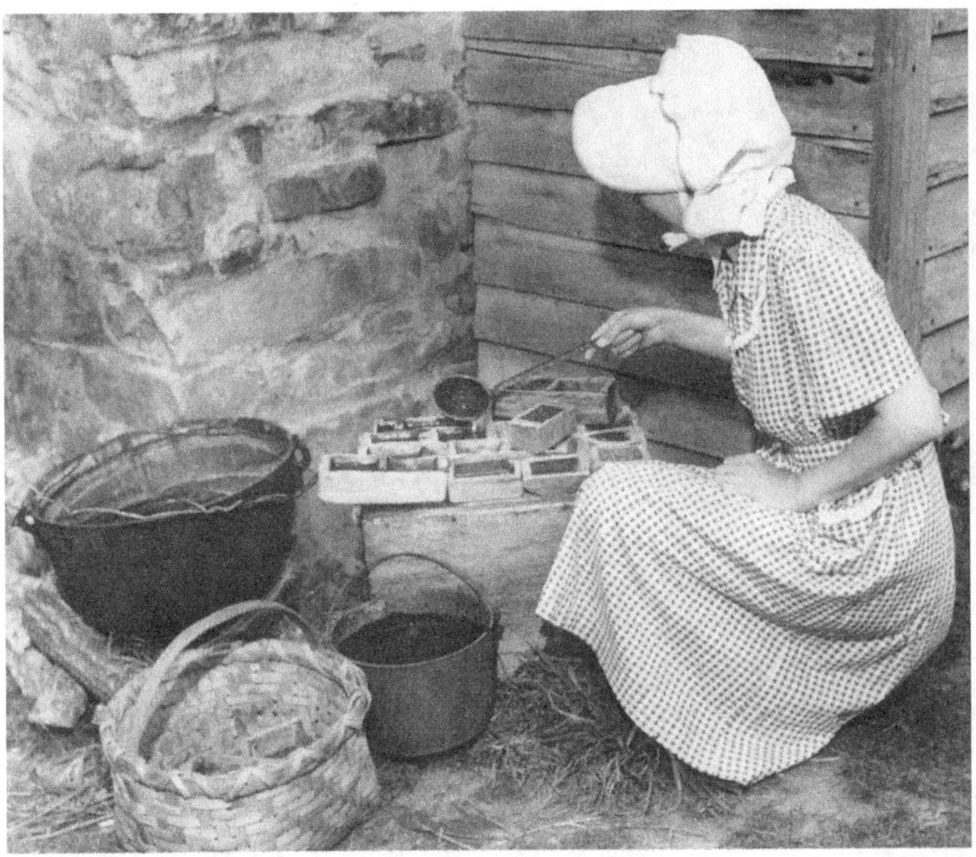

Raymond Ray's wife pours fire-hot maple syrup into wooden molds; it quickly crystallizes into cakes of maple sugar candy, sold to bolster the economy of many a mountain family.

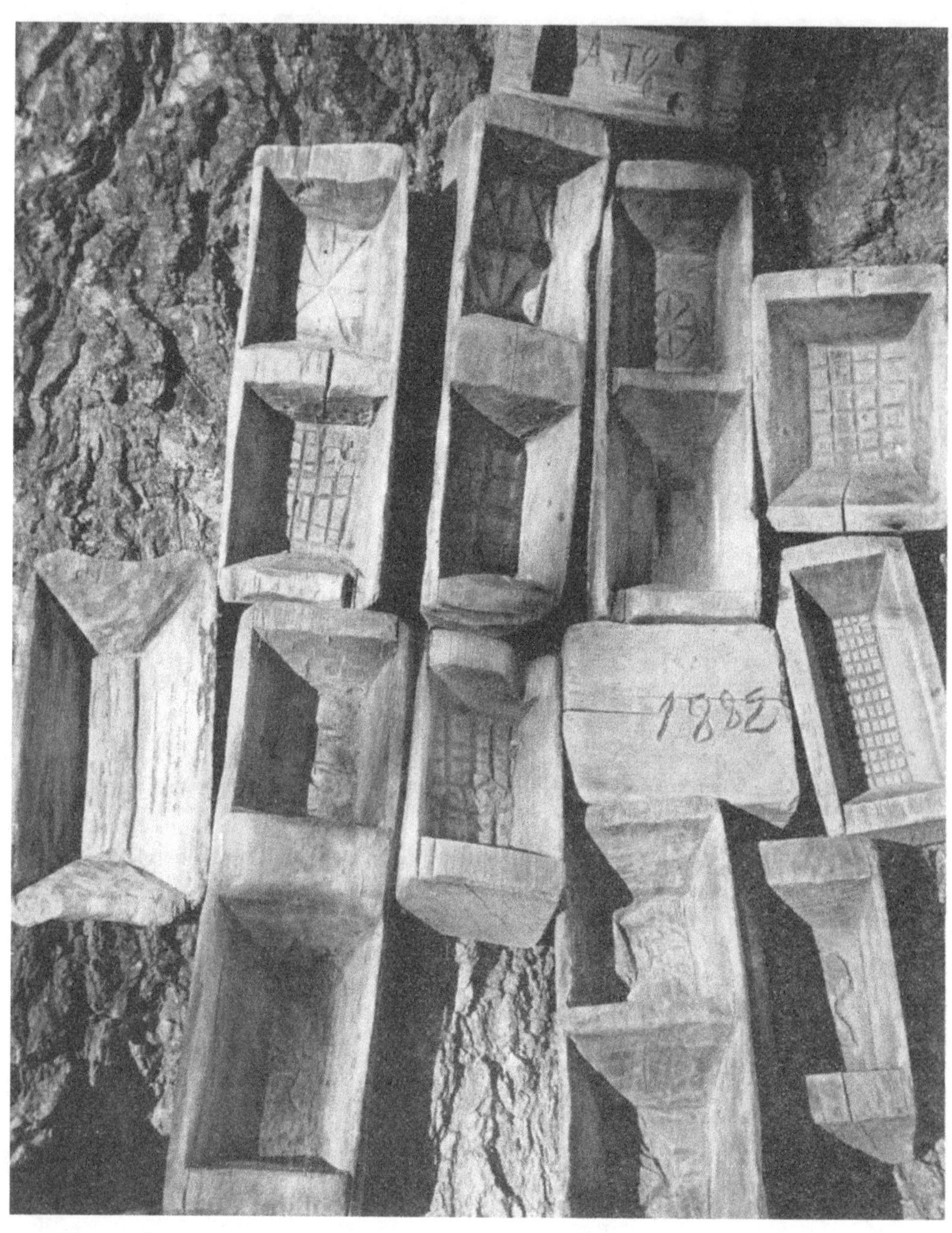

Hand carved wooden molds, whittled shortly after the Civil War from poplar and dogwood, have been used for generations to make maple sugar candy; they have a charm associated with fireside creations of a bygone day.

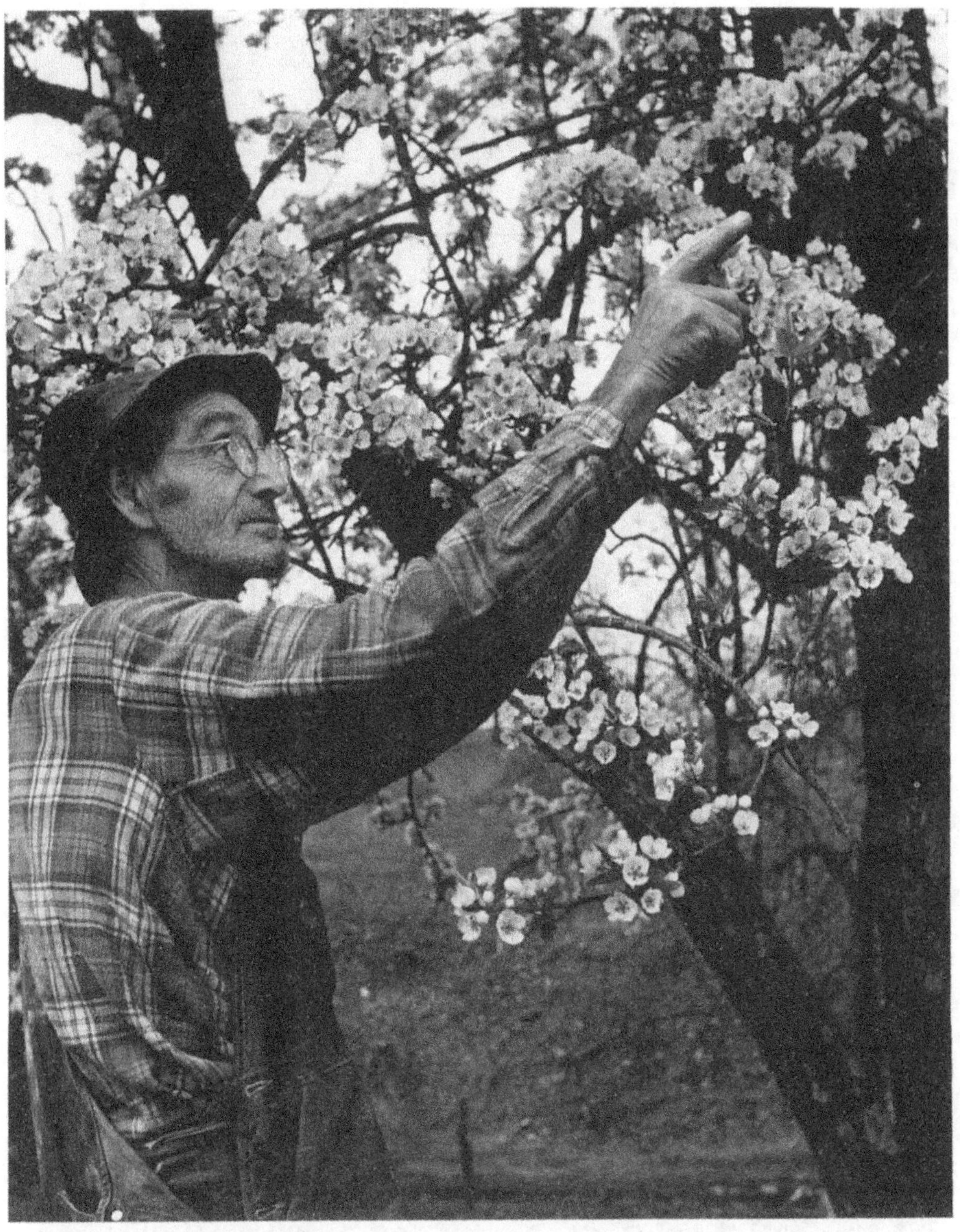

Bee-wise Abe Farley can course bees from their watering place to their swarm in a pear or apple tree. Then he smokes the swarm into a homemade hive and takes them to his house. [Montgomery County, Virginia, 1955.]

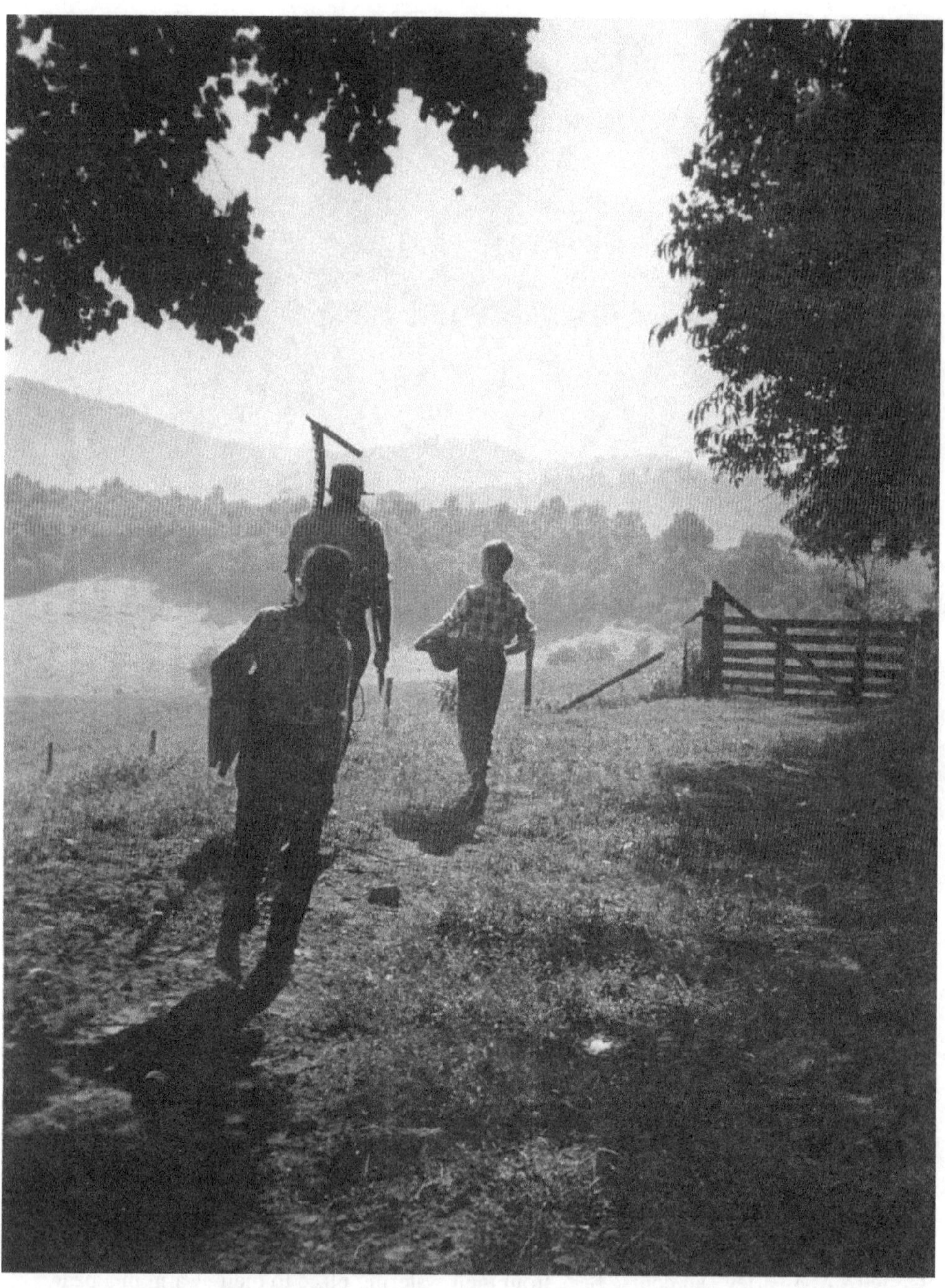

Bee-tree hunters set out early to find a hollow tree containing a swarm of sting-happy wild bees. After the tree is chopped or sawed down, a bee-smoker comes into play to smoke down the bees, rendering them stingless—you hope. Depending on the size of the tree, sometimes you are rewarded with several gallons of honey. At other times black ants, yellow jackets, or termites have taken over the colony and your work is all in vain.

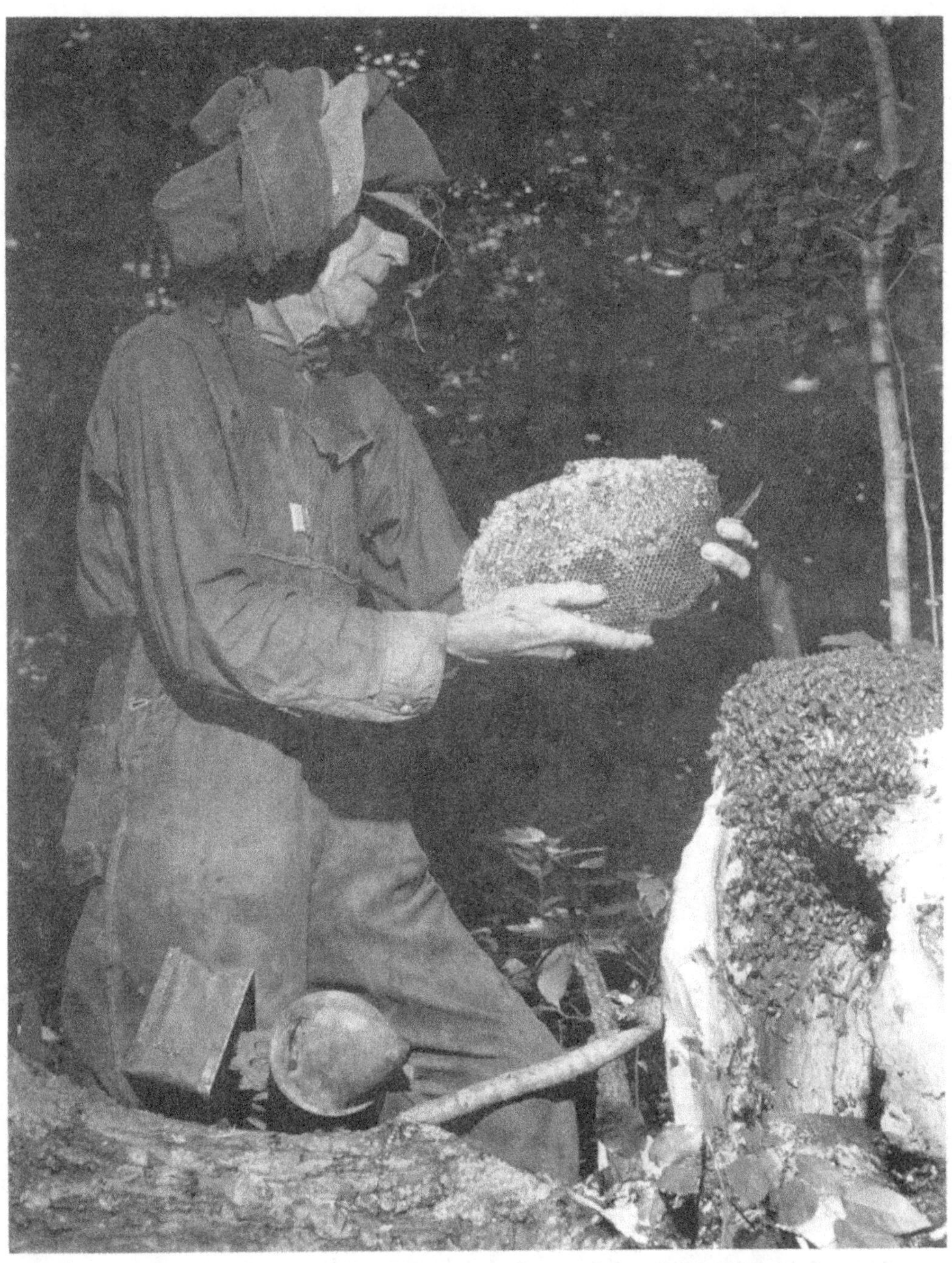

Takes right much know-how and nerve to rob a bee-tree of its honey. Pim Wheeling goes about his robbing bare-handed, singing "Don't you sting me, honey. . . . I just want to get your honey, honey" as he extracts the nectar-sweet honey from a hollow pin oak.

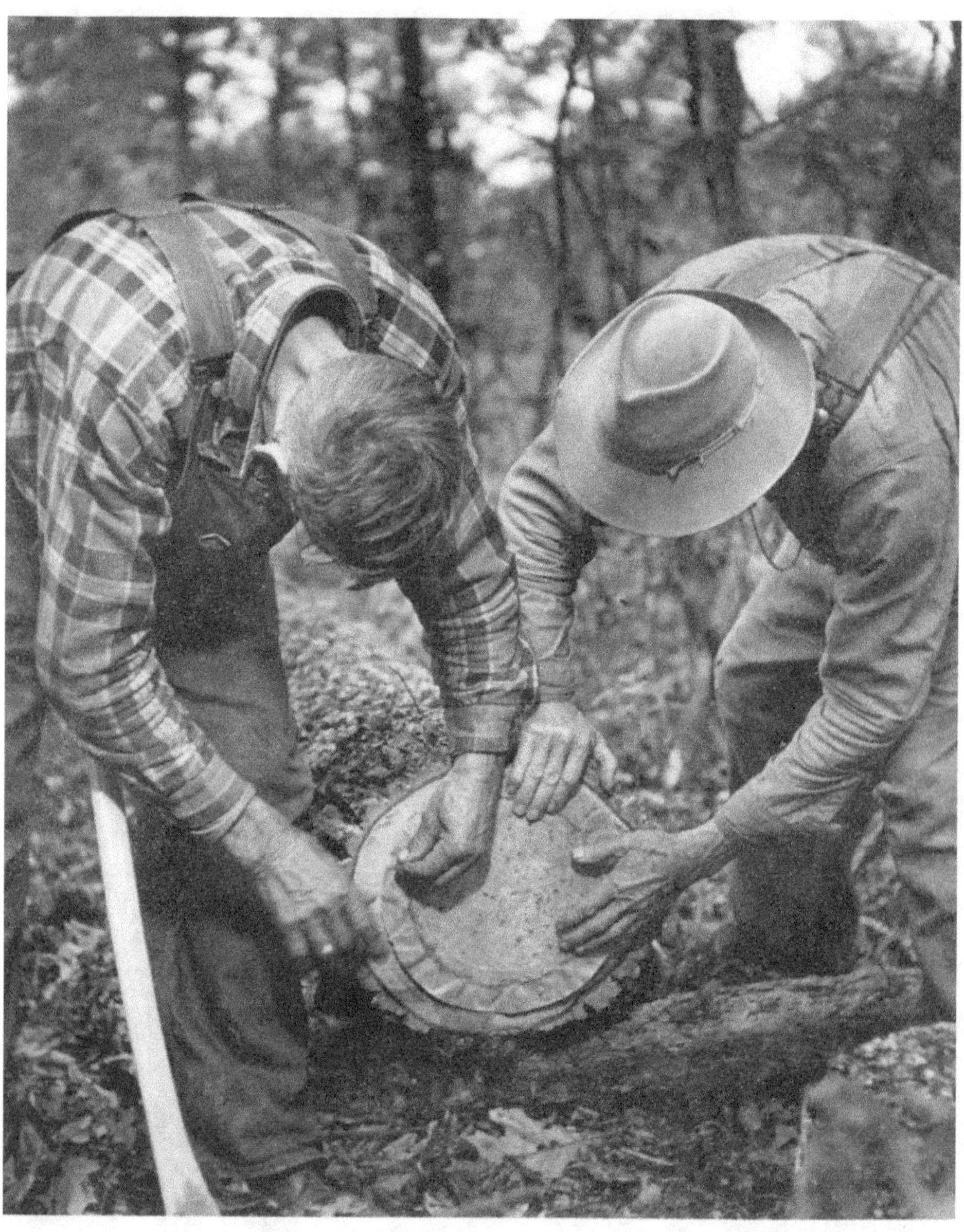

Sometimes a bee tree contains very little honey, so the hive is sealed to give the bees time to store up more honey. Then the hive will be reentered and some honey taken, making certain the bees have enough left to carry them over the winter until wildflowers bloom again. [Southwest Virginia, 1955.]

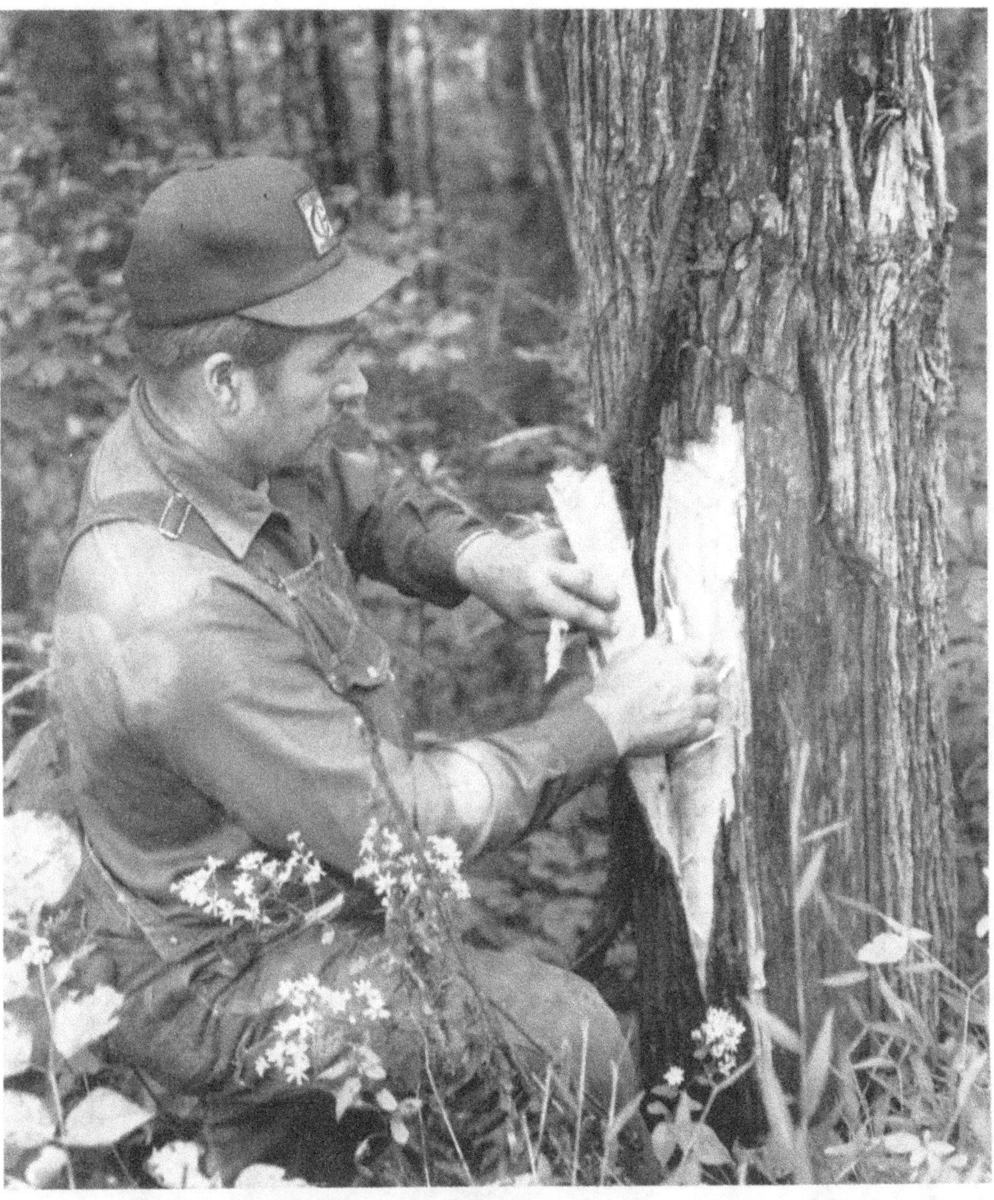

Sam "Thumpkeg" DeHart peels hisself some strips of slippery elm from a tree on his place on Shooting Creek in Franklin County [Virginia]. Among the many plant materials possessing therapeutic powers for man's feelin' just tollables and poorlys, the inner bark of the American sweet elm tree ranks high in use by many mountain folks. Many mountain-born and fetched-up people use a poultice of slippery elm bark to fetch boils into a head. Too, they use slippery elm's juice to cure throat ailments. [1954.]

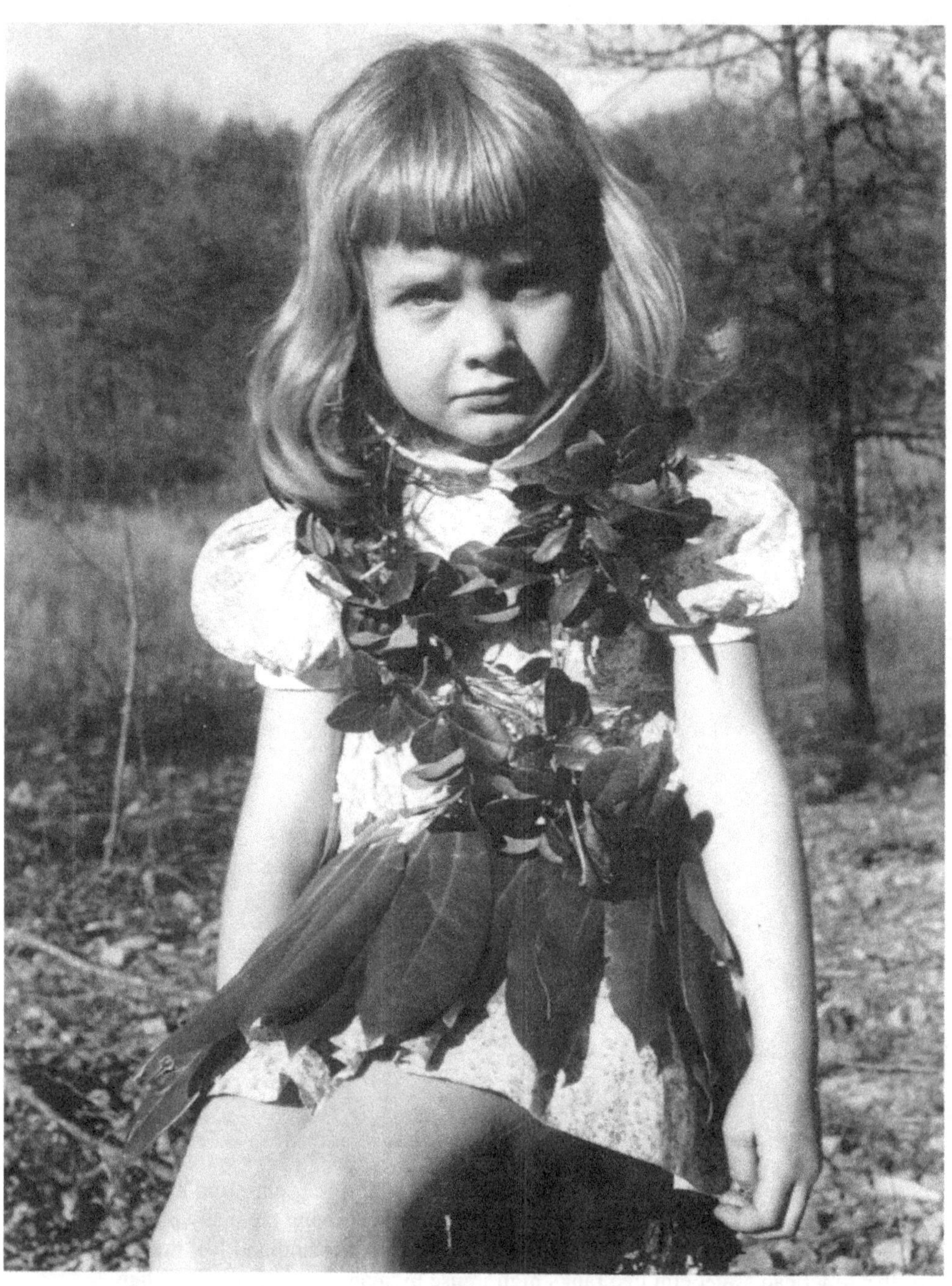

Vicky DeHart wears a necklace of rhododendron, believed to ward off disease and generally promote good health. Giant laurel and teaberry leaves worn as belts help provide young girls with good husbands, so the mountain folk say. [Patrick County, Virginia, 1954.]

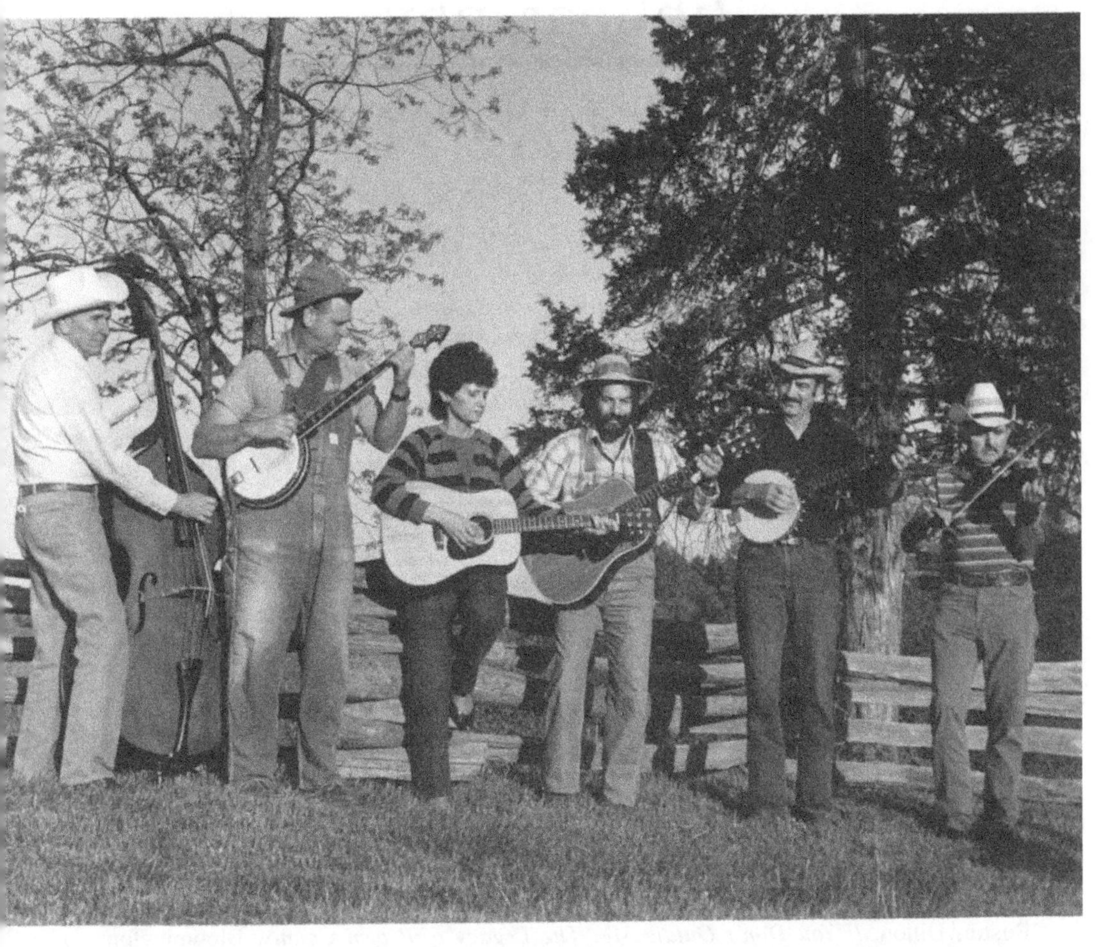

[Making music at Palmer's home to celebrate his eighty-second birthday, Christiansburg, Virginia, 1987.] The musicians are Olen Gardner and his Appalachian Ramblers band.

Bibliography

Aikman, Lonelle. *Nature's Healing Arts: From Folk Medicine to Modern Drugs*. Washington, D.C.: National Geographic Society, 1977.

American Photographers of the Depression: Farm Security Administration Photographs 1935-1943. New York: Pantheon Books, 1985.

Babcock-Abrahams, Barbara. "'A Tolerated Margin of Mess': The Trickster and His Tales Reconsidered." *Journal of the Folklore Institute* 11 (1975), 147-186.

Bake, William A. *The Blue Ridge*. Birmingham: Oxmoor House, 1977.

Barrow, Thomas F.; Armitage, Shelley; and Tydeman, William E., eds. *Reading Into Photography: Selected Essays, 1959-1980*. Albuquerque: University of New Mexico Press, 1982.

Barthes, Roland, "The Photographic Message." In *Photography in Print*, ed. by Vicki Goldberg. New York: Touchstone Books, 1981.

Bayer, Jonathan. *Reading Photographs: Understanding the Aesthetics of Photography*. New York: Pantheon Books, 1977.

Boddy, Julie M. "The Farm Security Administration Photographs of Marion Post Wolcott: A Cultural History." Ph.D. dissertation, State University of New York at Buffalo, 1982. (Published by University Microfilms International.)

Brannan, Beverly W. and Horvath, David, eds. *A Kentucky Album: Farm Security Administration Photographs, 1935-1943*. Lexington: The University Press of Kentucky, 1986.

Breckinridge, Mary. *Wide Neighborhoods*. New York: Harper and Brothers, 1952; reprint Lexington: University Press of Kentucky, 1981.

Bristol, Claude M. *The Magic of Believing*. New York: Prentice-Hall, 1948.

Bustin, Dillon. *If You Don't Outdie Me: The Legacy of Brown County*. Bloomington: Indiana University Press, 1982.

Clark, Joe. *Tennessee Hill Folk*. Nashville: Vanderbilt University Press, 1972.

Clark, Joe. *Up the Hollow from Lynchburg*. New York: McGraw-Hill, 1975.

Coe, Brian and Gates, Paul. *The Snapshot Photograph: The Rise of Popular Photography, 1888-1939*. London: Ash & Grant, 1977.

Eller, Ronald D. *Miners, Millhands, and Mountaineers: Industrialization of the Appalachian South, 1888-1930*. Knoxville: University of Tennessee Press, 1982.

Ewald, Wendy, ed. *Appalachia: A Self-Portrait*. Frankfort, KY: Gnomon Press for Appalshop, Inc., 1979.

Fassbender, Adolf, F.R.P.S. *Pictorial Artistry: The Dramatization of the Beautiful in Photography*. New York: B. Westerman, 1937.

Featherstone, David, *Doris Ulmann, American Portraits*. Albuquerque: University of New Mexico Press, 1985.

Featherstone, David, ed. *Observations: Essays on Documentary Photography*. Carmel: Friends of Photography, 1984.

Fetterman, John. *Stinking Creek: The Portrait of a Small Mountain Community in Appalachia*. New York: E. P. Dutton, 1970.

Fisher, Stephen W. *Identity as Symbolic Production: The Politics of Culture and Meaning in Appalachia*. Ph.D. dissertation, Princeton University, 1977. (University Microfilm International.)

Forsee, Aylesa. *William Henry Jackson: Pioneer Photographer of the West*. New York: Viking Press, 1964.

Gibbs, Lee W. and Stevenson, W. Taylor. *Myth and the Crisis of Historical Consciousness*. Missoula: Scholars Press, 1975.

Ginsberg, Louis. *Photographers in Virginia, 1839-1900: A Checklist*. Petersburg, Va.: published by the author, 1986.

Goldberg, Vicki, ed. *Photography in Print: Writings from 1816 to the Present*. New York: Simon and Schuster, 1981.

Hurley, F. Jack. *Portrait of a Decade: Roy Stryker and the Development of Documentary Photography in the Thirties*. Baton Rouge: Louisiana State University Press, 1972.

Hurley, F. Jack. *Russell Lee, Photographer.* Dobbs Ferry, NY: Morgan & Morgan, 1978.

Jeffers, Jack. *Appalachian Byways: A Photographic Documentary.* Bassett, Va.: published by the author, 1984.

Kephart, Horace. *Our Southern Highlanders*. New York: MacMillan, 1913; reprint ed., Knoxville: University of Tennessee Press, 1976.

Kirby, Jack Temple. *Rural Worlds Lost: The American South 1920-1960*. Baton Rouge: Louisiana State University Press, 1987.

Lesy, Michael. *Bearing Witness: A Photographic Chronicle of American Life, 1860-1945*. New York: Pantheon Books, 1982.

Lindley, Daniel A., Jr. "Walker Evans, Rhetoric, and Photography." *Reading Into Photography.* ed. Thomas F. Barrow; Shelley Armitage; William E. Tydeman. Albuquerque: University of New Mexico Press, 1982, pp. 161-179.

Lord, William G. *Blue Ridge Parkway Guide, Book Two*. Asheville: Hexagon, 1976.

Lyman, Christopher M. *The Vanishing Race and Other Illusions: Photographs of Indians by Edward S. Curtis*. Washington, D.C.: Smithsonian Institution Press, 1982.

Lyons, Nathan, ed. *Photographers on Photography.* Englewood Cliffs: Prentice-Hall, 1966.

Marling, Karal Ann. *Wall-to-Wall America: A Cultural History of Post-Office Murals in the Great Depression*. Minneapolis: University of Minnesota Press, 1982.

Miller, Jim Wayne. *The Mountains Have Come Closer.* Boone: Appalachian Consortium Press, 1980.

Murray, Kenneth. *Down to Earth: People of Appalachia*. Boone: Appalachian Consortium Press, 1974.

Murray, Kenneth. *A Portrait of Appalachia*. Boone: Appalachian Consortium Press, 1985.

National Geographic Society. *American Mountain People*. Photographed by Bruce Dale. Washington, D.C.: National Geographic Society, 1973.

Ogburn, Charlton. *The Southern Appalachians, A Wilderness Quest*. New York: William Morrow, 1975.

Ohrn, Karin Becker. *Dorothea Lange and the Documentary Tradition*. Baton Rouge: Louisiana State University Press, 1980.

Plattner, Steven W. *Roy Stryker: U.S.A., 1943-1950, The Standard Oil (New Jersey) Photography Project*. Austin: University of Texas Press, 1983.

Pratt, Davis, ed. *The Photographic Eye of Ben Shahn*. Cambridge: Harvard University Press, 1975.

Roberts, Bruce and Nancy. *Where Time Stood Still*. New York: Crowell-Collier Press, 1970.

Roskill, Mark and David Carrier. *Truth and Falsehood in Visual Images*. Amherst: University of Massachusetts Press, 1983.

Rothstein, Arthur. *Documentary Photography*. Boston: Focal Press, 1986.

Routzahn, Mary Swain. "Presenting mountain work to the public." *Mountain Life and Work* 4 (1928), 27-30.

Sekula, Allan. "On the Invention of Photographic Meaning." *Artforum*, January 1975.

Shapiro, Henry. "Appalachia and the Idea of America: The Problem of the Persisting Frontier." *An Appalachian Symposium*, ed. J.W. Williamson. Boone: Appalachian State University Press, 1977. Pp. 43-55.

Shapiro, Henry. *Appalachia on Our Mind: The Southern Mountains and Mountaineers in the American Consciousness, 1870-1920*. Chapel Hill: University of North Carolina Press, 1978.

Sheppard, Muriel Earley. *Cabins in the Laurel*. Chapel Hill: University of North Carolina Press, 1935.

Sontag, Susan. *On Photography*. New York: Delta Book, 1973.

Straw, Richard. "Early Regional Photographers: Margaret Morley and William Barnhill in Western North Carolina." *The Impact of Institutions in Appalachia*, ed. Jim Lloyd and Anne G. Campbell. Boone: Appalachian Consortium, 1986.

Stuart, Jesse. "It's Still 'Stick to your Bush.'" *Mountain Life and Work* 46 (May 1970), 8-11.

Stuart, Jesse. *Man With a Bull-Tongue Plow*. New York: E. P. Dutton, 1934.

Stuart, Jesse. *The World of Jesse Stuart: Selected Poems*. Ed. and with introduction by J. R. LeMaster. New York: McGraw-Hill, 1975.

Turner, Victor. *Process, Performance, and Pilgrimage*. New Delhi: Concept Publishing, 1979.

Turner, Victor. "Process, System, and Symbol: A New Anthropological Synthesis." *Daedalus* 106 (Winter 1977), 61-80.

Ulmann, Doris. *The Appalachian Photographs of Doris Ulmann*. Highlands, NC: The Jargon Society, 1971.

Watkins, Charles Alan. "Merchandising the Mountaineer: Photography, the Great Depression, and *Cabins in the Laurel*" *Appalachian Journal*, 12 (Spring 1985), 215-238.

West, John Foster and Roberts, Bruce. *This Proud Land: The Blue Ridge Mountains*. Charlotte: McNally and Loftin, 1974.

Whisnant, David. *All That Is Native and Fine: The Politics of Culture in an American Region*. Chapel Hill: University of North Carolina Press, 1983.

Williams, Cratis. "Subtlety in Mountain Speech XI." *Mountain Life and Work* 43 (Spring 1967), 14-16.

Wolcott, Marion Post. *FSA Photographs*. Carmel: The Friends of Photography, 1983.

Worth, Sol. *Studying Visual Communication*. Philadelphia: University of Pennsylvania Press, 1981.

Selected Publications by Earl Palmer

"Blue Ridge Broommakers." *Scenic South*, November 1954, pp. 16-19.

"Mountain Herbs (photographs)." *Scenic South*, March 1955, pp. 14-19.

"Apple Butter Time." *Scenic South*, November 1955, pp. 2-5.

"Hunting Wild Honey, Nature's Sweetest Sport." *Dodge News*, 1956, pp. 2-3.

"Bee-Tree Honey." *Frontiers, A Magazine of Natural History*, April 1956, pp. 112-13.

"Blue Ridge Mill." *Scenic South*, April 1956, pp. 16-19.

"This Is Country-Ham Country!" *Dodge News Magazine*, 1957, pp. 6-7.

"The Blue Ridge Countryside." *People and Places*, January 1957, pp. 10-15.

"Hunting Wild Honey." *American Bee Journal* 97 (April 1957), 146-48.

"Monument to a Tree." *Dodge News Magazine*, April 1957, pp. 2-3.

"Sunshine Preserves." *Scenic South*, June 1957, pp. 6-7.

"The Appalachians' Quiltin' Queens." *Dodge News Magazine*, October 1957, pp. 12-13.

"It's Forest Festival Time in Elkins!" *Dodge News Magazine*, October 1957, pp. 10-11.

"Autumn Treasure." *Scenic South*, October 1957, pp. 16-17.

"Virginia Creeper." *People and Places*, April 1958, pp. 3-6.

"Copper Valley Hams are Shipped Coast to Coast." *Spout*, May 1958, pp. 2-5.

"Mill-Day in the Mountains." *Dodge News Magazine*, October 1958, pp. 16-18.

"There's an Herb for Whatever Ails a Feller." *Dodge News*, 1959, pp. 12-13.

"Cumberland Gap." *Scenic South*, July 1959, pp. 2, 7.

"Drive-in Coal Mine." *People and Places*, August 1959, pp. 20-22.

"Bloody Harlan Revisited." *Dodge News Magazine*, October 1959, pp. 2-5. (Text by W. W. Diehl)

"Bad Days in Harlan." *The Cincinnati Pictorial Enquirer*, 31 January 1960.

"Aunt Lulu's Grit Bread." *Dodge News Magazine*, February 1960, p. 10.

"Good Olde Mountain Herbing." *Popular Gardening*, August 1960, pp. 38-39, 53.

"Blue Ridge Parkway—'Hit's a Bushel and a Peck o' Road from End to End.'" *Dodge News Magazine*, November 1960, pp. 11-13.

"Down Kentucky's Cumberland River." *Travel Magazine*, June 1961, pp. 37-39.

"Cradle of the Historic Potomac." *Dodge News Magazine*, March 1962, pp. 11-13.

"The Miracle of Spring." *Dodge News Magazine*, April 1962, pp. 2-3.

"America's Longest National Park?" *Dodge News Magazine*, August 1962, pp. 4-6.

"Comeback of the Folk Toys." *Dodge News Magazine*, December 1963, pp. 3-4.

"Next National Park?" *Travel Magazine*, August 1963, pp. 33-35.

"Never to Return . . ." *Mountain Life and Work*, Fall 1964, pp. 50-52.

"Mountain Whittler." *Scenic South*, October 1964, pp. 16-19.

"Herb Hunting in the Southern Appalachians." *Scenic South*, October 1965, pp. 14-19.

"Rx for the Boys in Gray." *The News Bag*, September 1966, pp. 1-5.
"Cumberland Gap." *Scenic South*, October 1966, pp. 2-7, 12, 14-15.
"Kingdom Come." *Scenic South*, October 1967, pp. 4-6.
"Swappin' Meetin'!" *Scenic South*, October 1967, pp. 2-3.
"Moonshining in Virginia." *Blue Ridge Institute 1983 Calendar.* Ferrum College.
"Steam on the Grade." *Blue Ridge Institute 1984 Calendar*, Ferrum College.
"Mountain Medicine." *The Virginian*, March-April 1986, pp. 84-86.

www.ingramcontent.com/pod-product-compliance
Lightning Source LLC
LaVergne TN
LVHW082001060826
844660LV00005B/270

* 9 7 8 0 8 1 3 1 1 6 9 5 2 *